GREENING THE PARANORMAL

PARANORMAL

EXPLORING THE ECOLOGY OF
EXTRAORDINARY EXPERIENCE

GREENING THE PARANORMAL

EXPLORING THE ECOLOGY OF EXTRAORDINARY EXPERIENCE

Edited by

JACK HUNTER, PhD

www.augustnightpress.com

Dedicated to the memory of animist thinker Dr. Brian Taylor. His chapter contribution 'is a true reflection of his deep thinking, sensitivity, humanity and love of nature.'

PRAISE FOR
GREENING THE PARANORMAL

This book does everything one can hope for. It begins with a shocking shared road encounter with what looks like, well, the Green Man of European folklore. It then travels through any number of well worn paranormal paths, each time, like the initial astonished encounter, spotting new (and yet very old) things and struggling mightily with the empirical highly strange aspects of the phenomena. The essayists do not flinch. They do not look away. They walk ahead, right into the dark green forest of religion, mythology, and folklore. What they bring back could signal major shifts in our intellectual, social, political, and moral landscapes with respect to a natural world that is really a super natural world, that is really us.

– **Jeffrey J. Kripal,** PhD.,
AUTHOR OF *Secret Body: Erotic and*
Esoteric Currents in the History of Religions

Having joined the Green movement in 1973 after reading Limits to Growth, which warned of potentially devastating climate change, I have supported Greenpeace, Friends of the Earth etc., since then. Recently I have become a Green Town Councillor to further help in changing the way in which we live our lives. However, my work has always been in Parapsychology, both as a teacher and a researcher. I have always seen Parapsychology as the spiritual aspect of the Green movement, and have given talks and written articles to that end. So I am absolutely delighted that Jack has brought out this compilation of the Green aspects of the Paranormal, written from a very diverse array of perspectives. I hope that it makes a great impact on our society which is in desperate need of changing its predominant world view.

– **Serena Roney-Dougal,** PhD.,
AUTHOR OF *Where Science and Magic Meet*

CONTENTS

FOREWORD

Paul Devereux

~

It is hard to know where to begin in dealing with a challenging topic like the greening of the paranormal. I suppose that for me, it has to be one overcast mid-afternoon in the west of Ireland about twenty years ago.

My wife Charla and I were driving along a lonely country road during a fieldwork research session for a planned book on worldwide lore relating to beliefs about spirit routes passing through the physical landscape (Devereux, 2001a/2003). We were trying to geographically map generations-old accounts of fairy paths we had uncovered in the verbatim folklore records of University College Dublin. We were on our way to the next location on our UCD list in County Mayo to see what we could find in the way of a local memory about a fairy path belief at a particular place there. We came to a Y-junction in the narrow road. There was no road sign and unsure of what direction to take, we slowed to a walking pace and proceeded cautiously onto the right-hand fork. A level sward of low grass occupied the triangle of land between this fork of the road and the left-hand one. Suddenly, standing on the grass, there was a figure, between two and three feet tall. It was anthropomorphic and fully three-dimensional (as we could clearly determine while we were drifting slowly past). It had sprung into appearance out of nowhere, and it caught my wife's and my own transfixed attentions simultaneously.

The figure was comprised of a jumble of very dark green tones, as if composed of a tight, dense tangle of foliage, rather like the stand of woodland a hundred yards or so beyond the sward of grass. It didn't seem to quite have a face, just a head with deep-set eyes peering out of the green tangle. It presented a distinctly forbidding appearance. As we crawled past in our car, the figure started to turn its head in our direction, but then vanished. Charla called out: 'Oh shit!' We looked at each other, both of us wide-eyed and thoroughly disconcerted. 'You saw *that*?' I asked rhetorically. The whole episode had lasted for only about half a minute or so, but it was unquestionably an actual, if transient, objective observation.

I found this experience to be especially disturbing, not to say inconvenient, as I had been conducting the research on the confident assumption that fairy lore was an artefact of cultural conditioning, predicated on a smattering of ultimately explicable experiences had by uncomplicated and superstitious rural people. But I can't explain this event, this 'other-than-human' encounter, to anyone, least of all to myself.[1] Indeed, how 'other' could one get? Had we just witnessed that ancient folkloric motif of the 'green man,' assumed to be a fertility symbol? Well, if so, it is no longer a mere motif to me. In the present context of this anthology, the combined experience of 'greening' and 'paranormal' had hit me squarely in the face. I had received a stern lesson.

I am ashamed to say that I was so ontologically discombobulated (a fancy way of saying I was scared) that I just put my foot down on the accelerator and drove away from the scene at speed, without staying to conduct further investigation. This was particularly shameful, because a few years before this experience, I had published Re-Visioning the Earth (1996), which discussed many of the topics addressed in this present volume. I now understood even better than I had before that for such a 're-visioning' to happen we will have to dig very deep indeed, for grasping the ecological dimensions of what our culture calls the 'paranormal' (or however else we wish to label those pulled threads in the fabric of reality) will require us to re-acquaint ourselves with some aspects of the worldviews of earlier and indigenous peoples. And what aspects would they be? Well, certain themes recur in various guises throughout the essays in this anthology, and in a foreword I can pick up on only a few examples that prompt some personal thoughts and reminiscences that I hope will be relevant.

Animism

Acceptance of this way of knowing is fundamental to a deep ecological sensibility, and it permeates the papers in this anthology in various ways. Animism is the 'Big Step' for our culture to make – acquiring the understanding, the sense, that the elements of the non-human world are animate in some way and have a spiritual nature: rocks, rivers, soil, not to mention all the other-than-human entities (which include not only plants and living organisms but also what are called 'spirits' in old parlance). It requires our mainstream cultural re-education as to the nature of reality, and the shedding of a number of received prejudices about the nature of mind. As it stands, animism is utter anathema to modern thought. But it has been a reality, a spiritual fact, to the countless ages of humanity that have preceded us.

Such mythopoetic relationship with the environment was one example of what the ethnologist Lucien Lévy-Bruhl called *participation mystique*. By this is meant a local relationship with the land that went beyond mere utility and subsistence. To the indigenous person, 'Earth and sea are to him as living books in which the myths are inscribed,' Levy-Bruhl stated (1935). Another anthropologist, A. P. Elkin, put it more specifically when writing about indigenous Australasian peoples: 'The bond between a person and his (or her) country is not merely geographical or fortuitous, but living and spiritual and sacred. His country ... is the symbol of, and gateway to, the great unseen world of heroes, ancestors, and life-giving powers which avail for man and nature' (cited in Lévy-Bruhl, 1935, p.43).

In the West, this kind of relationship was noted at least as long ago as ancient Greece, where there were two words for subtly different senses of place, *chora* and *topos*. Chora is the older of the two terms, and was an holistic reference to place: place as expressive, place as a keeper of memory, imagination and mythic presence. *Topos*, on the other hand, signified place in much the way we think of it nowadays – simple location, and the objective, physical features of a locale. Topography. But, ultimately, even sacred places have become *topoi*.

Place-names can often survive through countless generations, providing echoes of the animistic relationship that existed in ancient landscapes. In Greenland, for instance, Inuit (Eskimo) place-names include *Toornaarsutoq*, 'the place with lots of spirits,' and *Angakkussarfik*, 'the place of the initiation of the shaman.' In Celtic lands the word 'pap,' meaning female breast, was often applied to rounded hills and

xiii

mountains, recalling a perception of an Earth Mother goddess residing in the very landscape that goes back deep into prehistory. In every land that had an indigenous language, place-names can provide clues to former sacred cartography.

Concepts of animism can take various forms. For many ancient societies the land was so alive it had a voice in their dreams. A clear account of this was provided by a Paiute Indian, Hoavadunuki, who was a hundred years old by the time he was interviewed by ethnographers in the 1930s. The old Indian stated that a local peak, Birch Mountain, spoke to him in his dreams, urging him to become a 'doctor' (shaman). The Paiute resisted, he said, because he didn't want the pressures and problems that would come with that (Steward, 1934). Communication from this mountain occurred a number of times throughout the old man's long life and was not seen as strange or peculiar by him – indeed, the idea of the land being capable of speaking to humans was probably widespread in ancient sensibility.

Sacred soundscapes were simply a natural corollary of that sensibility. The basic notion of the land having speech, or of being read like a text, was lodged deeply in some schools of Japanese Buddhism – in early medieval Shingon Esoteric Buddhism, founded by Kūkai, for instance. He likened the natural landscape around Chuzenji temple and the lake at the foot of Mount Nantai, near Nikko, to descriptions in the Buddhist scriptures of the Pure Land, the habitation of the buddhas. Kūkai considered that the landscape not only symbolised but was *of the same essence* as the mind of the Buddha. Like the Buddha mind, the landscape spoke in a natural language, offering supernatural discourse. 'Thus, waves, pebbles, winds, and birds were the elementary and unconscious performers of the cosmic speech of buddhas and bodhisattvas,' explains Allan Grapard (1994).

This is reminiscent of the beliefs of the Kaluli and Umeda people in Papua New Guinea. To them, birdsong emanating out of the dense jungle foliage are the voices of the ancestors, the living birds are giving voice to the spirits of the dead. These peoples classified birds not by their plumage or appearance, but by the songs they produce. Anthropologist Alfred Gell came to realise that peoples like the Kaluli and Umeda, who live in dense forests, tended to be acoustic cultures, and make hearing and, in some cases, smell the primary sense, ahead of vision. (The Kaluli even have a verb, *dabuma*, that melds the taking in of sensory information by ear or nose). Gell observed that the Kalulis' spirit idea about birdsong was only one kind of 'coding of acoustic experience': the sounds produced by rivers, streams, waterfalls and other environmental sounds also enter the language of these New Guinea people by means of onomatopoeia. The Kaluli can 'sing places' like waterfalls, navigating a sonic cartography. 'Place, sound and social memory are fused together in Kaluli poetics,' Gell wrote (1995).

Throat singers in Tuvan, an autonomous republic within the Russian Federation, developed their vocal art originally as a means of communicating with their natural environment, not for entertainment. Throat singing involves the production of resonant sounds, overtones and whistles within the throat, nasal cavities, mouth and lips, and was used to provoke echoes or imitate natural sounds like waterfalls or wind. The master throat singers can select precise locations inside caves where the resonances are exactly right to maximise the reverberations of their songs. They even wait until atmospheric conditions are perfect for the greatest effect. It is in essence a technology of echoes. At one locale, where a singer called Kaigal-ool performed in front of a cliff-face, ethnomusicologist Theodore Levin reported that 'the cliff and surrounding features sing back to the musician in what Kaigal-ool calls "a kind of meditation – a conversation that I have with nature"' (Levin & Suzukei, 2006).

It is only in our modern culture that we have stopped listening to the land within a spiritual context. If we could fashion a modern, suitably culturally-ingrained animistic model, it is clear we would treat the environment with much more respect.

Vision Quest

The term 'vision quest' is referred to a number of times in these pages. We know about it primarily from the archaic practices of shamans in Native American and Palaeo-Siberian tribes. In a typical, traditional vision quest the individual journeys alone into the wilderness, perhaps to some special, sacred vision-questing site known to the tribe, and there fasts and goes without sleep for three or four days and nights in the hope of receiving a vision, which can be visual or auditory. (It is said that some traditional American Indian chants originated as auditory hallucinations during vision quests). Vision quests were, and are, also sometimes undertaken as rites of passage by young Indian braves.

Without using the term directly, Barry Lopez gives a wonderful account in his *The Rediscovery of North America* of one of his experiences. It is redolent with animistic elements:

The Rediscovery of North America

I remember a Kamba man in Kenya, Kamoya Kimeu, a companion in the stone desert west of Lake Turkana – and a dozen other men – telling me, you know how to see, how to *mark* country. And he and others teaching me to sit down in one place for two or three hours and look.

When we enter the landscape to learn something, we are obligated, I think, to pay attention rather than constantly pose questions. To approach the land as we would a person, by opening an intelligent conversation. And to stay in one place, to make of that one, long observation a fully-dilated experience. We will always be rewarded if we give the land credit for more than we imagine, and if we imagine it as being more complex even than language (Lopez, 1990).

This reminds me of one of my own experiences. I had spent years trying to 'read' the fairly well-preserved Neolithic landscape in Wiltshire, containing the mighty stone circle and henge of Avebury. I had been visiting there at all times of day and season with little success. On this particular occasion I decided to go in the very early morning and sit on the flat summit of Silbury Hill, the 130-foot (40m) tall artificial Neolithic mound near the centre of the Avebury monumental landscape.[2] It is exquisitely positioned within the natural contours of the landscape. Unknowingly, at the time, I was about to conduct *utiseta*, 'sitting out,' the pagan North European version of the vision quest.

I had arrived well before sunrise and the hill was shrouded in a dense mist. But this was hugging the ground, and on the top of Silbury I found it was thin enough to see the sky overhead. I sat on the circular summit as if on a grass island surrounded by a candy-floss sea, which, as the sky grew lighter, became tinted with the most delicate pastel colours. Suddenly, as if a voice spoke inside my right ear, I heard the statement, 'In this mystery shall we dwell.' Startled, I turned my head to look around, but even as I did so I knew that the voice had been a mental one, though of exceptional clarity and authority. The voice had carried a sense, an 'aura,' that it had emanated from Silbury itself. I felt that the great monument had actually spoken to me. A crazy, beyond rationalisation, animistic experience.

The great mound became my teacher and over a series of further visits I was led to uncover a number of the Avebury landscape's secrets – they were open secrets if one's eyes were correctly directed. After 5,000 years, they are now in the archaeological record (Devereux, 1991). But one secret didn't get into the official record – Silbury's final lesson.

I was standing on the mound's summit with my back to the sunrise.[3] I could see a striking golden glow radiating a long distance westwards from the tip of Silbury's extended shadow thrown by the rising sun. This was a 'glory' or 'Brocken's Spectre,' an optical phenomenon created by the myriad prisms formed by dewdrops on the grass and crops in the fields to the west of the mound. But it *felt* as if the great mound was casting a blessing across the land. In this role, Silbury is a harvest hill, and perhaps was seen as the representation of the Earth Mother goddess (Devereux 1992; 2000).

Liminal, 'Thin' and Sacred Places

Various authors here in these pages (including Simmonds-Moore; Glazier; Schroll) have referenced ancient sacred sites. Such places, natural or monumental, are a way we can key into ancient perceptions and knowledge. There are a variety of reasons why ancient sacred places were identified if natural, or created if monumental: sometimes quite pragmatic ones such as being hunting viewpoints, or places that were sources of ritual materials – certain minerals for paints, for instance. But many were venerated or located specifically at what were perceived as 'thin' and 'liminal' places – sites where 'breaking through' to otherworld realms or altered mind states (take your choice) were felt to be more easily accomplished than other places. Places redolent with *chora*. They are good places to absorb numinosity, to meditate, to dream.[4]

It is also possible to *listen* to ancient sacred sites: the sound the wind or nearby waters (rapids, waterfalls, springs) make at them, the echoes at or around them, and, particularly, the way their acoustics respond to sounds made around or within them (Jahn, Devereux & Ibison, 1996; Watson & Keating, 1999; 2000; Devereux, 2001b; Goldhahn, 2002). In some places the very stones can speak (Fagg, 1956; Dams, 1985; Hultman, 2010). We found that even the source area of the Stonehenge bluestones, around Carn Menyn in the Preseli Hills of South Wales, is a veritable soundscape, thanks to a preponderance of natural ringing rocks and lithophones (Devereux & Wozencroft, 2014).

Having spent half a century of my life on and off in the company of sacred places on three continents, I can vouch for their ability to promote transpersonal insights. And not just discrete places – entire sacred landscapes too. Just for example, Death Valley in California appears to the superficial eye to be simply a harsh if beautiful landscape, yet it

Death Valley

is also home to a host of shamanic features subtly emblazoned on the ground and was known to the Shoshone as *tiwiniyarivipi*, 'mythic land, sacred country' (Werlhof, 1987; Whitley, 1996; Devereux, 2002; 2010).

Interspecies communion

This is mentioned a few times in the following pages (Hunter; Luke; Foster) and involves the use of altered mind states of one kind or another. In his paper in this anthology, Luke recounts taking an indigenous psychoactive plant in Mexico that gave him the vivid sensation of becoming 'completely transformed' into a shrub. Was that simply an hallucination? Not in my opinion, because I experienced something similar under LSD, 'back in the day.' During the session, I became transfixed by a lone daffodil in an elegant vase on a table. This is how I have described the experience elsewhere:

> As I gazed at its yellow petals, I saw that they were moving in a subtle way. I looked closer: yes, the petals really were making miniature waving motions. It was like a more modest version of one of those time-lapse film sequences which massively speed up the opening and closing of a flower. For me, time was not yet settled into place, I recognised, and I was indeed watching the flower in a local, speeded-up time frame. I wanted to ensure that this was no hallucination. I changed my position and I was able to plot the movement of the petals' peripheries against the 'grid' formed by the window panes beyond the table...I was convinced then as now that I was making a true observation. I sat back in my chair and various events diverted my attention for a while. When my gaze reverted to the vase and daffodil, I became horrified because there seemed to be tiny bugs crawling up the flower's stem. I looked more closely. They were not bugs but very small droplets of moisture moving by capillary action up the inside of the stem. I realised with a shock that I could only perceive this because I had 'x-ray' vision. Is it possible for the visual cortex to process energy outside the visible spectrum? (I didn't know at the time that shamanic healers around the world claimed to be able to see into their patients' bodies while in trance states, nor had I at that time heard of the shamanic artform known as 'x-ray' in which [prehistoric] rock paintings of animals depict their insides). While I mentally stumbled to work out how this could happen, I lost the novel visual ability and the daffodil became just the daffodil once more.

But the interaction between myself and the flower wasn't yet over. Some time later, I entered into a most curious relationship with it. There was no visual component, it was strictly an empathic link. Without losing my own admittedly by now somewhat bruised and fragile sense of identity, I found my awareness slipping inside that of the daffodil. While still being conscious of sitting in a chair, I could also sense my petals! Then an exquisite sensation cascaded through me, and I knew I was experiencing light falling on those petals. It was virtually orgasmic...At every moment I felt, repeatedly, as if I was receiving the first ray of sunshine on the first morning in Eden. The world was unutterably new and innocent. I knew why one got such a refreshing, uplifting feeling being in a garden (Devereux, 1997/2008).

I have already intimated that animism is the big bridge for our modern collective cultural mind to cross. A bridge too far, in fact. But here's the thing: mind-altering substances of the appropriate kind can provide our minds with the ability to experience direct communion with the plant world while at the same time allowing us to explore the deep wells of our spiritual and 'paranormal' dimensions. Psychedelic substances are the tools to enable us to return directly to animistic perspectives and knowledge, even if only as temporary ecopsychic visitors. Why, as Luke points out in his paper, do some plants even 'produce such supposedly toxic compounds that have no apparent benefit to the plant/fungus and yet interact so sophisticatedly with our own minds?' Nature, it seems, may have a plan.

Currently a relatively small number of people like Luke are exploring this area of enquiry at university level now that scientific study of certain psychedelic substances has become legal in a few countries.[5] If this can be continued and expanded rapidly enough, it could offer the key for an exponential expansion of Western consciousness, allowing for the crucially required melding of mind and nature – a soul-to-soul interaction with anima mundi.

～

The authors in this anthology provide a pool of deep thought on the challenging matter of greening the paranormal, producing a welter of topic strands, some of which one would never expect, ranging from earth lights and cryptozoology to butterflies and 'soul birds' as psychopomps, and much else. I would like to wax on about them all, but I risk overstaying my welcome. The remarkably comprehensive paper here by contributing editor, Jack Hunter, defines the research arena in detail. He has performed a great service in pulling together this valuable volume. Let it just be the beginning, for the hour is late.

Notes

1. I mention this encounter in passing in the introduction to the book, but did not give many details, as I was concerned in not blowing my credibility. I have reached an age now where that matters less to me. I know for certain that those who disbelieve me are, ironically, the ones inadvertently trapped in a falsehood, not me. It is a fact that we share this planet with other entities of which we are hugely ignorant. It is all down to what one's cultural bubble allows one to perceive. It is exceedingly frustrating, nevertheless, for anyone who has had such an experience to be aware of a truth that could change our modern world going begging.

2. In the years since I conducted this work, serious erosion has occurred at Silbury Hill, largely due to excessive numbers of visitors, and it is now strictly forbidden to climb the mound.

3. Silbury Hill is tightly positioned within the contours of the natural landscape. Finding the reason for this requires focusing upon the riddle of why such a majestic mound was built immediately alongside Waden Hill, virtually the same height as itself. It turns out that in the late July-early August period, and in the early May period (Beltane in pagan Celtic tradition), when the sun rises along the same segment of the horizon, an observer on top of Silbury sees the sun rise first over the distant skyline and then by going down to a now eroded ledge about 5m down on the monument's slope, sees it rising a second time minutes later over the top of Waden Hill. Silbury is thus built to exactly the right height in precisely the right place to visually separate the two (near and far) eastern horizons allowing a celebratory 'double sunrise' at two key times of the ancient ceremonial and agricultural year.

4. I have been personally involved for several years in a major dreamwork project at selected ancient sites (see www.dragonprojecttrust.org), and am working on a concluding chapter about it in *The Powers of Ancient and Sacred Places* (in progress).

5. See https://beckleyfoundation.org

CHAPTER 1

GREENING THE PARANORMAL: RE-WILDING AND RE-ENCHANTMENT

Jack Hunter

This book is an exploration of the many threads subtly interconnecting what might at first seem to be unrelated fields: *anomalistics* (the study of the paranormal in all of its guises), and *ecology* (the study of the relationships between organisms in living systems). It has emerged at a critical moment in the history of humankind's relationship with the Earth, and all the species that co-inhabit with us. Throughout the twentieth century, and into the twenty-first, we have continually – and often deliberately – ignored the warning signs of the ecological catastrophe we are now facing. 2018, so the World Meteorological Organisation (WMO) recently announced, was the fourth hottest year on record, closely followed by 2017, 2016 and 2015. Indeed, the twenty warmest years since records began in 1850 have been in the last twenty-two years (WMO, 2018a). Who knows what 2019 will hold? On top of this, the WMO also reports that global greenhouse gas emissions are at their highest levels yet, in spite of the efforts and agreements of governments around the world to reduce them (WMO, 2018b). When this is combined with the dramatic loss of animal species over the last fifty years – up to as many as 60% of species according to the World Wildlife Fund (2018)[1] – and the continued deforestation of vast swathes of the world's ancient woodland (BBC, 2018), we are presented with a very grim picture indeed. Something needs to be done, or rather, something should have been done a long time ago. As sociologist Bruno Latour puts it: 'we haven't lacked for warnings. The sirens have been blaring all along' (2017, p. 9).

There are, however, some promising signs that we are collectively *beginning* to wake up to the reality we have created. From the bottom up perspective there are already hundreds of grass-roots regenerative ecology projects emerging all around the world (Rootes, 1999). The Youth Strikes for Climate that have been taking place on every continent, inspired by sixteen year-old Greta Thunberg's 'Skolstrejk för klimatet' outside the Swedish parliament, are also raising awareness of our ecological crisis on a massive scale, as are the growing number of Extinction Rebellion groups across the UK. Promising signs from the top-down perspective include the Paris Climate Accord, which was agreed in December 2015 and signed and ratified in April 2016 by 195 countries. This was a major stepping stone in that the agreement represents an international scientific consensus on climate change – that it is real, that human beings bear the brunt of responsibility, and that we need to (and can) do something about it. The agreement is aimed at:

> [keeping] global temperature rise this century well below 2 degrees Celsius above pre-industrial levels and to pursue efforts to limit the temperature increase even further to 1.5 degrees Celsius. Additionally, the agreement aims to strengthen the ability of countries to deal with the impacts of climate change (UNFCCC, 2018).

This is a process that will involve radical social, cultural and economic transformations. These changes will (at least to begin with), be driven by the need to reduce CO_2 emissions by 50% in the next decade, followed by similar 50% reductions in the following two decades. It will entail a total transformation of the way we live our lives – food, energy, transport, culture and society. By 2050 we should be living in a carbon negative world if we hope to have even a 66% chance of avoiding run-away climate change (Rockström *et al.*, 2017). Although it is true that no international agreement is ever going to solve the problems we face – we are talking about something much more than mere politics here – it is the overarching message of the Paris Agreement that is of greatest importance. In essence, the Paris Agreement calls on individual nations, communities, institutions and individuals to develop their own *localised responses to climate change*. In other words, *it is up to us* – in whatever capacity we can – to develop innovative new ways (or perhaps even return to some very old ways) of building resilient communities, regenerating ecosystems, enhancing biodiversity, mitigating climate change and meeting the targets of the Paris Agreement. It is an opportunity for creativity (Jones & Hunter, 2017; 2018).

All this talk of climate change, biodiversity loss and the urgent need for practical action might well seem a million miles away from the fringe topic of the paranormal, and it may at first be difficult to see any way that a re-engagement with the paranormal might help us to make sense of and overcome these terrifying global threats. In the spirit of creative exploration, however, this is precisely what I am suggesting with this book: that approaches emerging from the study of (and engagement with) the supernatural may ultimately help us to re-connect with the natural, and in so doing develop innovative approaches to confronting the eco-crisis. This book, then, will examine parallels between anomalistics (incorporating parapsychology, paranthropology, cryptozoology, religious studies, and so on), and ecology, not just for the sake of exploring interesting intersections (of which there are many), but for the essential task of contributing towards a much broader – *necessary* – change of perspective concerning our relationship to the living planet.

In a sense what I am suggesting is that the ontological assumptions underlying the rejection of the so-called paranormal by mainstream materialist science and culture are precisely the same as those that underlie the ecological crisis and our society's fractured relationship with the Earth. It is this book's contention that if we really want to change our behaviour we will have to *change the way we think* about our place in the cosmos. I am not the first person to suggest this kind of approach – see, for example, Jospeh K. Long's 'Extrasensory Ecology' (1977), Warwick Fox's (1990) work towards a 'transpersonal ecology,' Paul Devereux's (1996) 'Re-Visioning' of the Earth, and Mark A. Schroll's (2016; 2018) explorations of 'transpersonal ecosophy,' to name just a few. This book may be thought of as a contribution to these increasingly pertinent conversations.

The following introductory discussion will be broken down into four parts. Part 1, 'Belief, Experience and Behaviour' will look at how an engagement with alternative worldviews (such as religious and paranormal worldviews) might be useful for developing social, cultural and behavioural changes that can have a positive impact on the living planet. Part 2, 'Ecology and Anomalistics' lays out key concepts arising from these two fields of research and explores how they might relate. Part 3, 'Other Minds: Non-Human Intelligence' looks at some of the possible deeper ontological connections between ecology and the paranormal, specifically in relation to the notion of mind and intelligence in nature, and the processes by which it manifests and interacts with us. Finally, Part 4, 'Animism and Re-Connecting to Place,' considers animism as a model for engaging with the world and synthesising the ideas we have been exploring.

PART 1:

Belief, Experience and Behaviour

~

E nvironmental activists can sometimes be a bit squeamish about engaging with the faith communities of organised religions. Indeed, some scholars have argued that our current climate catastrophe has its roots in the doctrines of the major monotheistic denominations and their ideological influence on Western society and culture. In particular, commentators have highlighted the anthropocentric emphasis on human dominion over nature in monotheistic traditions (Toynbee, 1971). Religious worldviews have been used to justify human consumption of the Earth's finite resources. It is equally clear, however, that a large proportion of the blame for the ecological crisis also falls on the scientific and philosophical developments of the Enlightenment, and the technological and industrial developments of the eighteenth, nineteenth and twentieth centuries (Harding, 2009, pp. 31-35). Combined with the more recent digital revolutions of the twenty-first century, and our increasing absorption in screens of various kinds, we have long been on a trajectory of increasing *perceived* separation from nature.

Religion and science have both played their part in this unfortunate unfurling. As a category that effectively collapses the distinction between science and religion, however, the paranormal might suggest new directions for innovative thinking about our relationship with the ecological systems that surround, sustain and interpenetrate us – beyond mainstream scientific and religious perspectives. Indeed, Jeffrey Kripal suggests that the paranormal can be conceived as 'the *sacred* in transit

5

→ the social
in transit

from the religious and scientific registers into a parascientific or 'science mysticism' register' (Kripal, 2010). This 'middle-way' could provide new routes toward re-evaluating our relationship with the world around us. At any rate it is clear that there is an urgent need for this kind of boundary crossing work, especially if we hope to develop creative ways of reversing the damage that humanity has inflicted on the Earth. Neither science *nor* religion can tackle these problems alone. We will *all* have to pull together, across differences of culture and belief, if we are to stand a chance of keeping global temperatures below 1.5 degrees of change from pre-industrial levels, as research indicates that we must (IPCC, 2018).

The Greening of Religion

With approximately 2.2 billion Christians (32% of the world's population), 1.6 billion Muslims (23%), 1 billion Hindus (15%), nearly 500 million Buddhists (7%) and 14 million Jews (0.2%) (not to mention all those who participate in indigenous, folk, and new religious movements), by invoking the admittedly contested category of religion we are talking about vast numbers of people right across the planet – a demographic that encircles the entire globe (PEW, 2010). If even a fraction of these faith communities (as eclectic and diverse as they are) was to take up ecologically regenerative practices (such as permaculture, agroforestry, community garden projects, wildlife restoration, and so on) – *made meaningful to their lives by their respective cosmological models* – consider the huge impact it *could* have on the global system.

Fortunately, since the 1980s there has been a growing awareness of anthropogenic climate change among the major world religions, as well as a rise of religiously motivated ecological restoration projects. Some have referred to this phenomenon as the 'Greening of Religion' (Taylor, Wieren & Zaleha, 2016). In the build up to the United Nations Paris Climate Summit (COP21) in 2015, for example, statements were issued by representatives of the major world religions calling on members of their respective faith communities to take positive action on climate change (Chaplin, 2016). Pope Francis, for instance, announced his first encyclical – *Laudato Si'* ('Praise be to you') – which is expressly concerned with issues of sustainable development, runaway consumerism, global warming and environmental destruction. In the encyclical, Pope Francis (who takes his name from the patron saint of ecologists, St. Francis of Assisi) writes:

I urgently appeal ... for a new dialogue about how we are shaping the future of our planet. We need a conversation which includes everyone, since the environmental challenge we are undergoing, and its human roots, concern and affect us all (Pope Francis, 2015).

A central connecting feature of many of the statements issued by representatives of the major faith denominations is an emphasis on 'holistic, organic or relational images of the world' (Chaplin, 2016, p. 2), which highlight the interconnectedness of all life on Earth. The Hindu declaration on climate change, *Bumi Devi Yai Kah!*, for example, suggests that 'all elements of reality are 'organs of God's body ... the entire universe is to be looked upon as the energy of the Lord' (cited in Chaplin, 2016, p. 3). We will return to these themes throughout the chapters that follow, but suffice to say at this juncture that the potentials for both *affecting social and cultural change* and *practically regenerating ecosystems* framed in cosmological models such as these are enormous. Models of the universe as a living system imbued with intelligence and agency, of which we are all a part, are valuable alternatives to the mainstream models of reductionist and materialist science, which have actively contributed to the collapse of our global ecosystems (Plumwood, 2010).

Greening the Paranormal

Just as the faith communities of the world's religions represent an opportunity for climate change mitigation, so too might the 'paranormal milieu.' If recent surveys are anything to go by, belief in (and experiences of) the paranormal are remarkably common in the Western world (Castro, Burrows & Wooffitt, 2014; Bader, Mencken & Baker, 2017). The Chapman University Survey of American Fears (2018), for instance, suggests that paranormal beliefs are actually on the rise in the United States. The survey suggests that 57.7% of the US population believe that 'Places can be haunted by spirits,' an increase of 11.1% since 2016, and that 75.9% (approximately ¾) of the US population holds some form of paranormal belief. Interestingly, the Chapman Survey of American Fears also revealed that just 53% of the population is 'Afraid of Global Warming and Climate Change.' Based on these figures it would appear that there are more paranormal believers in the US than people worried about the damage we have inflicted on the global ecosystem. Is there

7

a way of redressing the balance somewhat? What if the paranormal demographic could also be tapped into for climate change mitigation?

Just as we might talk about the 'Greening of Religion,' maybe we could also talk of a 'Greening of the Paranormal'? What if every time Sasquatch research groups went on an expedition into the wilderness they also planted trees to rebuild habitat, or lake monster researchers worked to improve water quality, or when ghost hunting organisations conducted vigils in abandoned hospitals they also scattered wildflower seeds to enhance biodiversity? What if UFO spotters set up community gardens for late night star gazing? Consider the possibilities. On a very practical level, appealing to the sheer number of paranormal enthusiasts out there to get involved in regenerative efforts *could* yield very real positive outcomes. As fun as this sounds, however, this is not really what I am talking about – I am talking about something much *deeper*.

Religious spectrum – doctrine – experience

Personal Religion and Spirituality

There is also reason, I would suggest, to try to engage with the *other* end of the religious spectrum (if we consider religion as a spectrum of phenomena ranging from doctrine on the one hand, to religious experience on the other) – what the psychologist and philosopher William James (1842-1910) called 'personal religion,' or 'the feelings, acts, and experiences of individual[s] in their solitude, so far as they apprehend themselves to stand in relation to whatever they may consider the divine' (James, 2004, p. 39). The appeal of this broad definition of personal religion is that it also encompasses atheistic and non-religious worldviews, which may be conceived as a *rejection* of the divine (however it is defined). This element of religion (or the rejection thereof) does not rely on doctrine for its power, but rather draws its vitality from direct personal experience and individual introspection. Indeed, it is often the personal experience of religion that forms the basis of doctrine in the first place. Personal religion, therefore, provides a framework and a context through which *individuals understand their relationship with the world around them.* We could call it 'worldview.'

Another way of framing this element of religion (if we can even call it such) is 'spirituality.' A useful definition of spirituality is offered by David Hay and Rebecca Nye in their examination of children's spirituality, where they explain that spirituality is the 'potential to be much more deeply aware of ourselves and our intimate relationship with everything that is not ourselves' (2006, p. 22). More than doctrinal belief, spirituality and personal religion are informed by personal *experience*, and as a consequence take on a much more heterodox nature – often incorporating a range of different ideas and beliefs beyond those found in official religious texts and teachings. The sociologist Jeff Astley refers to this as an 'ordinary theology' (Astley, 2002). Framed in this way it is clear to see why it is so important that we try to connect the urgent need for ecological regeneration with the religious and spiritual level of thinking – it offers a very direct route toward re-dressing our *immediate relationship* with the world around us at a fundamental, highly personal level. It has the potential to re-frame our relationship with the world.

→ link to presence - (meditative)

Dark Green Religion

There is also a strand of the magico-religious that emerges not from the traditions of organised religion, but from direct engagement with ecology and environmental activism. Bron Taylor presents a thorough exploration of this phenomenon in his book *Dark Green Religion* (2010). Taylor explains that Dark Green Religion is 'generally deep ecological, biocentric, or ecocentric, considering all species to be intrinsically valuable ... apart from their usefulness to human beings.' He further writes:

> This value system is generally (1) based on a felt kinship with the rest of life, often derived from a Darwinian understanding that all forms of life have evolved from a common ancestor and are therefore related; (2) accompanied by feelings of humility and a corresponding critique of human moral superiority, often inspired or reinforced by a science-based cosmology that reveals how tiny human beings are in the universe; and (3) reinforced by a metaphysics of interconnection and the idea of interdependence (mutual influence and reciprocal dependence) found in the sciences, especially in ecology and physics (Taylor, 2010, p. 13).

Taylor goes on to distinguish between four dominant frameworks adopted by Dark Green Religionists:

9

	Animism	Gaian Earth Religion
Supernaturalism	Spiritual Animism.	Gaian Spirituality.
Naturalism	Naturalistic Animism.	Gaian Naturalism.

(TAYLOR, 2010, P. 15)

These categories are not always distinct, and frequently merge and overlap with one another, but they are useful in highlighting core perspectives of different camps within the environmental milieu. In this context 'animism' refers to 'a shared perception that beings or entities in nature have their own integrity, ways of being, personhood, and even intelligence,' which may be interpreted supernaturally (i.e. as spiritual beings), or naturalistically (as intelligence without supernatural connotations) (Taylor, 2010, p. 15). The reference to Gaia indicates an understanding of 'the biosphere (universe or cosmos) [as] alive or conscious, or at least by metaphor and analogy [resembling] organisms with their many interdependent parts' (2010, p. 16). Again, Gaia can be understood supernaturally (as a teleological Gaian consciousness), or naturalistically (as global homeostasis through material systems). We will return to a discussion of animism and the Gaia hypothesis later in this introduction.

Mystical Experience and the Numinous

Many (though by no means all) of those who Taylor gathers together under the banner of Dark Green Religion came to their respective positions through what *could* be described as peak, mystical, religious or paranormal experiences in nature. Aldo Leopold (1887-1948), widely regarded as the father of modern wildlife conservation, for example, experienced a radical transformation of perspective following an encounter with a wolf he had shot. As a wilderness warden, Leopold had been responsible for culling wolves and bears in national parks, a task he had not thought twice about until he came face to face with one of his victims:

We reached the old wolf in time to watch a fierce green fire dying in her eyes. I realized then, and have known ever since, that there was something new to me in those eyes – something known only to her and to the mountain. I was young then, and full of trigger-itch; I thought that because fewer wolves meant more deer, that no wolves would mean hunters' paradise. But after seeing the green fire die, I sensed that neither the wolf nor the mountain agreed with such a view (Leopold, 1949).

A connection between transformative religious and mystical experience and the natural world has long been recognised in the scholarly literature of religion (Marshall, 2005). Indeed, one of the major categories of mystical experience proposed by the scholar of mysticism W.T. Stace (1886-1967) – *extrovertive* mystical experience – specifically refers to mystical experiences that are either initiated by, or which transfigure, the natural landscape and environment in which the experiencer finds themselves:

extrovertive

> The extrovertive mystic with his physical senses continues to perceive the same world of trees and hills and tables and chairs as the rest of us. But he sees these objects transfigured in such manner that the Unity shines through them ... the extrovertive experience is sensory-intellectual in so far as it still perceives physical objects but is nonsensuous and nonintellectual in so far as it perceives them as "all one" (Stace, 1960, p. 15).

Very often these ecstatic experiences give rise to a renewed vision of the Earth and an enhanced sense of connection to the natural world, both physically and spiritually. The archives of the Alister Hardy Religious Experience Research Centre (RERC), housed at the University of Wales Trinity Saint David in Lampeter, contain over 6,000 accounts of self-submitted religious experiences. Sir Alister Hardy (1896-1985), himself a marine biologist and ecologist, was convinced of the importance of religious experience in the biological and cultural evolution of humankind, and originally established his research centre at Manchester College, Oxford, to collect first-hand reports for detailed study. Many of these accounts refer to 'extrovertive' experiences of transcendence and connection to the natural world. The following are just a couple of particularly vivid descriptions of self-reported religious experiences initiated through interaction with landscape and ecology from the archive:

As I watched, suddenly the whole countryside changed and everything in it, without exception, simply glowed with numinous light – it seemed no longer to be lit by the sun but by its own internal radiance. Sunlight was not reflected from it, but I myself and everything else seemed to have become light – which now inter-penetrated and shone through our previously dense physical forms ... The whole scene shone with an extraordinary golden glow, which included the sky and the atmosphere itself.

RERC Reference: 10003, Male, no details.

As we conversed the situation became unreal. The plants and shrubs and the three pine trees in a copse...became unreal. And yet they were more real than I had ever seen them in the 3 1/2 years I had lived there. Instead of merging into a general familiar pattern, each item of plant, shrub and tree, stood out singularly, vivid, vibrant...The whole area became something on its own, apart from the rest. The whole area became something I had never seen before. I became filled with a feeling of elation and well-being such as I have never before or since experienced ... I felt that I had seen Nature as it really is.

RERC Reference: 002780, Male, 1941

For more on mystical experiences in nature, and different frameworks for understanding them, see Paul Marshall's work for a comprehensive survey of the field (2005). With these extraordinary experiences we are entering the territory that German theologian Rudolf Otto (1869-1937) called the *numinous* – the non-dogmatic, non-rational, experiential, essence of religion (Otto, 1958). Famously, Otto made a distinction between two polarities of the numinous – the *mysterium fascinans* – the element of the numinous that is fascinating, beautiful, and draws us in – and the *mysterium tremendum* – the terrifying, repulsive and yet awe inspiring end of the numinous spectrum. The accounts of mystical experiences recounted above would certainly fall into the category of the *mysterium fascinans*, but many people also report darker and/or stranger experiences that, in the Western idiom, are often referred to as 'paranormal.'

12

Defining the Paranormal (Again): High Strangeness

I have explored definitions of the supernatural and paranormal in some depth elsewhere (Hunter, 2012, pp. 21-27), but generally take it in the sense of psychical researcher F.W.H. Myers' (1843-1901) term 'supernormal,' referring to phenomena 'beyond the scope of current scientific understanding.' For the purposes of the following discussion, however, it is worth noting that there are benefits in keeping the category of the paranormal as open and as broad as possible. If we are too restrictive in our definition and ignore the overlaps between, for example, the (relatively) scientifically acceptable phenomena associated with *psi* – a scientific term used in parapsychology to refer to telepathy (mind-to-mind communication) and psychokinesis (mind-matter interaction) – and the much less respectable phenomena associated with UFOs, cryptids, faeries, mediumship, religious miracles and the like, then we will inevitably be missing out on a large and significant part of the puzzle. Indeed, any perusal of the paranormal literature quickly reveals that all of these anomalous phenomena are inseparable components of a much deeper mystery. Journalist and Fortean writer John Keel (1930-2009) is famous amongst paranormal researchers for pointing out deep connections between different paranormal phenomena, which he suggests could indicate a 'trickster-like' consciousness underlying all manner of spectral manifestations:

> We are confronted with a series of manifestations that indicate that the human mind can be programmed and reprogrammed like a computer, that human senses can be made to see anything and hear anything at the whim of the phenomenon, that our reality itself can be distorted by some mysterious force. When you study all of the manifestations, it becomes clear that the force has a childlike intelligence – capricious, often irrational (Keel, 2013, p. 11).

Robbie Graham's (2017) recent edited collection, featuring diverse voices from the field of UFOlogy, also demonstrates a range of interconnections between UFO, alien abduction and other paranormal experiences and occult phenomena. UFO experiencers and alien abductees often report a whole array of other strange experiences following their encounters, including interactions with the dead, poltergeist activity, and telepathic dreams, and it is not uncommon for Bigfoot witnesses to report telepathic communication with the elusive hairy hominid, or to have UFO experiences of their own. Faery lore also seems to overlap with all of the above in a number of ways, a fact first alluded to in Jacques Vallee's 1969 *Passport to Magonia* (Vallee, 2015), and more recently taken up by Fortean folklorist Joshua Cutchin (2015). As if to make matters yet more complicated, encounters with all manner of alien entities are also very common in psychedelic experiences (Strassman, 2000), as are a variety of other psi phenomena, including telepathy, clairvoyance and psychokinesis (Luke & Kittenis, 2005; Locke & Kelly, 2009), and occasionally even mediumship and possession (Luke, 2014).

The list of thematic overlaps in the paranormal could go on. Suffice to say that if we want to understand the paranormal we need to embrace its *weirdness* and its *complexity*. A reductionist approach does not seem to work. Although it is tempting to try to split the paranormal up into academically acceptable and unacceptable portions, in reality it simply is not possible. One leads to the other. Cryptids, faeries, UFOs, telepathy, psychokinesis, religious and mystical experience, psychedelic entity encounters and so on, are all fundamentally interconnected elements of a broader phenomenon, and any approach that attempts to reduce this complexity can only move us further away from where we ultimately want to be. In other words, the paranormal is perhaps best understood in a wider comparative context (Kripal, 2018), and as something much greater than its individual component parts.

The term 'High Strangeness' is often employed in paranormal research to refer to experiences, events and phenomena that are so bizarre that they evade easy classification and explanation. The concept derives from the work of astronomer and pioneering UFOlogist Dr. J Allen Hynek (1910-1986). In his book *The UFO Experience: A Scientific Inquiry* (1974), Hynek explains his 'Strangeness Rating':

> A light seen in the night sky the trajectory of which cannot be ascribed to a balloon, aircraft, etc., would nonetheless have a low Strangeness Rating because there is only one strange thing about the report to explain: its motion. A report of a weird craft that descended within 100 feet of a car on a lonely road, caused the car's engine to die, its radio to stop, and its lights to go out, left marks on the nearby ground, and appeared to be under intelligent control receives a high Strangeness Rating because it contains a number of separate very strange items, each of which outrages common sense (Hynek, 1974, p. 42).

Computer scientist and UFOlogist Jacques Vallee later expanded Hynek's notion of a strangeness rating, elaborating as many as *seven* categories of strangeness (Vallee, 1977, pp. 114-119). It is this element of 'strangeness' that characterises paranormal experiences and phenomena. For the purposes of this book, then, we will take a very broad view of the paranormal – a *High Strangeness perspective* – taking in both those subjects which are more academically respectable, such as laboratory research on psi and research on mystical and religious experience, as well as those subjects that are right on the very fringes of academic thinking, such as alien abductions, cryptid encounters and more. Indeed, I would argue that it is precisely the *most unusual* (and so least respectable) – the *Highly Strange* – accounts of paranormal experiences that we should be investigating, because they raise the most questions and challenge our established worldviews most strongly. In other words, it is High Strangeness that stands the most chance of shaking up the *status quo*.

PART 2:

Ecology and Anomalistics

The Ecosystem

The field of ecology – defined as the study of the relationships between living organisms and their physical environment – is a relatively new area of scientific research. Its roots as a legitimate field of scientific study go back to the nineteenth century, though it did not reach maturity as a discipline in its own right until the middle of the twentieth century (Dickinson & Murphy, 2007, pp. 8-15). A key concept emerging from the study of ecology is the notion of the 'ecosystem.' We will be encountering this term frequently throughout the chapters that follow, so it is important that we take a moment to unpack it and consider its wider relevance to our discussion. Eugene Odum (1913-2002), one of the pioneers of the science of ecology, defines the ecosystem as referring to:

> ... a unit of biological organization made up of all of the organisms in a given area (that is, "community") interacting with the physical environment so that a flow of energy leads to characteristic trophic structure and material cycles within the system (Odum, 1966, p. 262).

In other words, an ecosystem is a complex system of interactions between living organisms (plants, animals, microbes, fungi and more), and the 'non-living' environment (water, minerals, gasses, sunlight, and so on). These interactions include the exchange of energy and nutrients through 'food webs' (Dickinson & Murphy, 2007, p. 11). Plants (whether we are talking about shrubs, trees, seaweed or phytoplankton) are known as 'primary producers' and capture energy from the sun by photosynthesis. It is through plants that energy enters into the food chain. Plants are consumed by herbivores, who in turn may be consumed by predators. Thus, the sun's energy is shared out amongst biological organisms in an ecosystem, gradually decreasing as it moves higher up the food chain (ibid., p. 13). Energy and nutrients are also constantly cycling around this system through processes of *growth* and *decay*. Energy, nutrients and carbon collected and stored by trees, plants and animals are slowly released back into the system through the action of decomposers such as bacteria and fungi. Above all, therefore, ecosystems are all about *relationships* – relationships between organisms, as well as relationships between organisms and the non-living environment. Everything is connected through networks of reciprocal exchange.

Another major concept in ecology is the notion of 'succession' in ecosystems. Succession refers to the processes by which living organisms colonise and transform environmental niches to suit their own needs, as well as the needs of successive species. Odum defines succession as referring to three key parameters:

> (i) It is an orderly process of community development that is reasonably directional...(ii) It results from modification of the physical environment by the community; that is, succession is community-controlled even though the physical environment...often sets limits as to how far development can go. (iii) It culminates in a stabilized ecosystem in which maximum biomass...and symbiotic function between organisms are maintained per unit of available energy flow (Odum, 1966, p. 263).

The organisms that make up an ecosystem are, therefore, active in transforming local environmental conditions to suit their own needs, as well as the needs of other species. Hardy pioneer species colonise bare land and transform the structure of soils, which in turn creates new conditions for other less hardy species to inhabit. *Co-operation* between species in an ecosystem, therefore, seems to be essential (though we cannot ignore the very real role of *competition*). Indeed, organisms often work *mutually* (where one species acts as a host for another, for example the remora fish, which feeds on the parasites of sharks), and sometimes *symbiotically* with one another (where two organisms live an entirely interconnected life, see below on mycorrhizal fungi) to create optimum conditions for *biodiversity*. This observation seems to run counter to the mainstream reductionist Darwinian concept of competition and 'survival of the fittest' as the sole drivers of evolution (Dickinson & Murphy, 2007, p. 24).

A classic example of this kind of interspecies co-operation is seen in the relationship between trees and mycorrhizal fungi in forest ecosystems. Mycorrhizal fungi (very fine filamentous fungi), are associated with the roots of 90% of all plant species. They interface with the root systems of trees and plants to essentially extend the tree's access to water and nutrients in the soil. The fungi help the tree to access these vital resources in exchange for sugars that the tree produces through photosynthesis, as fungi do not photosynthesize themselves. This is a reciprocal relationship that is mutually beneficial. Mycorrhizal fungi effectively form a network in the soil, enabling communication and nutrient transfer between trees and other plant species, sometimes referred to as the 'wood-wide web' (Bonfante & Genre, 2010). Mycologist Paul Stamets has suggested that the mycelial networks that interconnect woodland ecosystems provide a substrate for intelligence, much like the neurological structures of the brain and nervous system. He writes:

> I see mycelium as the living network that manifests the natural intelligence imagined by Gaia theorists. The mycelium is an exposed sentient membrane, aware and responsive to changes in its environment. As hikers, deer, or insects walk across these sensitive filamentous nets, they leave impressions, and mycelia sense and respond to these movements. A complex and resourceful structure for sharing information, mycelium can adapt and evolve through the ever-changing forces of nature (Stamets, 2005, p. 4-6).

Once optimum conditions have been achieved in a particular ecological niche, the ecosystem reaches a state of *climax*, which is maintained through cycles and feedback loops that lead to a relatively stable state of *homeostasis* (Dickinson & Murphy, 2007, p. 9). James Lovelock's famous 'Gaia hypothesis' is essentially an extension of this general observation about ecosystems to the whole Earth system. The Gaia hypothesis, developed by Lovelock in the 1970s, suggests that the Earth itself is a single living system, composed of multiple inter-related parts (including the chemical and mineral composition of the Earth, as well as all organic life forms) which work together to maintain a stable global system (Lovelock, 2000). In essence, Lovelock's hypothesis points to the idea that the Earth is a vast self-regulating organism. Ecopsychologist Theodore Roszak explains:

> ... living things, once they appeared on our planet, took charge of the global environment in a creative way. They became fully fledged partners in the shaping of the Earth, its rocks and water and soil ... The goal of life is global homeostasis, and toward this end it transforms the planet into what might be viewed as a single self-regulating organism (Roszak, 1993, p. 147).

Lovelock attracted a great deal of criticism from the scientific establishment because of his invocation of Gaia, the ancient Greek goddess embodying the Earth. In particular it was the teleological (purposeful) implications that go with the idea of Gaia as a *divine being* that the scientific community vehemently opposed – the idea that global homeostasis could be an expression of intelligence directing natural processes. In his 1982 book *The Extended Phenotype*, for example, outspoken atheist and evolutionary biologist Richard Dawkins argued against the Gaia hypothesis on the grounds that it seems to present a top-down teleological explanation for global homeostasis. He writes:

> A network of relationships there may be, but it is made up of small, self interested components. Entities that pay the costs of furthering the well being of the ecosystem as a whole will tend to reproduce themselves less successfully than rivals that exploit their public-spirited colleagues, and contribute nothing to the general welfare (Dawkins, 1982, p. 237).

Dawkins' view differs from that of Lovelock primarily on the grounds that the former presents a reductionist view based on the competition of selfishly motivated individuals, while the latter presents an holistic view based on top-down co-operation, directed towards a specific goal. This is an ongoing debate in ecological science, and is often referred to as the 'holism-reductionism debate' (Bergandi, 2011). To counter such criticisms Lovelock went to great pains to explain away Gaia's apparent teleological drive, by stating that Gaia was simply a metaphor, and

holism- reductionism debate

top down vs. self interest

certainly not a theological statement or indication that the Earth is in some sense a conscious living being:

> Neither Lynn Margulis nor I have ever proposed a teleological hypothesis. Nowhere in our writings do we express the idea that planetary self-regulation is purposeful, or involves foresight or planning by the biota. It is true that our early statements about Gaia were imprecise and open to misinterpretation, but this does not justify the persistent almost dogmatic, criticism that our hypothesis is teleological (Lovelock, 1990).

Nevertheless, the image of the Earth as Gaia – as a self-regulating intelligence of which we are all a part – has been hugely influential in popular ecological culture. As noted by Bron Taylor, the study of ecology tends to lead toward models of the environment that emphasise 'interconnection and the idea of interdependence (mutual influence and reciprocal dependence),' as essential features of the natural world (2010, p. 13). What ecology provides, therefore, is a scientific bedrock on which we might be able to construct a 'new vision of reality.' Fritjof Capra explains that this new vision of reality is 'based on an awareness of the essential interrelatedness and interdependence of all phenomena – physical, biological, psychological, social and cultural. It transcends current disciplinary boundaries and will be pursued within new institutions' (Capra, 1985, p 285).

We do not have the space here to delve more fully into the science of ecology and its implications for our worldview (this will be taken up more fully in Hunter, 2019), but suffice to say that the picture of interrelatedness and interdependence provided by the observation of ecosystems serves the vital function of reminding us (as human beings) that we are also enmeshed within the vast living system of the Earth – that we are inseparable components of the global system, and that our actions have a very real impact on everything else that shares the planet with us. Ecological thinking effectively breaks down the Cartesian separation of the observer and the observed, which has dominated Western science since the seventeenth century, and relocates us within a wider network of relationships. This would seem to be a good point to shift our focus towards anomalistics, and to begin drawing in the threads.

Anomalistics

It is a commonly reported consequence of several different types of extraordinary experience that the experiencer comes away from their encounter with an enhanced sense of connection to the environment and the world around them. Harvard psychiatrist John Mack's (1929-2004) work on the alien abduction phenomenon, as just one example of a particular variety of extraordinary experience, highlighted the frequent centrality of the eco-crisis theme in many abduction experience narratives (echoing the earlier concern of the 'Space Brothers' for global destruction, as communicated to the contactees of the 1950s). Summarising the prevalence of ecological themes in the abduction narratives he investigated, Mack writes:

> It seems impossible to avoid the observation that the alien abduction phenomenon is occurring in the context of a planetary ecological crisis that is reaching critical proportions and that information about this situation is often powerfully conveyed by the alien beings to the experiencers (Mack, 1995, pp. 434-435).

Individuals who claim to have had contact with extra-terrestrial intelligences, therefore, may go on to develop a closer relationship to their terrestrial ecology, and to develop a new sense of their place in the cosmos following their experience. Similarly, Ring & Valarino (2006) have noted parallel effects amongst Near-Death Experiencers, who often develop a 'heightened sensitivity to the ecological health of the planet' (p. 125) following their experience. Changing patterns of behaviour and worldview have also been noted following other forms of extraordinary experience, for example: 'lifetime experience with psychedelics in particular may ... contribute to people's pro-environmental behavior by changing their self-construal in terms of an incorporation of the natural world' (Forstmann & Sagioglou, 2017). At face value, then, there appears to be a connection between anomalous and extraordinary experiences of various kinds and the development of ecological consciousness.

After over 130 years of concerted scientific research into the paranormal, beginning with the foundation of the Society for Psychical Research in 1882, we are now in the position to draw together several important observations about the nature of paranormal experiences and phenomena. They do not, however, present a particularly neat or tidy picture of the paranormal. What they do seem to suggest is that what we call the paranormal arises through complex interactions between numerous different biological, physical, psychological, social, cultural and non-physical processes. In other words, that the paranormal, like the elements of an ecosystem, is interconnected with countless other subtle processes. The following points briefly summarise some of the key findings from parapsychology, which could be revealing of how ecology and the paranormal intersect:

- The evidence for the existence of psi (telepathy, clairvoyance, precognition and psychokinesis) is highly statistically significant (Radin, 1997; 2006). If these phenomena and faculties are *real*, then our models of reality should reflect this fact. If they exist, then we would expect them to occur in other areas of ecology, beyond the human sphere. The work of Rupert Sheldrake (2000) is suggestive that psi is not confined to human beings, but may also be a capacity possessed by the animal and plant kingdoms as well.

- Dream states have been found to facilitate psi functioning in human subjects (Ullman *et al.*, 1977). What happens when we add into this mix recent findings that 'sleep-like' states have been detected in species as different from humans as cuttlefish (Frank *et al.*, 2012), and trees (Wohlleben, 2016, pp. 43-44), amongst others. If these non-humans sleep, might they not also dream, and if they dream can they also communicate using psi? What are the implications here for understanding societies that communicate with plants and animals through dreams and other non-ordinary states of consciousness?

- Intention seems to play significant roles in the production of psi effects under laboratory conditions (Radin, 1997; 2006; 2013). Belief, expectation and culture also play a role in modulating – but not necessarily creating – paranormal experiences (de Martino, 1975; Batcheldor, 1984). Cultures with different expectations may, therefore, make certain kinds of experiences more or less common for people living within those cultures. A culture that holds open the possibility of communion between human and non-human intelligence may, therefore, facilitate such experiences, while a culture that denies the possibility will stifle such experiences.

- Anomalous experiences have distinctive neurophysiological correlates. Researchers have long known of the role of altered states of consciousness in the mediation of religious and paranormal experiences (Luke & Kittenis, 2005), but recent developments in brain imaging technologies are beginning to reveal clear neurophysiological differences between different altered states, enabling us to differentiate between pathological conditions and mediumship, for example (Krippner & Friedman, 2009). These findings reveal that whether or not mediums, shamans, psychics, or other magico-religious practitioners are in communication with 'real spirits,' they are undergoing genuine neurophysiological changes when they enter into their trance states. *Something is going on.*

- Anomalous Information Reception (AIR) does seem to take place with certain individuals – mediums, psychics – even under rigidly controlled experimental conditions (Beischel *et al.,* 2015). This raises the question of where this information comes from – could it be information from discarnate sources (i.e. spirits), or is it the product of some kind of 'super-psi' ability? If there *are* discarnate sources of information, and if human personality really does survive the death of the physical body, then what are the implications for the other forms of life – animals, plants, fungi, bacteria – that share the Earth with us? Do they also have spirits, or souls? Is it possible to establish communication?

There are also insights from the social-scientific study of the paranormal that are of relevance to our discussion. Although parapsychological research does seem to indicate the existence of objective psi phenomena (i.e. of something more than delusion that can be objectively investigated in the laboratory), it is also clear that the expression of psi *is* mediated by psychological, social and cultural factors. There is always, therefore, a subjective element to psi phenomena as they manifest in the real world.

In my own research on trance and physical mediumship in Bristol (Hunter, 2018a), I came to the conclusion that the séance is a ritualised performance through which aspects of 'non-human intelligence' are recognised and developed into communicating entities. Unusual behaviours exhibited while the medium is in an altered state of consciousness (trance), such as spasmodic movements, twitches, and so on, are picked up by the circle leader as evidence of an intelligence

23

attempting to communicate. These behaviours are given attention and nurtured until a dialogue is established, and over a period of weeks or months the intelligence is able to express its personhood more fully and distinct from the medium, becoming a real social agent in the process. In a sense, we could say that the process of manifesting spirits in the séance is the equivalent to permaculture principle number 1: 'Observe and Interact,' and this has implications for our understanding of the way that non-human intelligences can be known and interacted with in other areas of the natural world. It is through *interaction* that non-human intelligences manifest and become communicable with. We have to look for the signs and nurture a conversation.

The paranormal is, then, *co-created*. It is an interaction between an objective other and a participating subjectivity. With these key points in mind, the next sensible step would seem to be to further contextualise the paranormal in the wider perspective of ecological systems (of which we are all a part), and to further enmesh the paranormal into the systems of plant, animal and 'other' life and intelligence that surround us. This further contextualisation of paranormal research is not necessarily a new idea, and certainly has precedents in the history of parapsychology. For example, Franz Anton Mesmer's (1784-1814) notion of 'animal magnetism' as a force that flows through and connects all lifeforms (Alvarado, 2010), biologist Hans Driesch's (1867-1941) vitalist interpretation of parapsychological phenomena (Driesch, 1933), and Rupert Sheldrake's research on morphic fields and his 'New Science of Life' (Sheldrake, 2009), to name just a few. My hope in attempting to re-focus on the wider ecological context of the paranormal is that this discussion might serve to provide a fresh perspective for those engaged in the study of the paranormal (in whatever capacity), while also presenting new avenues for those involved in the study of ecology and the application of ecological thinking to tackling the planetary eco-crisis.

PART 3:

Other Minds: The Non-Human

~

We should ... make a distinction between alien intelligence and intelligent aliens ... That alien intelligence exists is indisputable ... and although whether intelligent aliens exist or not in some other part of the cosmos is another question, the demonstrable existence of such intelligence at least opens one's mind to the *idea* of the existence of intelligent aliens (Holroyd, 1979, p. 10).

Acommon thread underlying both anomalistics and ecology is the issue of trying to comprehend non-human intelligence. Both research areas are confronted with the challenge of understanding different forms of mind and intelligence and making sense of their motivations – from gods, goddesses, angels, poltergeists, faeries, UFOnauts, spirits of the dead, and DMT entities in the context of anomalistics (to name just a few), through to animal and plant sentience, the long-range strategies of trees, fungi and mycelium networks, the self-regulating capabilities of the global ecosystem, and so on in ecology. Is it a co-incidence that paranormal researchers such as Charles Fort (1874-1932) and John Keel (1930-2009), who spent their lives and careers investigating the anomalous, came to consider that there might be a greater intelligence underlying the many diverse manifestations of paranormal phenomena, while researchers in the parallel field of ecology also point to similar ideas in their interpretations of ecosystem dynamics – especially in the context of Gaia hypothesis

> Trickster
Intelligence –
see Antistructure

25

and its various interpretations? Consider, for example, the similarities between the following extract from John Keel and the explanation of the Gaia hypothesis presented above:

> It is quite possible – even probable – that the Earth is really a living organism, and that it in turn is a part of an even larger organism, that whole constellations are alive, transmitting and receiving energy to and from other celestial energy sources. Up and down the energy scale the whole macrocosm is functioning on levels of reality that will always be totally beyond our comprehension. We are a part of it all, just as the microbe swimming on the microscope slide is unknowingly a part of our dismal reality, and, like the microbe, we lack the perceptive equipment necessary to view the larger whole. Even if we could view it, we could not understand it (Keel, 2013, p. 248).

Could the insights of paranormal researchers like John Keel be glimpses of the same vast intelligence revealed by ecology? If the Earth really is a vast living organism with some form of intelligence, agency and intentionality, then it is worth taking a moment to examine a little more deeply what we mean by these terms. In particular we will focus on the question of intelligence – what it is, and how we recognise and interact with it.

In his book *Intelligence in Nature* (2006), anthropologist Jeremy Narby points out that definitions of intelligence have tended to be anthropocentric – defined in terms of human capacities such as problem solving, tool use, symbolic thought, culture, and so on (Narby, 2006, p. 43). Research is increasingly demonstrating, however, that members of non-human species also possess similar attributes. These similarities are all the more impressive when found in species that are very distantly removed from us. Tool use, for example, has been observed amongst a diverse range of marine animals, including 'fish, cephalopods, mammals, crabs, urchins and possibly gastropods' (Mann & Patterson, 2013). Evidence of socially learned culture has been found amongst 'humans plus a handful of species of birds, one or two whales, and two species of fish' (Laland & Hoppitt, 2003, p. 151). Findings such as these suggest that attributes we have associated with intelligence are much more ubiquitous throughout nature than we have often wanted to admit. In keeping with my suggestion that we should look to High Strangeness to revitalise our worldviews, the new science of plant intelligence – which presents such a *radically*

[handwritten marginal note: Anthropocentric views of intelligence]

26

different understanding to the popular mainstream view of plants – could well lead to a total re-evaluation of our relationship with our 'primary producers.'

Plant Intelligence

> The study of plant intelligence points up a very interesting aspect of research on intelligence in general: how difficult it is for us humans to understand living systems that think differently from us. Indeed, we only seem able to appreciate intelligences very similar to ours (Mancuso & Viola, 2015, p. 146)

In spite of the dependence of the animal kingdom upon plant life on Earth – it is plants, after all, who draw down energy from the sun making it usable by animals and humans alike, and who maintain stable atmospheric conditions for us to breath – humankind has had a tendency (at least in the dominant Western culture) to disregard plants as unconscious *objects* – devoid of subjectivity and personhood – which we have a right to dominate and bend to our will. In their book *Brilliant Green* (2015), plant intelligence researchers Mancuso and Viola call for a radical shift in the way we think about plants. They explain:

> ... a compelling body of research shows that higher-order plants really are "intelligent": able to receive signals from their environment, process the information, and devise solutions adaptive to their own survival. What's more they manifest a kind of "swarm intelligence" that enables them to behave not as an individual but as a multitude (Mancuso & Viola, 2015, p. 5).

Indeed, plants perform all manner of behaviours that were previously assumed to be hallmarks of the so-called 'higher animals.' Peter Wohlleben's book *The Hidden Life of Trees* (2016), for example, collects together evidence suggesting that trees are in fact social beings who live in communities. They look after their young and elderly by sharing out nutrients amongst themselves (even the stumps of long fallen trees continue to be supported with nutrients by the rest of the community), and communicate with one another through complex chemical signalling and mycorrhizal networks.

In a remarkable book that very clearly blurs the boundaries between shamanism, the paranormal and the science of plant intelligence, Monica Gagliano's *Thus Spoke the Plant* (2018) documents and details how her own interactions with plant consciousness – through dreams, ritual dieting and vision quests – have guided her mainstream scientific research on plant intelligence into novel, even revolutionary, new domains. Gagliano's research has demonstrated, for example, that plants are capable of learning and remembering (Gagliano *et al.*, 2014), that plants have the capacity to hear sounds (Gagliano *et al.*, 2017), and that they might also use sound for communication (Gagliano, 2013). Gagliano's research has helped to solidify the newly emerging field of 'plant neurobiology' (Brenner *et al.*, 2006), a field of research that was (much as with parapsychology's relationship with academic psychology), considered 'fringe' research by mainstream biology, until recently.

Findings such as these, not to mention Gagliano's experiential communication with members of what she calls 'the vegetal kingdom' (2018, p. 1), point towards interesting new ways of thinking about the plant-human communications reported by groups such as the Findhorn Foundation in Scotland. The Findhorn Garden is an organic garden established in the late 1960s by a group who claimed to be in communication with supernatural beings variously conceived as God, *devas* and elemental spirits (each with their own role and function), who guided the planting and maintenance of the garden with extraordinary results. Despite being situated on relatively poor growing land, the Findhorn garden was abundant with fruit and (often oversized) vegetables, which the group attributed to their guidance from the devas and elementals:

> While the devas may be considered the "architects" of plant forms, the nature spirits or elementals, such as gnomes and fairies, may be seen as the "craftsmen," using the blueprint and energy channelled to them by the devas to build up the plant form (The Findhorn Foundation, 1975, pp. 58-59)

The findings emerging from the new field of plant neurobiology also call for a re-appraisal of the work of polygrapher Cleve Backster (1924-2013) and his investigations into plant consciousness. Backster's interest began in 1966 when he recorded polygraph (lie-detector) readings indicative of emotional arousal in house plants after watering a *dracaena massangeara* pot-plant in his office, to which he had attached electrodes

28

and a galvanometer (Tompkins & Bird, 2002, p. 4). Backster was so intrigued by his findings that he went on to develop numerous innovative experiments to test for further emotional states in plants, culminating in 1968 with the publication of his influential paper 'Evidence of Primary Perception in Plant Life' in the *International Journal of Parapsychology* (Backster, 1968). In the paper Backster summarises his methods and findings, and presents his primary perception hypothesis:

> The author proposes that there exists a yet undefined primary perception in plant life … and that this perception facility in plants can be shown to function independently of human involvement … this perception facility may be part of a primary sensory system capable of functioning at cell level (Backster, 1968, pp. 333-345).

As if to make matters yet more complicated, Backster also claimed that his experiments provided clear evidence of mind-to-mind communication between humans and plants. Backster's plants seemed to react to his thoughts, emotions and intentions even before they had been expressed in the physical world. Peter Tompkins and Christopher Bird (2018) provide a thorough overview of the pioneering work of researchers at the borderlands of parapsychology and plant physiology in the 1960s and 70s. Could it be possible that research in plant neurobiology, the experiments in plant memory and communication of Monica Gagliano, the polygraph experiments of Cleve Backster, the long shamanistic traditions of plant communication, and the early work of the Findhorn Foundation are all pointing towards a single truth? That plants are radically more conscious than we have given them credit for in the materialist west.

The Paranormal Mind

Both anomalistics and ecology are concerned with trying to develop ways of thinking *beyond the human* (a task that anthropology is now also embracing with the so-called 'Non-human turn,' see, for example, Kohn, 2013), so that we can better understand and co-exist with the non-human (in whatever form it takes). What lessons can we learn from these other forms of consciousness? Is there anything that might be added to our understanding of, for example, the unusual phenomena associated with so-called 'window areas,' such as the Skinwalker Ranch

window areas— I mod zones

in Utah (Kelleher & Knapp, 2005), where numerous incomprehensible paranormal phenomena – ranging from apparitions of therianthropes to UFO encounters and manifesting interdimenstional doorways – are associated with an area of approximately 500 acres? Maybe – through demonstrating just how little we actually know about non-human intelligence, even about the plants that have sustained us since time immemorial. If we cannot comprehend the consciousnesses of organisms that have been evolving alongside us for millions of years, what hope do we have of understanding extraterretrial, let alone extra-dimensional, intelligence?

Time-scales may be particularly important factors in making sense of the incomprehensibility of other forms of intelligence. Fungi, plants, trees, bacteria and animals all express their consciousness and intelligence over very different time-scales. We find it easy to relate to the intelligence of dogs and cats, for example, because they express their consciousness along time-scales similar to our own – we are more or less synchronised with them. We relate much less to the rapid time-scale of the fruitfly, than we do to larger mammals. At the other end of the spectrum there are trees. Trees express their intelligence over decades, centuries and even millennia. Yew trees, for instance, exhibit particularly long range thinking in their strategy in the forest fight for sunlight:

> Living to be a thousand years old or more, they easily outstrip the closest competition, and over the course of centuries, they increasingly get to bask in the sun whenever an old tree growing above them breathes its last (Wohlleben, 2017, p. 77).

Yews wait patiently, for hundreds of years at a time, before making their move. What time-scale could the intelligences that appear to manifest through all manner of paranormal phenomena be working on? Their incomprehensibility could, in part, be a product of how *out of synch* we are with the time-scales of their expression. This is precisely the reason that humankind, especially in the Western world, has so often ignored and denied the intelligence of plants, which science is only now beginning to rediscover (Mancuso & Viola, 2015; Gagliano, 2018). Could this also be one of the reasons why it is often so difficult to make sense of the intelligence that seems to be behind paranormal phenomena? That it is an intelligence that expresses itself over hundreds, if not millions, of years?

PART 4:

Animism and
Re-Connecting with Place

The term animism derives from the Latin root word *anima*, meaning soul, and in its scholarly usage has referred to the *belief* that the world is populated by 'spirits,' or, to use a more recent (and somewhat more encompassing) term, 'other-than-human persons' (both empirical/physical and non-empirical/non-physical). For an animist the world is alive, so that rocks, trees, animals, plants, mountains and rivers could all posses personal attributes, desires, fears and needs, just like human persons. From an animist perspective, ecosystems can be understood as complex *communities of persons in reciprocal dialogue* with one another, and we are participants in this dialogue as well.

Animism was first popularised as a scholarly category by the anthropologist Edward Burnett Tylor (1832-1917), who saw the belief in spiritual beings as the very earliest expression of religious thought. Indeed, for Tylor there was little distinction between traditional indigenous religions and the major world religions – he considered that *all* religions, from tribal religions to Catholicism, could in their essence simply be defined as the 'belief in spiritual beings.' Tylor's version of anthropology, however, was closely wedded to a form of social evolutionism known as developmentalism, that was particularly popular during the latter half of the nineteenth century (Stocking Jr, 1982, p.

97-100). According to this view, European (and especially British) culture was understood to be the pinnacle of social and cultural development, while other non-western and indigenous cultures were seen as somewhat backward, irrational and misguided, but that nevertheless had somehow survived into the modern day. Sadly, such a view ultimately distorted Tylor's perception of the animistic worldview(s) he wrote about in his books, and it wasn't until much later that scholars began to re-engage with animism without such developmentalist (maybe even colonialist) attitudes.

In his 1960 publication 'Ojibwa Ontology, Behavior and World View,' the American anthropologist Alfred Iriving Hallowell (1892-1974) instigated a renewed interest in animism in his writings on the Ojibwa people of central Canada. For the Ojibwa the world is populated by *persons* 'not all of whom are human.' Hallowell famously gives the example of his conversation with an old Ojibwa man: 'I once asked an old man: Are all the stones we see about us here alive? He reflected a long while and then replied, 'No!' But some are' (Hallowell, 1960). The old man's answer had a lasting impact on the anthropologist. His response suggests that for the Ojibwa people, stones have the *capacity for life*, even if it is not always manifest or obvious – their worldview leaves open the *possibility* that stones, trees, mountains and so on *can* be persons, and as such ought to be granted the same respect as human persons, *just in case*. From this perspective, interactions with certain objects, as well as with features of the landscape, must be understood as *interactions between persons*, or as *relationships between persons*, even if their intelligence is not outwardly expressed. On occasion, however, this capacity for life becomes expresses itself as true animation:

> Associated with the Midewiwin in the past there were other types of large boulders with animate properties. My friend Chief Berens had one of these, but it no longer possessed these attributes. It had contours that suggested eyes and mouth. When Yellow Legs, Chief Berens' great-grandfather, was a leader of the Midewiwin he used to tap this stone with a new knife. It would then open its mouth, Yellow Legs would insert his fingers and take out a small leather sack with medicine in it. Mixing some of this medicine with water, he would pass the decoction around (Hallowell, 1969).

In accounts such as these the connections between animism and High Strangeness become abundantly clear. We are also reminded of the suggestion in Part 2 of this introduction that cultural expectation plays an important role in facilitating extraordinary experiences. If a worldview holds open the possibility of communication with plants, animals, rocks and other features of the natural environment, then it may in turn facilitate just such communications. Furthermore, we are also reminded of the role of participation and interaction in facilitating extraordinary experiences and enabling the expression of non-human intelligence. In the case of Chief Berens discussed above, ritual interaction with the boulder enabled reciprocal communication and the exchange of medicine.

More recently, scholar of religions Graham Harvey has taken up the themes of Tylor and Hallowell's work (amongst others), with the formulation of his 'New Animism.' New animism differs from Tylor's 'old' animism firstly through rejecting the social developmentalist perspective that sees animistic beliefs as symptoms of primitive and irrational thinking, and secondly by shifting its focus away from the somewhat problematic notion of 'spirits,' towards the much more encompassing idea of 'persons,' which may include persons who are 'other-than-human.' Harvey writes:

> Animists are people who recognise that the world is full of persons, only some of whom are human, and that life is always lived in relationship with others. Animism is lived out in various ways that are all about learning to act respectfully (carefully and constructively) towards and among other persons. Persons are beings, rather than objects, who are animated and social towards others (even if they are not always sociable). Animism ... is more accurately understood as being concerned with learning how to be a good person in respectful relationships with other persons (Harvey, 2005, p. xi).

The underlying relational philosophy of the new animism (which is only 'new' to academia), represents the antithesis of the materialistic-industrial-consumer philosophy that has dominated Euro-American attitudes to the environment for the last two hundred years, and would seem to offer a route towards the kind of 'Deep Ecology' advocated by Arne Naess (2009). *Deep ecology.*

Many in our post-industrial society are likely to feel uncomfortable with the notion of attributing personhood to the various components of our ecosystems (recall the scientific establishment's backlash against Gaia theory). As we have seen, however, the growing body of research

33

on plant and animal cognition suggests that non-human personhood *is* something we will increasingly have to take seriously. If we are unwilling to take it all the way then perhaps we can take a hint from the Ojibwa and treat ecology *as if* it possesses personhood, without necessarily believing that it does – just in case. If we were to adopt a relational attitude, and interact with rivers, streams, trees, animals, soils and so on as if they are persons, our behaviours and actions would also necessarily be altered as a consequence. We wouldn't want to pump sewage into another person, for example, or destroy the home of another person, or abuse, misuse or exploit another person. When we think in terms of relationships, we realise that we need to develop *good relationships* with the other persons in our ecosystem – prosperous, mutually beneficial relationships. A relational worldview makes us aware of our own interconnected and interdependent relationship with the world around us. So, even if we don't *believe* that the tree in our garden is a person, or the river in our village, or the sky above our heads, we can still *behave* as if they are – our actions can be informed by a relational ecocentric perspective, rather than a purely anthropocentric one.

Granting Personhood Status to Ecosystems

An interesting recent development is the gradual granting of legal personhood status to key ecosystems by some of the world's governments. For example, the Whanganui River in New Zealand, known as *Te Awa Tupa* amongst the indigenous Maori people, was the first river to be granted the legal status of personhood. The Wahanganui people, whose lives are dependent on the river system, and who have always thought of the river as an ancestor, have been fighting for the last 140 years for the river to be treated with the respect that it deserves as an ancestor and living entity, a request that was finally granted on Wednesday 15th March 2017. Gerard Albert, the lead negotiator on behalf of the Whanganui tribe explains:

> We can trace our genealogy to the origins of the universe, and therefore rather than us being masters of the natural world, we are part of it. We want to live like that as our starting point. And that is not an anti-development, or anti-economic use of the river but to begin with the view that it is a living being, and then consider its future from that central belief.

What this means for the Whanganui River is that, as a legal person, any damage inflicted on it is legally equivalent to damaging a human being. What if we could do this for our own local rivers, forests and mountains? What impact would it have on our relationship with our local ecosystem? Would it encourage us to behave more responsibly? To change our use of chemical fertilisers, for example, which may leach into the river from farmlands? I think it would.

Within days of the New Zealand government's decision to grant personhood status to the Whanganui River, a court in Northern India ordered that the sacred River Ganges, and its primary tributary the Yamuna, also be granted the legal status of personhood, as well as glaciers and other ecosystems connected to the Ganges, precisely so that they can be protected and preserved for the benefit of future generations, and for our global system as whole.

It is important at this point to note that I am not talking about a wholesale importation or appropriation, of any particular worldview or culture. It would not necessarily work, for example, to transport a shamanistic cosmological model that emerged in the Amazonian Rainforest over onto to the hills of rural Mid-Wales. The spirits would be different (though I wouldn't want to rule out overlaps). What I am suggesting, rather, is something more like Arne Naess' notion of *ecosophy*, or a philosophy of place, which emerges naturally from participative interaction with a particular location. In other words, we need *to re-connect with the 'spirits' of our particular place* – re-connect with what is directly around us, right now, wherever we are.

Indeed, we might be surprised to find that many of the most familiar features of our own local environments have *already* had their personhood recognised by our ancestors, which may make this re-connection slightly easier. In my local area, in rural Mid-Wales, for example, I can point to Llyn Tegid (Bala Lake), the deepest natural lake in Wales in the midst of the Berwyn mountains, which is rumoured to be inhabited by the great monster Tegid (and in fact is also the endemic home of the Gwyniad, a small prehistoric fish). The River Severn, which meanders along the Wales/England border, was known by the Romans as the goddess Sabrina and was venerated as such with shrines along its banks. What about other local rivers? What forms of 'other-than-human' consciousness did our forebears discern in our familiar surroundings? Have we been treating them with the respect they deserve? Could animist principles be a catalyst for the change in thinking required by the Paris Climate Agreement? Perhaps we should consider lobbying to have our rivers recognised as persons, and our ecosystems as complex communities of these 'other-than-human persons,' just as the Whanganui people have been doing for the last 140 years.

Magical Animals

Holmes, Smith & Ward (2017) have put forward a compelling argument for the possible role of 'magical animals' in the struggle to conserve biodiversity and protect ecosystems. They take the concept of magical animals broadly, as referring to 'both mythical animals not recognized by science and extant animals that are recognized by science but have magical properties.' Their discussion on the links between magical creatures and conservation includes everything from the *Huldufólk* of Iceland (the elves who still today have the power to influence urban planning, see *The Guardian*, 2013 and *The Irish Times*, 1999 for an Irish analogue), through Lake monsters as eco-tourist attractions at Loch Ness and elsewhere, and on to magical beliefs surrounding various animals in Madagascar, which fundamentally affect how humans perceive and interact with these creatures and the landscapes they inhabit. They write that:

> ... magical animals can have positive and negative consequences for conservation, and ... the relationship between magical animals, human beliefs and behaviour, and extant biodiversity is complex ... we argue that conservation needs to interrogate the interaction of magical animals, extant animals and biodiversity conservation goals ... It should see these animals as part of broader systems, be it of cultures, rationalities or belief systems, and acknowledge that beliefs and values around magical animals are dynamic ... Ultimately, by understanding human interactions with magical animals, conservation could create successful coexistence between humans and non-humans (Holmes, Smith & Ward, 2017, p. 237).

It is an interesting recent development that the Loch Ness monster has been recognised as a Naga, a Hindu and Buddhist serpent deity, or spirit, often associated with water. Lama Gelongmo Zangmo, director of the Samye Ling Buddhist Monastery in Dumfries, Scotland explains that 'Nessie is a naga. We build the relationship with the naga, try to please them and don't abuse the environment. If Nessie is treated well she will bring prosperity' (*The Scotsman*, 2014). In a similar blending of the paranormal and the ecological, Joshua Cutchin has suggested that Bigfoot might best be understood as a sort of wilderness poltergeist (*wildnisgeist*), owing to frequent reports of disembodied voices, stone throwing, rapping, orbs of light, and so on in Bigfoot encounters (Cutchin, 2018). From an animist perspective there is nothing anomalous about these paranormal creatures, indeed we would expect them to be there. Approaching the natural environment from an animistic perspective may take us some way towards fostering a much healthier relationship with our living planet, and the various forms of 'other-than-human-consciousness' that co-inhabit with us.

Extraordinary Experience and Ecological Interaction: A Feedback Loop

In 2018 I conducted an informal online survey of permaculture practitioners to uncover possible connections between practical engagement with ecology and paranormal experience. This is not the place to go into a full examination of what the survey found (see Hunter, 2018), but suffice to say here that the perceived connections between permaculture and extraordinary experience recounted by my survey respondents point towards an interesting correlation between *interacting* with the natural world (whether through observation of ecosystems, or the practical tending of gardens) and *extraordinary experience* (feelings of connectedness to nature, communication with plants and animals, and so on). Through fostering a closer relationship with our ecology (through implementation of the permaculture principle of 'observe and interact,' for example), we may also open ourselves up to extraordinary experiences in nature. The work of Botelho *et al.* (2016) supports this suggestion. In their study of Brazilian agroforestry (a combination of agriculture and forestry techniques to promote biodiversity while also generating large crop yields) they found that:

> ... through the adoption and collaborative development of the agroforestry system, farmers have begun to conduct intense observations of the environment in relation to plants, animals, water, and soil and to shape and renew the use of traditional knowledge in their production methods. Furthermore, because the farmers

now verbalize their reflections and exchange their observations and knowledge with others, they are internalizing the idea that a profound change is occurring in their conceptions of nature. This process is similar to the process that deep ecologists describe as a metaphysical reconfiguration of the self and the ecosystem (Botelho *et al.*, 2016, p. 218).

The work of anthropologist James Woolley on dowsers in the UK (2018) also has relevance here, particularly in relation to the role of participation and interaction with ecology and the fostering of ecological consciousness. Woolley concludes that the practice of dowsing, which we might consider as a practice that blurs the boundary between the paranormal and ecological engagement, leads to a deeper intuitive connection to the land:

Anthropologists have carefully explored the importance of non-scientific ways of knowing, particularly with regard to understanding and engaging people about climate and conservation ... the subtle power of dowsing, I argue, lies in more than mere illusion and bias; rather, its power comes in part from the strength of engaging bodily and pragmatically with one's surroundings (Woolley, 2018, p. 25).

We can also look to research on mystical, peak and ecstatic experiences in wilderness, which further supports the idea that opening ourselves up to, and interacting with, the ecological conditions in which we find ourselves can lead to extraordinary experiences of connection with the natural world (McDonald *et al.*, 2009). It is also important to point out at this juncture that the ethnographic and theoretical literature on animism also emphasises the significance of participation and interaction with local ecosystems, and the formation of reciprocal relationships between humans and other-than-human persons, in animistic societies (Bird-David, 1999; Harvey, 2005). Ecopsychologist Theodore Roszak has even gone so far as to suggest that animism has 'a proven ecological utility,' in that 'it disciplines the relationship of humans to their environment, imposing an ethical restraint upon exploitation and abuse (Roszak, 1993, p. 84). Given that we are facing unprecedented ecological collapse on a global scale, this would seem to be a particularly pertinent area for future research, and it is my hope that this book might contribute to it.

Our Haunted Planet: Re-Wilding and Re-Enchantment

If the world truly is radically more alive (conscious) than we have tended to give it credit for in the post-modern, post-industrial Western world, then we are right to call the Earth a 'haunted planet' – a term coined by John Keel in his 1971 book of the same name. Waking up to this expanded view of reality – to the many different forms of consciousness and intelligence that surround us, and with which we are constantly interacting (whether we are aware of it or not) – may be understood through the lens of 're-enchantment.' In recent years there has been a growing sense of dissatisfaction with the dominant materialist paradigms of academia, which leave very little room for the mythic, mystical and imaginal in academic scholarship, and which could also (as we have already discussed), be held at least partially responsible for the ecological crisis we are currently facing. Re-enchantment offers an alternative perspective. In their recent edited book *Re-Enchanting the Academy* (2017), Angela Voss and Simon Wilson write:

> To feel enchanted is to step through a hidden portal into another way of seeing, into a new reality, where the reasonable, the certain, the measurable, and the predictable give way to the awesome, the wonderful, the delightful, the paradoxical, and the uncertain – and perhaps even the longing of the soul for some other kind of life beyond the exigencies of the everyday (Voss & Wilson, 2017, p. 13).

The rediscovery of the sense of awe and wonder in nature is really what this whole introductory essay has been homing in on. By transforming the way we think about and experience the natural world we can also change the way we behave in relation to it. If we understand the world to be imbued with consciousness and intelligence, then by enhancing biodiversity we are also enhancing *psychodiversity* – the measure of the total diversity of thought within a system. Every plant and animal, as conscious entities, contribute to the 'psychosphere' of the Earth. With every biological species that we lose (or worse, eradicate through human activity), we also lose vital forms of non-human consciousness and cognition, from which we have much to learn. The biodiversity crisis is also a psychodiversity crisis. In this case, re-wilding is extremely important. George Monbiot elaborates on the concept of re-wilding:

Rewilding, to me, is about resisting the urge to control nature and allowing it to down the fences, blocking the drainage ditches, but otherwise stepping back. At sea, it means excluding commercial fishing and other forms of exploitation. The ecosystems that result are best described not as wilderness, but as self-willed: governed not by human management but by their own processes (Monbiot, 2014, p. 9-10).

Re-wilding and re-enchantment go hand in hand. Drawing from the ideas we have been exploring throughout this introduction, the process of re-wilding – of allowing natural systems to regenerate without human interference – provides a space for non-human intelligence to flourish, unfurl, and reach its full expression.

Let's Explore ...

Now that we have tentatively mapped some of the territory connecting anomalistics, anthropology and ecology, it is time to focus in on some particular niches within this network of interconnected ideas. Contributors to this volume come from diverse backgrounds, both academic and non-academic, so present a range of different perspectives on the greening of the paranormal. Following each chapter (including this one), our intrepid authors have included 3-4 questions that can be used to guide further thinking in the classroom (or indeed anywhere that the book might be read). These are ideas that need thinking through.

To begin, Cody Meyocks presents a critique of civilisation and explores how anomalous phenomena destabilize social structures and offer the hope of breakthrough to something new. Amba Sepie's chapter draws on the message of the Kogi Mamas for guidance in bringing about a cultural shift towards Earth-Mindedness, with a particular emphasis on the messages contained in the enigmatic documentaries of Alan Ereira. Nancy Wissers introduces the Native American Lenape idea of 'recruitment by the Earth' – something that often occurs as the result of childhood experiences of connection to nature – and surveys writers and thinkers who have received the calling. Lance Foster, a member of the Ioway tribe, then contributes a chapter on the 'Invisible Ecosystem,' and Native American perspectives on the so-called paranormal. His chapter includes a wonderful re-telling of the story of Plenty Coups, which has many lessons for how we can go about reconciling anomalous phenomena and the natural world.

Jacob Glazier's chapter argues for the Trickster archetype as an ontological framework for the interpretation of both psi and nature, while Christine Simmonds-Moore's contribution surveys research on the cognitive and neuropsychological correlates of psi experiences and suggests that extraordinary experiences arise as 'conversations between liminal people and places with liminal properties.' Mark Schroll's chapter continues with the theme of sacred spaces as he examines the role of the interaction of human consciousness with sacred space in the development of 'transpersonal ecosophical consciousness.' Simon Wilson's chapter then surveys the pioneering work of Paul Devereux on 'Earth Lights,' and suggests that paranormal experiences (such as UFO sightings) are co-created as imaginal consciousness interacts with landscape. Next, Viktória Duda illuminates the networks in nature and human nature, and speculates on the internet as an externalisation of much more ancient psychic connections.

Psychedelic parapsychologist David Luke surveys the range of current research on eco-consciousness and its relationship to the psychedelic experience, including fascinating insights into his own experiences of interspecies communication on psychedelics. This is followed by Brian Taylor's contribution, which looks at the phenomenon of after death communication from an animist perspective, with particular emphasis on butterflies and 'soul-birds' as mediators between the living and the dead. Maya Ward's chapter then proceeds to present a 'secret history of listening,' exploring how deep listening becomes deep feeling, which in turn leads to ecological knowing.

Silvia Mutterle's chapter focusses on the Wild Earth Animal Essences – a modern re-imagining of the spirit animal concept – which are currently used in the context of therapy and healing. Continuing with the animal theme, Susan Marsh then examines the implications for cryptozoological research of our rapidly changing world, including an intriguing peek into her own search for the mysterious dragon-like Ninki Nanka in Gambia.

Timothy Grieve-Carlson's chapter then expores 'The Hidden Predator' and probes the ecological subtext of Whitley Strieber's infamous alien abduction experiences, as well as his engagement with ecological themes in his novels and writing. Finally, Elorah Fangrad, Rick Fehr and Christopher Laursen delineate a new methodological framework – which they term 'Psychic Naturalism' – for investigating paranormal experiences, phenomena and narratives in their deep ecological context.

I sincerely hope you find the chapters that follow of interest, and that they encourage readers to think differently about the paranormal, ecology and our place in the cosmos.

Acknowledgements

Thanks to Dr. Nicholas Campion, Dr. Fiona Bowie, and Dr. Maya Ward for useful comments on this introduction. Thanks also to the audience at the 'Umoja Spring Garden Party: Exploring 2050' in Conwy for serving as a sounding board for the ideas presented in this introduction.

Questions

1. What role can religion and spirituality play in tackling the eco-crisis?

2. In what ways do the sciences of ecology and parapsychology make us reconsider our relationship with the living Earth?

3. How can an understanding of non-human consciousness help us change our behavior?

4. What is the relationship between re-enchantment and re-wilding, and how do they sustain one another?

CHAPTER 2

THE ANARCHIST AND THE UNICORN: ON SCIENCE, SPIRIT, AND CIVILIZATION

Cody Meyocks

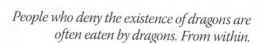

People who deny the existence of dragons are often eaten by dragons. From within.

—Ursula K. Le Guin

Paranormal research as a field crystalized with Charles Fort's 1919 work *The Book of the Damned*, published just months after the close of the First World War, as the world staggered away from the trenches and wastelands of the battlefield into a new age. These two events, though one tragic and one fairly comic, are not unrelated. Fort's exhaustingly researched volume of empirical oddities, foraged from archives where science had 'damned' them to obscurity for not fitting in with prevailing theories, was a whimsical retort to what he saw as scientific pretence and hypocrisy. 'We shall have a procession of the damned which science has excluded,' he began. Light-hearted as it was, it would prove as grave an omen for the fate of life in the new era as the Great War itself. The modern age had arrived, and with the dispassionate logic of science at its core and the ravenous appetite of the technological economy at its vanguard, it began its megalithic corrosion of the natural world.

The First World War cemented the sombre reality that technologically advanced nations could readily demolish others who lagged behind in their command of manufacturing, infrastructure, and the sciences. The Industrial Revolution had reached a critical tipping point in the importance of technical affluence for military superiority. Far from stemming from simply a crisis of international alliances, World War One was the inevitable culmination of an international landscape re-shaped by the industrial age.

To A.J.P. Taylor (1969) the First World War was 'imposed on the statesmen of Europe by railway timetables.' Taylor found that the meticulous, rigid scheduling necessary to mobilize troops via railcar – a system meant to deter war with the threat of rapid troop deployment – ended up boxing the great powers into hair-trigger responses and forcing an otherwise unwanted war. The tsar of Russia, for instance, on the day he mobilized troops to the German border, wrote in his diary about spending a warm day bathing in the sea, but said nothing about the mobilization in his journal. A devastating international conflict seemed the furthest thing from his mind. Mobilization after all was just a threat, if a serious one.

Germany, on the other hand, was trapped between two fronts – France and Russia – and if they failed to strike France quickly, risked a crucial delay in mobilizing to meet a Russian offensive. When Russia refused Germany's order to demobilize, Germany had to pre-emptively invade France before any other country had taken a definitive step towards war – or else compromise its entire defence strategy, which was based around its inflexible rail timetables. 'It was an unexpected climax to the railway age,' Taylor concluded.

Decades later, the fate of the Second World War would likewise be dictated by industrial factors. The new Bonneville and Gran Coulee dams on Oregon's colossal Columbia River would decide the war by providing Boeing enough electricity to smelt unprecedented amounts of aluminium – ultimately accounting for about a third of all planes in the Second World War, plus 750 large boats and twenty-seven percent of the U.S. naval fleet. Truman recalled in 1948, 'Had we not had that power source, it would have been almost impossible to win this war.' The Bureau of Reclamations had found an actual purpose for the dams they were obsessed with building, one to replace their ill-fated mission to remake the arid American West into a verdant agricultural Eden – rivers could become weapons.

John Zerzan (1988) speculates that the First World War was caused by a fermenting social unrest aimed at dissatisfaction with the constricting grasp of European industrialism. Total war was the blow necessary to retain state hegemony in the face of a mounting general rebellion. He called it the 'most significant stroke of counterrevolution in modern world history ... The scale and conditions of the war had to be equal to the force straining against society, in order to replace this challenge with the horror and despair that spread from the battlefields to darken the mind of the twentieth century West.'

No single underlying cause could ever suffice, but the dying rumble of artillery signalled a bleak post-war social reality, in which the core purpose of whole societies definitively shifted to embrace the primacy of industrialism. As the power of nation-states increasingly waxed and waned in step with their mastery of the industries and sciences—which became the central focus of production—so the values of societies came to align with these institutions. As if the trauma of the war had left an existential abyss gaping at the heart of the modern world, the zeitgeist of science stepped in to offer a rational and mechanical cosmology for a new rational and mechanical economy.

Just six years after *The Book of the Damned* was published, in 1925, the *Tennessee v Scopes* trial saw the U.S. Supreme Court rule in favour of John Scopes' right to teach an evolutionary account of history from the textbook *Civic Biology* (1914), symbolically passing the torch from Christianity to scientism as the officially sanctioned cosmology of the state. The chief prosecutor for Tennessee, Senator William Jennings Bryan, wrote in his proposed summation, 'Science is a magnificent force, but it is not a teacher of morals. It can perfect machinery, but it adds no moral restraints to protect society from the misuse of the machine. In war, science has proven itself an evil genius; it has made war more terrible than it ever was before.'

Although often remembered as a watershed victory for rational society, the evolutionary ideas in *Civic Biology* are repugnant by today's standards. For example, a pseudoscientific section titled 'Races of Man' concludes its list of races by vaunting, 'the highest type of all, the Caucasians, represented by the civilized white inhabitants of Europe and America,' and ominously concludes its 'Evolution' section with the suggestion that the 'beginnings of civilization were long ago, but even to-day the earth is not entirely civilized,' meaning not entirely colonized. Another section on eugenics deals with the bloodlines of 'social parasites' and their hindrance to building a 'stronger race,' saying regretfully, 'If such people were lower animals we would probably kill them off to keep them from spreading.' And in a section tellingly titled 'The Human Machine,' 'Man is the thinking animal, and as such is master of the earth.'

Such were the ideals of evolution championed by scientists at the time. This blatantly genocidal social Darwinism has remained embedded at the core of modern civilization's mythos, covered by a thin veneer of political correctness which nevertheless sees technical superiority as the zenith of evolution, beside which all other life is inferior.

Paul Feyerabend (1978), anarchist epistemologist, would observe half a century after Scopes, 'Science is no longer a particular institution; it is now part of the basic fabric of democracy just as the Church was once a part of the basic fabric of society.' Vine Deloria (2002), Native American scholar, would concur: 'When evolution replaced the concept of creation... it became an inviolable law in the eyes of Western people in much the same way that the...biblical story had been accepted by Western people in former centuries.' In order to fully indulge the post-WWI economy of profound mechanisation and its new dominance as a political, social, and moral force at the centre of life, a hard scrabble philosophy was necessary – a rational, mechanical, law-of-the-jungle philosophy. Evolution and scientism, which had allied itself with state and powers since its infancy, fit the bill to justify the new modern landscape perfectly.

This aptitude of Darwin's theory of evolution to give capitalism a philosophical posture is likely why the theories of anarchist biologist Pyotr Kropotkin never caught on. Kropotkin was born a Russian prince in 1842 but renounced his title, fled into exile, and went on to write *Mutual Aid: A Factor of Evolution* (1902) in opposition to Darwin's vision of nature as a war of all against all. A hardy man with smiling eyes and a large untamed beard, he wrote, 'Sociability is as much a law of nature as mutual struggle,' laying the foundation for his theory of cooperative evolution.

Despite dying a national hero after returning to Russia (Lenin even allowed imprisoned anarchists to attend his funeral – amazingly letting them carry anti-Bolshevik banners – as long as they promised to return to jail that evening), Kropotkin's ideas on human nature were blandly received by scientists. While his work has found praise in more recent times, his ideas of kindness, generosity, and egalitarianism as innate human social traits have been astronomically overshadowed by Darwin's 'survival of the fittest' style evolution, which has become an almost metaphysical cultural truism.

The early Enlightenment philosopher Baruch Spinoza wrote, 'Let a man only consider what a difference there is between the life of men in the most civilised province of Europe, and in the wildest and most barbarous districts of New India; he will feel it be great enough to justify the saying that, *man is a god to man*,' envisioning the evolutionary paradigm centuries before Darwin. Conversely, in 1921 the anarchist Bartolomeo Vanzetti, in his last speech to the court before being sentenced to death on false charges alongside his friend Nicola Sacco, would paraphrase the ancient Greek phrase *Homo homi lupus* into broken English: 'Sacco's name will live in the hearts of the people and in their gratitude when Katzmann's bones and yours will be dispersed by time; when your name, his name, your laws, constitutions and your false god are but a dim remembering of a cursed past in which man was wolf to the man ...'

Adolf Hitler (1927) himself said, 'The earth has been acquired on the basis of the right of the stronger,' echoing Darwin in his belief in the 'law of the eternal struggle.' Zygmunt Bauman (1989), meditating on the hyper-bureaucratic social engineering of the Holocaust, argued that rather than representing a regression into barbarism, the Holocaust 'arrived in a factory-produced vehicle, wielding weapons only the most advanced science could supply, and following an itinerary designed by scientifically managed organization.' He rightly concluded that modernity was the Holocaust's 'necessary condition ... It was the rational world of modern civilization that made the Holocaust thinkable.'

Francis Bacon, a founding father of science and darling of English royalty, firmly believed in man's dominion over nature, and government's dominion over man. He once personally tortured Edward Peacham, an elderly preacher charged with treason, in the Tower of London. Peacham allegedly wrote a sermon urging rebellion against the crown and the government. Although Peacham 'doggedly' maintained his innocence, even under torture, Bacon lobbied for his execution. Poor Peacham was sentenced to death but the frail old man, worn thin from his ordeal, died in jail before the execution.

Bacon (1620) wrote that the highest ideal for man was to, 'Endeavor to establish and extend the power and dominion of the human race itself over the universe.' He put this ideal, ironically, even over service to the nation or its empire. Bacon was a shameless jockey for status in the court. He saw early on that science was immensely palatable to power structures. He continued triumphantly, 'The empire of man over things depends wholly on the arts and sciences.' Pondering Bacon,

[handwritten margin note: × law of eternal struggle]

Adorno and Horkheimer would bluntly conclude, 'What human beings seek to learn from nature is how to dominate wholly both it and human beings. Nothing else counts.'

Bacon's philosophy of dominion over nature, which would ultimately lead to scientific modernity, wasn't a new position, however. Using human superiority to justify the exploitation of the natural world has been a theme running through civilised cultures, as far back as Genesis and Gilgamesh. Scientism is only the most advanced manifestation of the same impulse, which lies at the heart of the civilising project – the end of which is control, and the means of which is the objectification of living processes, the transformation of patterns in nature into a cultural map of controllable, exploitable symbols.

Scientific thinking is based around arbitrarily defined, symbolic segments of the universe. The way in which scientists break up the world's interrelated wholeness into concepts is a learned linguistic and conceptual activity, from which stem taxonomies capable of transforming the raw stuff of *sunsets* into *data sets*. Symbolic thinking compartmentalizes similarities, classifies and quantifies these symbols, and validates the resulting metrics as veritable truths. If conflicting evidence threatens a symbol, that experience is discarded (as Fort sorely noted), because otherwise the symbol itself would prove arbitrary.

The common complaint against scientific thought is that it is stubbornly materialistic, but while its empiricism is preoccupied with what is readily observable, scientific *reasoning* itself is a retreat into the symbolic, in which objective thinking means exactly objectifying the natural world – turning ongoing natural processes into static symbols which are capable of becoming variables and values in equations. 'Ostensibly,' Edward Sapir (1968) wrote of such symbols, 'they mark off specific concepts, concepts that lay claim to a rigorously objective validity. In practice, they label vague terrains of thought that shift or narrow or widen with the point of view of whoso makes use of them.' Or, as the *Tao Te Ching* – considered perhaps the oldest anarchist text – simply puts it: 'The Way that can be named is not the eternal Way.'

Far from being a material, sensual, specific experience, science relies on symbolic ideals which at once constitute the variables for experiments, the content of theories, and the linguistic relationship between the specialists who use them. It is no coincidence that in biology Latin still serves as an elite language for the intelligentsia, much as it did for the priests of earlier centuries.

48

The language of mathematics further acts as universal modifier for these abstractions. Wolfi Landstreicher (2001) observed, 'It should come as no surprise then that the language of science is the same as the language of the economy and of bureaucracy, a language devoid of passion and any concrete connection to life, the language of mathematics. What better language could one find for ruling the universe – a language that is at the same time utterly arbitrary and utterly rational?'

The concept of positivistic 'existence' itself serves as the bedrock for scientific belief – affirming that symbols are immutable and that phenomena (which actually move in and out of being like trees growing and decaying), are actually symbols. 'Existence' is the hallowed cartography of a positivistic universe, which trades the interrelated, dynamic patterns and cycles of the natural world for a static map of quantifiable objects. 'Existence' is the totality of possibility objectified, a foundation for a cohesive cosmology capable of excluding both subjectivity and anomalies, or as Nabokov (1962) wrote poetically, 'Existence is a series of footnotes to a vast, obscure, unfinished masterpiece.' It is the very selectivity of this positivism that drove Charles Fort crazy. He wrote, 'The state that is commonly and absurdly called 'existence' is a rhythm of heaven and hells.' Fort had a distaste for the 'Dominant' scientific institution 'and its suppression of all things and thoughts that endanger its supremacy ... I have often noted how, when they approach forbidden – or irreconcilable – subjects, the discussions were thrown into confusion and ramification...as if by something directive, hovering over them. Of course I mean only the Spirit of all Development.'

For Hegel, the artefacts of material culture – from spoons, chairs, and houses, to cities, political systems, and economies – are the physical embodiments, or objectifications, of human Reason. He saw history as the progressive architecture of this objectification, and alienation as the inevitable estrangement felt as artefacts become so ubiquitous as to seem natural, obvious, and inevitable. In forgetting their source within the human mind, the objectifiers find themselves surrounded by an artificial landscape of their own design, hopelessly unaware that it is artificial. Although Hegel believed that Reason would eventually come to its senses, the self-perpetuating landscape of commodity culture shows no sign of abating, and civilisation has become a global habitat of artifice claiming to be the crescendo of natural achievement.

In modernity, Lukaks (1923) concluded, 'Reification requires that a society should learn to satisfy all its needs in terms of commodity

49

exchange,' and Guy Debord (1967) opened his tirade against mediated existence, *Society of the Spectacle*, with the bitter line, 'In societies dominated by modern conditions of production, all life is presented as an immense accumulation of spectacles. Everything that was directly lived has receded into a representation.' Zerzan (2003) likewise observed, 'Although still touted as the precondition for 'objectivity,' human reason is no longer neutral. It has somehow become deformed, with devastating impact: our reason imprisons our true humanity, while destroying the natural world.'

This cycle of objectification, the making of a world of objects, didn't begin with the modern or even industrial eras, however. The transition from nomadic hunter-gatherer societies to agrarian cultures was likewise defined by a slow descent into reification. The increasing complexity of languages, rituals, and technologies all point to the primacy of the symbol in laying the foundations for labour specialization, domestication, and ultimately agrarian life. Although evolutionary logic sees modern civilisation as the highest rung reached on the ladder of human perfection, the advances of civilisation from the outset have been compelled by the artificial, dissociated, and intangible.

The vast majority of human history has been spent outside of symbolic confines. For perhaps two-million years, wild hunter-gatherer bands lived remarkably unmediated lives in direct communion with each other and the natural world. With increased symbolic culture in the Upper Paleolithic, however, we begin to see the rudiments of stratified society, and with it a gradual decline in human health and happiness, the dawn of hierarchy and warfare, and the blueprints for environmental ruin.

Rather than a 'Great Leap Forward,' the development of symbolic, reified culture appears more like a primordial spiritual trauma. As Chellis Glendenning (1994) said poignantly: 'Original trauma ... is the psychic displacement, the exile, that is inherent in civilized life. It is our homelessness.' Freud (1930) would be astonished by a similar conclusion: 'What we call our civilization is largely responsible for our misery, and that we should be much happier if we gave it up and returned to primitive conditions.'

Evolution's common mythology paints civilisation as the triumph of humanity's innate genius, elevating us out of the toil and brutality of our animal condition, but for every glorious advance attributed to civilisation, the anthropological record reveals deepening psychic and environmental trauma. As Freud observed, one 'gets an impression that civilization is something which was imposed on a resisting majority by a minority which understood how to obtain possession of the means to power and coercion.' Civilisation was a bitterly resented and repressive force from its outset.

Far from being 'nasty brutish and short,' Marshal Sahlins (1972) dubbed hunter-gatherers the 'original affluent society,' because their material needs were so readily satisfied by the natural world. They were also the original anarchist society. The lack of specialisation made each member of a band an autonomous unit, capable of moving freely to satisfy their needs. Bands were formed by voluntary affinity, consensus, and mutual aid. Autonomy shaped band society's ethos of egalitarianism, sharing and cooperation – all words which are synonymous with foragers in the anthropological literature. Sahlins contrasted this to modern civilisation, writing, 'The present human condition of man slaving to bridge the gap between his unlimited wants and his insufficient means is a tragedy of modern times.'

The concept of work as an institution is itself wholly absent in band society, and the myth that agriculture reduced humanity's workload has been turned upside down by recent studies. Sahlins estimated that extant hunter-gatherers only labour an average of three to five hours a day to meet their needs. Even among Kung Bushmen, in their harsh desert landscape, Richard Lee (1979) estimated twelve to nineteen hours a week satisfied their needs. Compared to the labour required to raise crops, it is little wonder that when Lee asked one Bushman why he didn't adopt planting, he replied, 'Why should we plant, when there are so many mongongo nuts in the world?' The often-observed sense of playfulness in foraging bands follows from their freedom from social obligation, and their pursuit of unmediated fulfilment of their immediate needs.

With the dawning of agriculture, symbolic culture and toil became cemented as means of livelihood. The separation and cultivation of land shows how sharply the agrarian concept of self contrasts with the far more ancient sense of transcendental fluency and kinship foragers enjoyed with the land. Rather than acting as a safeguard against famine, homogenized, domesticated crops actually proved much more susceptible to disease and failure than the diverse supply of wild foods foragers enjoyed. Life expectancy likewise actually declined with the emergence of agriculture, as did bone density, height, and dental health. Although it is a common myth that agriculture was an adaptation to growing population size, the opposite was true – population size increased only after agriculture developed. All these conundrums turn the popular myths of the Agricultural Revolution on their heads, and suggest that rather than the symbolic working to advance human life, human life became increasingly ritualised in service of the symbolic.

The pressures of cultivation, irrigation, and deforestation which accompany civilisation quickly exhausts land bases, forcing collapses, expansions, resource wars, or mixtures of these to inevitably follow domestication. Civilisation builds cities and leaves deserts in its wake. The barren hills of Lebanon – once covered in lush cedar forests – and the wastes of the once bountiful Tigris-Euphrates valley, where irrigation with saline river water slowly toxified the topsoil leaving it unproductive to this day, are famous and enduring examples.

Nietzsche (1885) wrote, 'Man is the most domesticated animal of all.' Herre & Rohres (1989) found that 'mental and behavioral deterioration' accompanies a decrease in brain weight and cortex volume in captive (domesticated) animals. They noted: 'Mammals are capable of memory and planned actions, and it is entirely justified to describe the intraspecific communication systems of mammals as species-specific 'languages.' In captivity, intraspecific communication is reduced.' Domestic dogs, for instance, have nowhere near the vocal complexity of wolves – the result of diminished nervous systems capabilities. Perhaps the rise of language as a dominant and defining cultural force coinciding with the rise of civilisation should be understood not as an advancement of our power to communicate but a remnant of a much fuller capacity for communion – not just among humans, but with the totality of being.

Freud (1933) suggests that telepathy is 'the original, archaic method of communication,' and Pobers (1956), after observing supernormal communications during natural disasters, suggested that for so-called 'primitive' people, telepathy 'remains an archaic means of communication in critical and conflictual situations.' He worried that 'the penetration of technological progress is faster than we think. In a few years' time there may be very little left of the phenomena.'

Pobers heard of a woman who asked a cotton tree to psychically contact her children – apparently the children responded in kind. When questioned, she replied, 'Rich people have telephones. I am poor. I have no telephone. I have to try it that way.' Laurens van der Post (1958) also observed telepathy among the Kalahari Kung, and when he inquired how this was possible a Bushman tapped his chest and said, 'We Bushmen have a wire here ... it brings us news.'

The telephone metaphors are telling. Who hasn't had a distant friend wander into their thoughts just before they call? This intuition may be just a shadow of its former potential. As Marshall McLuhan (1964) wrote, 'With the arrival of electric technology, man has extended, or set outside himself, a live model of the central nervous system itself. To the degree that this is so, it is a development that suggests a desperate suicidal autoamputation, as if the central nervous system could no longer depend on the physical organs to be protective buffers against the slings and arrows of outrageous mechanism.'

Technology, from the earliest stages of the division of labour, has always resulted in atrophy. Any specialisation naturally fragments wholesome autonomy, and creates inherent social imbalances around the division of labour. Shamans are considered the original specialists – in fact the first cultural practitioners at all – and their appearance in the archaeological record is the first clear seed of socio-economic stratification.

Along with the advent of shamanism – which suggests by nature that the trauma at the centre of the shift to advanced symbolism was a deeply spiritual one – also came the first rumblings of ritual and ideology – the seeds of cultural obligation, myth, and hierarchy. Chiefdoms soon follow, structuralizing and perpetuating wealth imbalances, and even in early chiefdoms anthropologists identify a bureaucratic class.

Another symbolic relic from the transition to agrarian life is the number. The need to quantify developed only with specialized trades, which required a way to standardize commodity exchange – a problem which had been absent in the hunter-gatherer gift economy. As Zerzan (1988) explains in Number: Its Origin and Evolution, 'Where articles are made, animals killed or plants collected for domestic use and not for exchange, there is no demand for standardized numbers or measurements. Measuring and weighing possessions develops later, along with the measurement and definition of property rights and duties to authority.'

Some of the earliest cave paintings – created by shamans – were stunningly fluid and expressive, but these impressionistic representations gradually formalized into simpler systems devoid of that earlier vitality, showing the tendency of symbols to lose their emotive power as they reach cultural stasis. Likewise, the earliest languages are rich in verbs but give way to nouns during agrarian settlement, where their prevalence suggests a worldview of fixed objectivity and domination long before modernity. The advent of writing later cemented

[handwritten marginal note:] Language structure → Commodity

53

the quasi-realities of language, time and number. From there they take their places in administrating wealth and debt – the cornerstones of complex material culture.

From the point where a quantified economy is the central axis which civilized life revolves around, it is an inevitable progression to the numerical cosmology of Descartes (1659), where, 'everything happens in nature in a mathematical way, and there is no quantity that is not divisible into an infinity of parts,' and the body is 'just a statue or a machine made of earth.' Our inheritance of this lineage – of the symbolic subsuming all nature under its authority – leaves little wonder as to the impoverishment and despair of the modern world.

Modern cosmology declares life is the product of chemical chance in a mechanical universe – a fluke on a meaningless planet which is inevitably dissipating into the black vacuum of entropy anyhow. As Deloria (2002) lamented, 'Science is our religion today. Because it officially produces no concept of divinity, it is regarded as neutral on the question of origins. But science is firmly grounded in a crude materialism that precludes the possibility of divinity, indeed even rejects any hint of teleology – the sense of purpose and meaning – in its explanation of the world we live in.' It is no wonder that postmodern culture is rife with nihilism, narcissism, irony, and depression – the authenticity and meaningfulness inherent in nature are buried under the wasteland of artifice. Horkheimer (1947) summarized, 'On the one hand, nature has been stripped of all intrinsic value or meaning. On the other, man has been stripped of all aims except self-preservation. He tries to transform everything within reach into a means to that end.'

Presently, the evolutionary myth is striving towards literal alienation – proclaiming that the ultimate destiny of civilization is to (somehow) colonize space. The fact that this ideal came from cultural osmosis of UFO lore (Vallee, 1969) is an irony worth pondering, and offers troubling revelations about both the myths of civilization and the ambitions of otherworldly visitors, but even on a mundane level, the myth that space colonization is the destiny of humanity's evolution is the epitome of shameless alienation, showing a naive and dangerous antipathy towards the earth and laying bare global civilization's omnicidal indifference towards life's inherent value.

Yet of course hope remains in the margins. As Fort proved by so joyously flaunting the 'damned' in the face of science's pretensions, the symbolic can never fully encompass a universe which defies parameters. Landstreicher (ibid) said it well, 'The scientific accountants with their calculations, graphs, charts and ledgers are perpetually confronted with a recalcitrant reality comprised of entities that don't conform to numbers or measurements, of individuals who resist interchangeability, of phenomena that cannot be repeated – in other words, of things that incessantly unbalance the accounts. Scientists may attempt to retreat to the laboratory, to the thought experiment, to virtual reality, but beyond the door, beyond their minds, beyond the realm of cyberspace, the unaccountable still waits.'

Instead of trying to corral anomalies into the packing plant of scientific consensus, perhaps it is better to directly seek the wondrous, untamable wisdom which anomalies and wildlings alike assert must await beyond the fences of objective control – to immerse ourselves in the 'rhythm of heavens and hells,' to rediscover our interconnectedness and the unfolding of eternity in each moment. As Yeats (1893) wrote, 'How do we not know but that our own unreason may be better than another's truth? for it has been warmed in our hearths and in our souls, and is ready for the wild bees of truth to hive in it, and make their sweet honey. Come into this world again, wild bees, wild bees!'

Or in Job: 39, where the whirlwind taunts Job with the unbridled strength of the wild and mystical: 'Canst thou bind the unicorn with his band in the furrow? or will he harrow the valleys after thee? Wilt thou trust him, because his strength is great? or wilt thou leave thy labour to him? Wilt thou believe him, that he will bring home thy seed, and gather it into thy barn?' Like Chang Tzu's gnarled, crooked tree which is blessed because no carpenter can square its strange wood, the anomalous defies objectification.

Mystical and mythical traditions offer a breadcrumb trail of de-civilizing reverse psychology. That love is often prescribed by mystics as an antidote to the trauma of ego separation – the reification of the self – is more than a banal moralism. 'Against all the evidence of his senses, a man who is in love declares that 'I' and 'you' are one, and is prepared to behave as if it were a fact,' wrote Freud in *Civilization and its Discontents*. Zerzan (1988) found, 'There is a profound truth to the notion that 'lovers need no words.' The point is that we must have a world of lovers, a world of the face-to-face, in which even names can be forgotten, a world which knows that enchantment is the opposite of ignorance.' Love in the mystical sense is neither a pacifying platitude nor a warm cocoon against the cold of sorrow. It is the intimacy that comes with the limitlessness of the self, and the sensuality of subjectivity. It is a living way to embrace, transcend, and travel among the stars – because we already do.

Questions

1. What are some moral dilemmas that accompany a critique of civilization? What are some moral dilemmas that accompany a defense of civilization?

2. Freud predicted that neurosis, anxiety, and depression would increase along with the advance of civilization. Was he correct? What does this imply about the nature of modern civilization?

3. Charles Fort, in despair, sometimes attempted to destroy his 48,000 handwritten notes on anomalous phenomena, which took him years to collect from manual library research. He was an outcast, and likely seriously depressed. Why might outcasts experience depression in modern society? Is depression an appropriate response to modernity?

4. The UFO theorist Jacques Vallee, at the end of his final book in the Alien Contact Trilogy (*Revelations*, 1991), wrote that the prospect of advancing technological society 'comes with a darker, disquieting side. There is more danger, crime, environmental damage, misery, and hunger around us than ever before. It will take a superhuman effort to reconcile the glittering promises of technology with the utterly disheartening dilemma, the wretched reality, of human despair.' He found troubling connections between the stories told by New-Age UFO contactees and some far-right extremist groups, both of whom focus on the utopian promises of alleged UFO technology. What political or social purposes could the popular UFO narrative serve? What does the belief in an advanced extraterrestrial origin of UFOs say about modern cultures? How does Vallee's idea that the UFO phenomena is trying to socially engineer its own mythos by giving messages to contactees shed new light on the modern extraterrestrial narrative?

5. Conceptually, the number 0 may exist, but 1 implies a distinct entity which is separate from, but contingent on 0. For the number 1 to stand out on this page, it is contingent on the blank space behind it to manifest. Therefore the number 1 conceptually implies 2 – the form and the background. Think of the yin-yang,

and this line from the Tao Te Ching: 'The Tao that is unnameable is the Source of the Heaven and the Earth. The name, once introduced, becomes the Mother of the Ten Thousand Things.' Does the number 1 exist? How are you, in physics, separate from the universe?

CHAPTER 3

LISTENING TO THE ELDERS: EARTH CONSCIOUSNESS AND ECOLOGY

Amba J. Sepie

In the old times the Kogi Mámas had great wisdom, given to us by Mother. We had the knowledge of everything we were and are. We knew, according to our law, not to kill too many animals, and not to cut down too many trees. We knew what complies with the law bequeathed us. The law is not written in books but in nature, which is itself a book ... The Mámas used to say that Serankua [Mother/Father] told them, five thousand years ago: "The younger brother is going to come and harm us. They younger brother will come as a blind man; in his blindness, he will disrespect. For the sake of his business, he will use machetes, metals, and enterprises to change what's proper... Another time will come, however, and they will see what they did. Then they will want to learn the word of old. It will be time to make it known."

— RAMON GILL BARROS (2009, P. 24)[1]

---

[1] *Máma* (sometimes rendered as *Mamo* or *Momo*) means 'of the Sun' or 'enlightened.' They are the Elders of the Kogi/Kaggaba (also, Kogui, Cogui, Kágaba, Cágaba), Wiwa, Arhuaco and Kankuama peoples of the Sierra

The Kogi Mámas (Elder Brothers) of the Sierra Nevada, speak from what they call Gonawindua, or the *Heart of the World*. In the Kogi world, planetary equilibrium is entirely dependent on the moral and spiritual integrity of these Mámas, a highly-trained, specialist group of Elders who guide Kogi life. The Mámas live in accordance with their duty to Earth and are compelled to maintain their sacred obligations to ensure Her ongoing flourishing (Davis, 2001, p. 42). *Jaba Aluna* is their name for the consciousness of Earth. She is not some distant god or goddess, but the mind of nature, with whom they are in constant conversation.

Five thousand years is a long time to wait for a prophecy – a direct revelation – to come to pass. Despite being forced upwards into the Sierra during the horrors of colonial invasion, the Kogi re-established themselves and continued with life as usual. The Mámas were patient; and then they were not. Watching in horror at the changes in their ecosystem, as the water at the very top of the mountains failed to thrive and feed the ocean, the Mámas, were initially perplexed. The time had arrived. They consulted *aluna* and asked her guidance on these distressing events. They determined that they must get a message to Younger Brother – their name for those westernised folk who know no better than to 'mutilate' the world, and who do not remember how to live properly with/in Earth.[2]

In the late 1980s, the Mámas called upon Alan Ereira, a British documentary maker, to come to their home and document their message. Ereira obliged; invited, as he was, into a community where no strangers were permitted, he made a film that set out their concerns in stark terms. The Mámas spoke knowledgably of Younger Brother in their film:

> It is very difficult for Younger Brother to listen, and to hear. It will be even harder for him to give things up. But he's going to have to learn. Younger Brother is going to have to listen carefully to the histories of the Mama, the Law of the Mama, the beliefs of the Mama...If we act well the world can go on (Ereira, 1990).

Nevada de Santa Marta in Colombia. Ramon Gil Barros (Kangemna) is a spiritual and political leader who was selected by Elders to be educated in Spanish, in order to liaise on behalf of the Kogi Mámas (Barros, 2009, pp. 23-24).

[2] Younger Brother appears in origin stories as an individual named Kasuaka who had to be sent away from Kogi lands because of his 'liking' for invention.

They were satisfied with the result. Ereira wrote a book to go with the little-known film, whilst the Mámas watched, waited, and listened to nature: 'They witnessed landslides, floods, deforestation, the drying up of lakes and rivers, the stripping bare of mountain tops, the dying of trees' (Reddy, 2013). They remained distressed. The Mámas told Ereira that they worked for not only the Kogi, but all people of the world. They explained that they were not angry with Younger Brother, but that they had a duty to care. They had spoken the truth. They did not know why their words had gone unheeded. The Mámas summoned (the now retired) Ereira to film with them a second time (Ereira, 2012).

> We have not spoken clearly. Our deep analysis has repeatedly confirmed the need for Alan to make a new film. The earth is a living body, it has veins and blood. Damaging certain places is like cutting off a limb. It damages the whole body ... Younger Brother must listen and stop causing damage or Nature herself will finish us off. We must renew this message to our English brother so that he will explain it to the world (Ereira, 2012).

Younger Brother was still choosing self interest over respect and care for the systems of Earth. They reiterated that he must see the damage he is creating, understand, and assume responsibility.

In this film, appropriately titled *Aluna*, the Mámas explain the Law that guides all aspects of Kogi life, prescribes human conduct, and gives direct guidance as to how to interact with the living world (Ereira 2012). They argue that the key to healing the world comes from understanding that what happens in one specific place has an effect somewhere else, precisely because it is all connected. Humans keep the balance, because humans are the custodians of Earth. The Mámas place great emphasis on special places that are sacred to maintaining life, animals, and plants in particular; they explained that all living things have their 'root' that must be protected.

To demonstrate this, the Mámas make a long journey that circumnavigates their home region and, accompanied by a weary Ereira, trace out the 'the Black Thread' they call Shikaka. She connects all key places, or *esuamas*, in the Sierra, linking coast to glaciated mountaintops. The Mámas concentrate on an *esuama* in order to establish how and where to make payments to 'keep the balance' of nature. The payments they make, as they trace the line, are an expression of reciprocal relations and maintaining responsibilities, and these payments represent a set of obligations or negotiations. Providence is assured by the maintenance of protocols, by adhering to Law, and by making payments to keep the balance. As the Mámas put it:

> We, the Mámas, know that there are special sites and they are threaded together. We're explaining this to our brothers across the sea so we can work with them and show the connection between places ... Shikaka is the Black Thread. Shi means thread. It connects everything. Important sites along the Line on the coast are connected to *esuamas* in the mountain. We collect materials here on the shore to make payments in the mountains and we bring materials from the mountain to make payments down here ... [Eriera speaks] *Esuama* means place of authority, the Kogi believe that's how nature operates. *Esuamas* in the mountains have direct linkage to places on the shore (Ereira 2012).[3]

The Mámas then travel with Ereira, boarding planes to speak with scientists around the world. They go to share their sciences, to 'prove' their ecological observations, and to encourage Younger Brother to think differently about nature. In Eriera's words: 'To show *our* scientists the way nature interconnects' (Ereira, 2012).

Far away, in England, the Mámas meet with surprised astronomers and discuss a star they know very well; a star that is not visible to the naked eye. Ecologists confirm the Mámas knowledge regarding how the

---

[3]   The Gamo People in the highlands of Ethiopia also know this. Settlement in the Gamo territories is at least several thousand years old, as with the Kogi. Both are sustainable and productive, both have supported large populations, and both use Earth protocols based on Law and balance, albeit rendered in different forms. Gamo customary laws, called *wagas*, dictate the correct management of all human-Earth relations: to maintain everything in balance, which in their communities includes an extensive agricultural base and a very large population. As all *wagas* are interconnected and dependent, a lack of balance puts the entire system at risk. Payments are made in order to secure balance for necessities, such as harvest protection or yields, and enacted through various kinds of exchange. Gamo Elder, Kapo Kansa, expresses the rule in this way: "It is not permitted among Gamoans to take out whatever one likes from the ground. There is a limit. You are taking grasses which you need. You don't destroy others. You are taking trees for your consumption. Not to destroy others. You want to pass a resource on for the coming generation" (Global Oneness Project, 2009).

different parts of Shikaka connect to one another. *If there is a scientist like the Máma who knows the earth,* they say, then, perhaps he can verify what we say. Frustratingly, they are mostly met with raised eyebrows. One such scientist, Professor Jonathan Baillie from the Zoological Society of London, responds in the film with the following:

> I don't find it such a surprise really at all, people living with nature understand a lot more about it obviously than a world that has become much, really disconnected from it. Living with nature you realise that certain species have certain strongholds, or certain refuge areas, that are essential to them ... I think it is very important to have that message, they are the ones who are going to know these particular areas in the forest that will be important to the long-term survival of species. So I think we have much to learn from them (Ereira, 2012).

No disrespect to Professor Baillie (who seems quite open-minded), but one has to wonder how it is that the scientific community translate all this into the language of 'strongholds and refuge areas.' Ereira did not fail to convey their message. The point is clearly made. All his commentary could be summarised to suggest there is something profound that we should *learn* from these people. And yet, high in the Sierra, is a group of Elders, still watching, still concerned. They do not think it is too late, *yet.* They hold out hope that there are 'Kogi in other lands' who will open their eyes, who will hear the Mámas Law and story, and understand how things really are (Ereira, 1990).

The Mámas' predictions are not 'fixed,' except in one critical sense. They say that if the Elder Brothers are no more, and Younger Brother does not change (which includes looking after the Elder Brothers, and listening to them), the world will end: The Mother said to the Younger Brother long ago, 'One day, you will look after the Older Brother. One day' (Ereira, 1992, p. 214). The Mámas are not yet sure if this will ever happen.

How Do They Know?

The Kogi are not 'religious' or 'cultural' in any way that can be set apart and analysed according to the pieces (although some have tried), and what they know is the direct result of centuries of highly tuned interaction with a sentient Mother and her enspirited kin, in ways that are specifically ritualised and refined over generations. The Mámas 'proved' their knowledge could be tested by reference to scientific means, as do many indigenous and traditional communities. Yet *how* they come to know can be immediately 'falsified' by its so-called 'supernatural' methods when these are held up against modern scientific standards. One can almost hear the confounded voices of explorers, anthropologists, and scientists echoing through time: How can they possibly claim to know that? That can't be correct. There is no evidence for that. There must be some other explanation.

How they come to know presents a problem.

There *are* explanations, and they appear in various forms and at a range of depths throughout ethnographic literature on indigenous and traditional peoples, and within their oralture. The explanations rely on an understanding of indigenous and traditional metaphysics and the practices which extend from these, as concretely linked to the realisation that Earth and other beings are kin (meant literally), that relationships are not abstract but personal, and that consciousness is not limited to a single human mind, but rather is something all life is *internal* to.

The core message in the films is very obvious: Mother knows more than humans, Mother cares, we are responsible to Mother, you are failing Mother, it is our job to tell you this and try to correct things. Their core message is not about 'the environment,' or 'nature,' and it cannot be reduced to terms like that without losing its orientation. When the Mámas plead with us to sort it out, they seem to assume that Younger Brother knows *why* it might be important to leave the oil and gold in Earth. However, it is not apparent whether Younger Brother *can* actually know this from the intensely dispirited, if not entirely secular, perspective that is now dominating westernised societies. To borrow from the late naturalist and author, Peter Matthiessen (2009), westernised peoples, when viewed through indigenous eyes, seem to have mislaid an entire dimension of existence.

Younger Brother is, for the most part, living without any deep relationship to place, and even in those rare corners where he tries to, references to what might be termed the supernatural are still set apart as novel. Our collective gestures towards anomalistics of various kinds are disorganised, at best, and generally not accepted as part of the 'normal' repertoire of human experience with/in Earth. Furthermore, our diverse modes of interpretation and insistence on the 'regulation' of experiences seem to get in the way. A flash of random lightning for one human, might be a ghostly appearance for another; a conversation with a spirit might be also interpreted as 'a delusion.' In accordance with our socio-cultural norms, we seek consensus as to what interpretation is most likely 'true,' yet our vastly different, highly individualised, symbolic registers conflict with one another in discerning the shape of this truth.

The problem does not end there, however. Emplaced communities of shared inheritance and belief are now so very rare, that individuals who stumble upon such experiences have no collective reference available to them, and can make up their own version of 'what is really going on,' sometimes entirely independently and with mixed results. There is no index for discerning the difference between an attuned communication with spirit, or Earth, and the very human, very random 'thoughts' of an arcane or anomalous nature. The Mámas train for years to cultivate this discernment, just as Buddhists and others in monastic traditions tame the 'chatter' with focus and meditation. Westernised societies offer no institutionalised training of this nature, which puts the individual out on a limb when it comes to learning the difference.

It is quite possible that the absence of a referential body of knowledge for situating anomalous experience can be a significant factor in creating potentially dangerous conditions for the individual, can attract diagnoses of various persuasions, and can be a powerful motivator for exclusion from a community. Our total incapacity to accommodate unseen dimensions also underscores the severe inadequacies of a societal system with no framework for understanding how an attuned human-Earth multispecies interface operates. If we are to do what the Mámas ask, we are going to need to remember how, and in what context, the human functions, and this appears impossible without reference to, and relationship with/in, our sentient, conscious Earth. As put forward by Paul Devereux (with co-authors):

> For a long time now, we have been unable to remember our former closeness with Earth. Due to this amnesia, the ecological problems now thrust upon us have come as a shock ... We notice the emergence of an amnesia that is really a double forgetting, wherein a culture forgets, and then forgets that it has forgotten (Devereux *et al.*, 1992, pp. 2-3).

What if Earth, as the ground and origin of all living beings, is *not* a benign resource, nor a collection of organic matter, but a site of continual conscious interactions (which our collective ancestors and many traditional and indigenous peoples are well aware of)? What if Earth is alive, in the same sense that we unquestionably count ourselves as alive? I frame this as an irreducible truth and, with Devereux, would say this is indeed a truth we have *forgotten*.[4] If we were to accept this premise, and drop the metaphysical bonds which prevent us from properly engaging with the invisible aspects of this ancient relationship, it may yet be possible to reckon with, and even overcome, our present socio-ecological circumstance. What if there is a way to live together, well, with/in Earth? What if we simply need to 'get over it and get on with it' when it comes to accepting Earth sentience?

The Elders invite us all – westernised, indigenous, colonised, and others – to apprentice to Earth-minded traditions in service to our collective futures. If we do this, as the Mámas remind us, it is not yet too late. Earth can be nourished toward proper balance and fertility if Younger Brother starts paying attention to what the Elders say.

Coming-to-Knowing Who and What We Are

The late physicist, F. David Peat, wrote that 'when a person comes into relationship with certain knowledge he or she is not only transformed by it but must also assume responsibility for it' (1994, p. 65). *Coming-to-knowing*, as he called this, is a journey from innocence (or ignorance) to ever-greater responsibilities, which balances the power inherent in knowledge and governs the potential for its misuse. Indigenous and traditional Elders, well-versed in the Laws that govern us all, express the wisdom of a whole lifetime of coming-to-knowing.

Reckoning with this begins with the decision to take indigenous and traditional worldviews seriously, and face up to the implications of doing so. Encounters with what we problematically call the paranormal are respected within indigenous and traditional Earth-focused communities, and misaligned communication (including

---

4   Further support for this line of thinking can be found in John Mohawk (1978), Jerry Mander (1991) Thomas Cooper (1998), Ralph Metzner (1999), Jane Jacobs (2004), Thom Hartmann (2009), Four Arrows (2016c), and Rajani Kanth (2017).

charlatanism) is easy to identify. When an attuned communication or experience is unclear, or results in a meaning that is hard to determine, then the process is mediated by elders and others in the community. Dreams, visions, coincidences, and encounters with 'the numinous' (in whatever form) are all 'data,' and no data is excluded from validity. *A priori* dismissal just does not make sense when Earth is known to be sentient and communicative. If it happens to be a rock that is speaking, well that's just fine. Humans do not determine the vehicle by which guidance arrives.

Consensus, when sought via the context of a group discussion, is not focused on the specifics of 'what happened,' but what was felt, or thought, or seen, and what that experience might *mean*, albeit for the individual or the collective. Although such communities may acknowledge an unseen 'spirit' or relational dimension, our demarcation of this dimension as 'paranormal' would make little sense. Spirit and Earth are entwined with/in Earth-focused communities, and this tends to complicate academic (and other) attempts to study such communities in 'parts.' All elements of social organisation, from kinship, to health practices, to cultivation and preparation of food, education, and work have aspects that, in some way, reference this relationship. The absence of a category or word for 'nature' amongst many traditional and indigenous peoples, the inappropriateness of words such as 'religion' and 'animism,' and other quandaries that have long-occupied academics become un-interesting when a sentient Earth ethic is really understood.

Furthermore, because our academic distinctions between indigenous and westernised worldviews are so entrenched as to often be unconscious, indigenous academics have to argue hard for basic acknowledgment for ways of being that are infinitely richer than those to which they are constantly asked to adapt. In the wake of repeated blows from colonial violences, the legacies of which are ongoing, indigenous and traditional communities deserve legitimacy beyond tokenistic indulgence. Whilst many westernised peoples experience a feeling of freedom without responsibility, Earth-oriented indigenous and traditional peoples have, for over five hundred years now, maintained this sense of responsibility without their freedom. As Pi'ilani-Kahakumakaliua scholar, Haunani-Kay Trask, has written:

> As indigenous peoples, we must fight for Papahānamoku, even as she – and we – are dying. But where do people in the industrial countries draw their battle lines? … If human beings, Native and non-Native alike,

are to create an alternative to the planned New World Order, then those who live in the First World must change their culture, not only their leaders. Who, then, bears primary responsibility? Who carries the burden of obligation? Who will protect mother earth? (1999, p. 62)

This is what it means to have kinship with Earth in these times: to stay with the trouble, even in the darkest of moments. The poignancy of her plea implores us to act differently with/in our world, and to take a journey into our hearts to consult deeply with Earth in an intuitive and emplaced manner.

These Earth sentient models can be consistently identified in both historical and contemporary contexts throughout the world, and the Kogi example is but one of many that might serve as instructional. If a sentient Earth ethic and belief demands a very deliberate reference to, and deep cognisance of, anomalistic phenomena that we might call the 'supernatural' or 'paranormal,' then I would argue that ecology, as concept and praxis, must be incomplete without reference to this dimension. Ecology requires an understanding of Earth as sentient – moreso, as specifically and viscerally *conscious* – in order to be truly effective. What is so often missing in ecological thinking and theory is an overarching, organising principle that transcends the particularities of an interpretative response, and science (as a body of knowledge and set of beliefs) does not provide this. Science alone is too clinical to sustain a really cohesive ecological vision for securing our shared future.

As is evidenced by the Mámas' frustrations, those things that are simple and understood clearly across many, many communities of indigenous and traditional peoples – that Earth is our Mother and is conscious and sentient; that everything is connected and everyone is related; that guidance is available and this guidance is reliable – have to be explained, defended, verified, supported, and clarified many times over when engaging with the westernised, scientific, reductionist worldview.

So, how might we bear witness and take seriously these words that are offered (and insisted upon) as authoritative, as truth? How might we conceive of a collective future, if we cannot (or will not) hear what is being said? The late historian, theologian, and novelist, C.S. Lewis, writing here in a mode of deep reflection following the death of his wife, challenges us to interrogate the very foundations upon which we build our reality. As he writes:

You never know how much you really believe anything until its truth or falsehood becomes a matter of life and death to you. It is easy to say you believe a rope to be strong and sound as long as you are merely using it to cord a box. But suppose you had to hang by that rope over a precipice. Wouldn't you then first discover how much you really trusted it? (1964, p. 64).

What I read in his words is the mandate to question our worldview, those orientations, orderings, and commitments to the un-thought cosmos that, nonetheless, manifest in the largest and smallest elements of daily life. In specifically academic terms, what are the effects of the long-standing impetus to exclude certain things from our collective knowledge bases, often in the pursuit of an ever-more sterile objectivity? What if there are other questions we could be asking, but refuse to consider, due to inherited precepts and biases that we may not even be consciously aware of?

The Mámas are not alone in voicing their concerns. Elders from across the globe have come forward to speak, often affectionately, to Younger Brother.5 Their instructions are clear. Accept the invitation we are extending. Drop the westernised worldview, learn the land, and learn the Laws of the Mother. Make relationships, follow your heart, and learn to walk the right road of respect, responsibility, reciprocity, redistribution, and reverence, *together*. Thankfully, as expressed by Potawatomi educator and botanist, Robin Wall Kimmerer, we are not being asked to do this alone: 'In this time of the sixth extinction, we could use some teachers – it's a good thing we don't have to figure everything out for ourselves' (2015).

The Mámas are asking us to hear their message, which requires that we transform our understanding of who and what we are. Their beliefs and practices are not 'incidental' to their depth of knowledge, nor novel, but illuminate the path we might follow to engage a kind of ecological understanding that is, perhaps, incomprehensible to us just now. They are waiting for Younger Brother to awaken, and say that he holds the remedy for our collective spiritual and ecological ills: a remedy that

---

5   The Council of Thirteen Indigenous Grandmothers, the San Bushmen, Australian Aboriginal Elders, and a host of wisdomkeepers from Turtle Island all point to the same key ideas regarding what is wrong with modern civilisation and how to fix it. These instructions are described in detail in the author's doctoral thesis, specifically chapters four and five (Sepie, 2018).

does not end with our generation, but compels us to be good ancestors to those who will come after. We must learn how to be 'Kogi in other lands,' and to consult directly with the mind of nature, with *aluna*, or by whatever name makes sense in our local tongues. Their final bid regarding our responsibilities was from the Kogi women:

> Our message is not only for people here but people all over the world ... When a baby is born, the Mother is rejuvenated ... The Mother is the owner of everything. All the rivers, all the mountains ... When a baby is born you must have good thoughts. Teach the example of others who have lived well. If we don't teach this baby anything he will not know how to think. This baby will teach the next generation. She will carry on the thread (Ereira, 2012).

Questions

1. The Kogi Mámas are often referred to as 'traditional' and 'religious.' How might these labels result in their knowledge being discredited or not taken seriously?

2. A sentient Earth ethic can alter how we interact with animals and nature. Think about the various ways in which this might affect your own interactions with animals and plants and make a list of how these might change if you were to follow the advice of the Mámas. What challenges would this raise for you in your everyday life?

3. What would scientists and ecologists have to change about how they think about nature and how they undertake their work in order to take the advice they were given in the films?

4. Prophecy and premonitions are often dismissed as 'paranormal' or 'fantasy' by westernised peoples, but they are taken very seriously by indigenous and traditional communities. How does the concept of a prophecy or premonition challenge our ideas of time, space, and the privacy of our own minds?

CHAPTER 4

THIS MOMENT RETURNS TO ME: CHILDHOOD REVERIE AND A LENAPE IDEA OF RECRUITMENT BY THE EARTH

Nancy Wissers

The Way It Started

You know, I think if people stay somewhere long enough – even white people – the spirits will begin to speak to them. It's the power of the spirits coming up from the land. The spirits and the old powers aren't lost, they just need people to be around long enough and the spirits will begin to influence them.

—Crow elder as quoted by poet and writer Gary Snyder (1990, p. 42).

It is hard to know where to start this story. Every time I think of a beginning, I think of something that came before it, but the section of the story that is relevant here began when I was painting a picture. I was in therapy for clinical depression, and I told my therapist I would paint a picture depicting what I encountered when I went for my walks in the woods, the one refuge in my darkening life. The painting is large and I am looking at it now, although it was never finished. It is a life-size depiction of a Pan-like being, a boy, maybe fifteen or sixteen, with dreadlocks, horns, green, slitted eyes, and fur from the waist down. He has a bemused look on his face, and would be carrying a wooden flute if I had filled in the blank space where the flute was going to be.

I just meant it as a metaphor, a picture of something I could not put into words, the reason I was so attached to nature, to bird watching and hiking and anything that meant being out where things grew and lived on their own. I do not see it as coincidence, though, that the phone call that began a new and fascinating part of my life came while I was painting him. The caller on the phone was a local magazine editor I had written for once or twice. She asked if I would be interested in writing an article about the indigenous people of our area, the Lenape people. Up until then I had done only nature writing, but since as far as I knew there were no Lenape anymore, I thought the Lenape article would require little more than reading a few books and contacting a few historical societies. I said yes, never suspecting I had just received what would become 'The Assignment That Ate My Life.'

Trying to be thorough in my research, I went online and sent out a few queries about matters connected to the Lenape and their connection to the supposed pre-Columbian stone work in Pennsylvania, rumors of which reached the newspapers from time to time. I thought it would make an interesting sideline to what otherwise looked to be a dry historical account of a robbed people. Then one night, as if I had walked into a novel, I received a call from a man named Fred Werkheiser, inviting me to come to dinner with him and a friend of his, their treat, to discuss matters concerning the Lenape and the stone work. Several people who had received my email inquiries had passed them on to him, and he wanted to learn what kind of person was inquiring into what apparently was a more delicate matter than I knew. Curious but a little nervous, I agreed to meet with them.

A few nights later, I was seated at a restaurant with two men I did not know, being interviewed to determine whether I was worthy to be given some knowledge, the nature of which I could not divine. They were good company, of wry humor and penetrating intelligence, so the evening would not be wasted even if I failed their test. At the end of the meal they conferred and decided I would be let into at least part of their secret. They could show me *some* of the stone work, and they would introduce me to *some* of the local Lenape people.

Only a little of the adventure I entered into that night is relevant here. I was, of course, skeptical about the people who called themselves Lenape. Most of the people I met did not 'look Indian,' and anyway, there weren't supposed to be any Lenape anymore, except on a reservation in Oklahoma. Only after having talked with them for a while did I become certain that, whatever their story was, these people had been brought up thinking differently than anyone I knew.

The first lead-in to our topic here was a comment by one of them, a young man named Jim Beer. We were talking about non-Indian people who worked to protect the earth and living things – environmentalists and the like – and he made the comment that people who work to protect the Earth, no matter what race they are, were selected or recruited in some way by the Earth itself, that the spirits had spoken to them.

It was an odd thing to say, and it struck me as one of those dreamy things that romantically-minded people like to believe. How could it be true? I mean, how would that work? I had put together a nature newsletter for a year, and distributed it for free. I couldn't remember any kind of recruitment. Everything else he was saying to me seemed thoughtful and insightful, so I allowed Jim this little quirk. Looking back, I can remember discussing Mesingwe with him, too. Mesingwe is the name of a spirit important to the Lenape. I was interested because after reading about him in my early research I had dreamed about him. Even though he was facing away from me in the dream, the moment of seeing him was memorable.

The second thing that led me into this pursuit was a later conversation I had with the man who was then chief, Bob Red Hawk Ruth. Fred Werkheiser's inspiration for his work concerning the stone work and the Lenape was a friend of his, Mark, who had died before I met Fred. Mark was an archaeologist who over time became convinced that some stone structures in the northeast had astronomical alignments and had been built before Columbus 'discovered' America, not by earlier sailors from Europe, but by the indigenous people. He also believed that some sites were still being used surreptitiously for rituals by descendants of the builders. While Fred was an amateur archaeologist, Mark had academic credentials and had to bear the derision of his colleagues, who embraced the orthodox assumption that the natives here did not build in stone, despite the fact that indigenous peoples everywhere else in the Americas did. Rather than back off, however, Mark remained fervent in his conviction until the end of his short life, even though no native people came out in his support. He said that one native man told him privately that the stone work remained hidden by the white man's inability to see, and the fact that Mark could see them meant something special about him.

Fred owned a copy of an unpublished novel by Mark, and he loaned it to me to read. In the novel, Mark brought up in several places something he called 'language in memory,' an experience he had had as a child which he felt was connected with the stone work and the landscape in some way. I recognized in his description an experience I myself had as a child, too, a golden timeless moment while alone in the tall weeds at the back of my parents' property, an experience I had never discussed with anyone.

In Mark's book, it was clear that this experience had shaped his relationship with the land and his own life. Having glimpsed what he glimpsed then, he could never see the land without knowing there was a living mystery contained within it. Thinking about it, I realized that the same was true for me. You could say that that moment had shaped much of my life, and even who I was. It was as if, in those moments, the earth really had recruited us.

I asked Bob Red Hawk whether, according to his way of understanding things, he would say that Mark had been contacted by spirits, whether he would see that as the source of Mark's vision and courage. Bob said yes. And suddenly I got it. This had nothing to do with the article I was working on at the time, but when I got off the phone I was elated. Maybe, I thought, I had never before had any idea what 'spirits' were. Maybe when these people used the word, they meant something *different* from what I thought it meant. Maybe they meant something that was real in my world, too. I lay back on the bed and kicked my feet in the air. I knew something, but right then I couldn't have told you exactly what it was.

But What?

In that childhood moment, I now realized, the sensation had been much like being with and communicating with someone, except that there was no tangible someone. It was as if there were something or some things out in the landscape with psychologically active properties, but no detectable physical properties – spirits. If this was what some people meant by spirits, they were nothing like what I had imagined spirits to be. The best way I can put it, I suppose, is that there was no outward localised presence, just the effect – a sense of inward presence and communication – which one cannot examine at the time, caught up in a sort of mystical ecstasy, but which is evident afterward, as Mark had put it, in memory.

Inward effect with no physical presence – that description captures the essence of the experience and shows why it is so hard to talk about, especially because that sense of an inwardly communicating presence is often apparent only in retrospect. Since we have little context for something from the outside touching the self without words, other than those provided by religion and culture, someone knowing only the Western worldview is likely to conceive of these golden moments as internal events of the self, or perhaps even as the presence of God. This experience happens to the religious and non-religious alike, however, generating the same life-long effects.

Words fail when we try to recreate it, and it is impossible to convey to someone who has not had it what the experience itself is like. Even when I have been writing about it, if I, in the course of other activities, experience some of it, my first thought when it is over is that it is not like what I am imagining during the writing. It is closer, more immediate, more private and personal than I can convey in any way I can think of. Good poetry comes closest, and I have to think that many poets have at least one of these experiences in their pasts. It occurred to me that people in our culture who had this experience would be forced to make up metaphors. The passage containing Pan in *The Wind in the Willows,* and Debussy's *Prelude to the Afternoon of a Faun,* seemed now like attempts to depict this intangible reality that had qualities of man and of nature, just as I had attempted it in my painting without knowing why.

I began to search for words for what I conceived it to be. I started with 'entity,' 'being,' 'consciousness,' 'psyche,' and the thesaurus soon had me off to 'wight,' 'fairy,' 'angel,' 'deva,' 'genius loci.' There was no word with the meaning I was looking for, exactly. Why would there be if our culture didn't have the concept? I ran across the word 'manitou,' a related Algonquin word, and that got me thinking about the Lenape again, who speak one of many Algonquian languages. Mesingwe, who I mentioned earlier, is an important figure in their spiritual world. They depict him as a human/animal mix, a hairy man like a Sasquatch. In an important story told about him he takes pity on and appears to two boys who were abused or neglected by their parents. He helps them and teaches them, eventually enabling them to return and help the whole village in a time of crisis.

I learned that sometimes before a Lenape child went out for vision quest, the parents and people of the village would pretend to abuse and neglect him, so that spirits like Mesingwe might take pity on him and choose to become his helper or guide. Was what happened to Mark and me similar to a vision quest? What would a vision quest be like if it happened by accident to someone who was completely unprepared for it? I knew that Mark had resorted to the outdoors as a refuge from serious abuse. While I hadn't been abused, I spent time outdoors as a young girl to escape a rough older brother and the strong emotions of my parents' failing marriage. Maybe the spirits took pity on us.

Then there was the issue of helper or guardian spirits. I knew nothing about them at first, but they were what vision quests were often about, and the qualities they added to a person who gained one were just the qualities that made someone like Mark stand out. Not just Mark, but people through history who had contributed to our culture showed many of the qualities attributed to people who had guardian or helper spirits.

The word *genius* as we commonly use it originally meant the helper spirit the outstanding person was thought to have. *Inspiration* means the arrival of a spirit. To be *dispirited* means to have lost your spirit. Language is like an archaeological site that is always at hand, and vestiges of many old ways of thinking remain buried in it.

I had never read about shamanism, for years dismissing it as just another way for some New Age crackpots to draw attention and money to themselves. But now I discovered that shamanism was all about spirits. Most of it seemed pretty far out, even though I was more prepared than I used to be to entertain new notions. Then I ran across something in one of the books that helped popularize shamanism in the West, *The Way of the Shaman* by Michael Harner. It said:

> To a shaman it is readily apparent that many Westerners have guardian spirits, as evidenced by their energy, good health, and other outward manifestations of their power. It is tragic, from the point of view of such a shaman that even these power-full people are nonetheless ignorant of the source of their power and thus do not know how to utilize it fully. A related tragedy, from the same

point of view, is that lethargic, ill, and dispirited Western adults have obviously lost the guardian spirits that protected them through childhood. Worse, they do not even know that there is a method to regain them (Harner, 1990, p. 65).

Tears came to my eyes when I found that. I was pretty sure I knew how at least some of those Westerners had acquired their guardian spirits. Records of those experiences had to be buried throughout Western literature. Time to take a look around.

Tracks of the Spirits

First, what is the nature of the experience we are talking about? How will we know it if someone describes it? For someone who has experienced it, it is easy to recognize, but here are some aspects that are common in descriptions of the experience. Most descriptions will include some of these characteristics. Few will have all.

1. The moment is *memorable*. Decades later, the person can usually tell you exactly where he or she was, and often can describe details: flowers that were blooming, the sound of bees or the colors of butterflies, even the quality or angle of the light.

2. The realizations that came with the moment have the sense of being *absolutely true*. One is seized with certainty and may believe he or she has had a vision of the inner workings of the world, the true essence of being. Most people come away from it with a strong feeling of awe and of having encountered a, or perhaps *the*, great mystery.

3. Subjects may experience a sense of *timelessness*, as if the experience somehow took place outside of regular time, in an eternal moment of what some might call blessing. While it is happening there is no chance that another person will come along and interrupt, as if you have stepped into an adjacent version of the world where others are invisible to you and you to them, or as if the power that is reaching you also has the power to divert anyone from that spot.

4. The world or the place seems *indescribably beautiful*, perfect in every detail, even in the characteristics that have always seemed like faults or wrongs. Beyond a shadow of a doubt and despite anything else that may be going on, everything is good and right.

5. This world that is good and right may have characteristics of a *being* or *person*, as if the place where you are, or the planet or world itself is some*one* rather than something.

6. Subjects may feel *personally blessed* by this perfect beautiful world, or befriended by this great being. The experience seems to be happening, not randomly because you happen to be there, but particularly and especially to you – who you are in the deepest and most personal sense. It knows you.

7. Subjects may have the feeling or realization that they are *one* with this perfect beautiful world, that all apparent separation is an illusion.

8. Subjects may be seized with the feeling or realization that the world, and therefore they who are one with it, are *eternal*, incapable of being destroyed.

9. Subjects may perceive everything around them as having a profound *meaning*, or feel they are receiving something like speech without words, language or communication of an esoteric nature, which tells them deep and absolute truths. Sometimes this may seem to be communicated through the behavior of some creature or through the wind, or by the sun moving on the leaves, in other words through some natural agent that has taken on, for that time, a supernatural significance.

10. Subjects are frequently taken up in a feeling of joy, elation or *ecstasy.*

These are the primary characteristics, but having listed them I have not described the experience. Those who have had it know that the experience is whole, immediate, intensely personal and ineffable. One is in the moment and in the world in a different way from normal, and the difference is inexpressible. These characteristics can only be separated and described with much thought later.

All of this makes it fascinating to search for and read accounts of these experiences in literature. Since there is no consensus name for it and the writers are attempting to describe the indescribable, they resort to creativity to express what they have experienced. I found some of the following descriptions myself, and others had already been collected by people who were exploring the topic for other reasons. Here is a good one to start with. I quote it from Tobin Hart's *The Secret Spiritual World of Children*. The girl who had it is simply known as Debbie:

> At age eleven, Debbie was by herself, lying back on her swing set. As she described, 'I was looking at the sky, just watching. I don't know how it happened but it all opened up to me. I don't know how to say it, but I felt everything was perfect and connected. I can't say I was thinking about anything – it's like there was no room even to think. It felt like my chest could just burst open and fly into a million pieces. It felt like I could explode and be the sun and the clouds' (Hart, 2003, p. 11).

Here is a passage from Thom Hartmann's *The Last Hours of Ancient Sunlight*, which it is worth quoting at length:

> I remember a summer when I was five years old. My parents had recently purchased a hammock and put it in our back yard, and I was lying on it on a bright sunny afternoon. The sky was a deep blue, with thin wispy clouds, and I could smell the fresh-mowed grass crushed by the green-painted yellow frame of the hammock. I could feel the ropes of the hammock against my back, through my T-shirt and pressing against my bare legs below my shorts, and hear the melodic sounds of birds singing in the trees that surrounded the yard. One of the birds was repeating over and over a three note call, while others chirped randomly.
>
> I stared at the sky, noticing little specks in my field of vision and how they'd jump when I moved my eyes and then slowly settle when I held my sight on a particular bit of cloud. There was a gentle wind blowing, and I could hear it rustling the leaves of the huge old maple tree about thirty feet from me; the hammock rocked very slightly, a soothing motion that made the sky seem to tilt slightly from side to side.

Turning my head to the left, I noticed that I was ten feet from a stand of pink, white, and yellow hollyhocks, covered with blossoms and standing five feet tall. The thick white stamens erupted from the waxy, colored petals, and honeybees and bumblebees moved lazily from flower to flower gathering pollen. I could hear them buzzing, as if they were humming their pleasure in finding the pollen.

As I looked at the way colors flowed from pink to white on the flower petals, noticed how the sounds of birds had changed with the movement of my head, felt the sun now full-warm on the right side of my face, I was washed over with a sense of total Now. I saw that the flowers were alive, the bees were alive, the tree and the birds were alive, and I was alive. The air was crystal clear, and I noticed the empty space between me and the flowers, the distance between me and the grass, the next house over, and the tree. Even the empty spaces vibrated with life.

"Wow," I said softly, then heard the sound of my own voice, and that was another miracle, amazing me all over again. It was a perfectly ordinary moment, but filled with Spirit (Hartmann, 2000, p. 254).

The Irish poet and mystic A.E. Russell describes an encounter he had while taking walks in the countryside during his adolescence:

The tinted air glowed before me with intelligible significance like a face, a voice. The visible world became like a tapestry blown and stirred by winds behind it. If it would raise for just an instant I knew I would be in paradise. Every form on that tapestry appeared to be the work of gods. Every flower was a word, a thought. The grass was speech; the trees were speech; the waters were speech; the winds were speech. They were the Army of the Voice ... I listened with my whole being, and then these apparitions would fade away and I would be the mean and miserable boy once more (Russell, 1918, pp. 4-5).

Albert Hofman's description of his experience is particularly beautiful and apt:

One enchantment of that kind, which I experienced in childhood, has remained remarkably vivid in my memory ever since. It happened on a May morning – I have forgotten the year – but I can still point to the exact spot where it occurred, on a forest path on Martinsberg above Baden, Switzerland. As I strolled through the freshly greened woods filled with bird song and lit up by the morning sun, all at once everything appeared in an uncommonly clear light.

Was this something I had simply failed to notice before? Was I suddenly discovering the spring forest as it actually looked? It shone with the most beautiful radiance, speaking to the heart, as though it wanted to encompass me in its majesty. I was filled with an indescribable sensation of joy, oneness, and blissful security.

I have no idea how long I stood there spellbound. But I recall the anxious concern I felt as the radiance slowly dissolved and I hiked on: how could a vision that was so real and convincing, so directly and deeply felt – how could it end so soon? And how could I tell anyone about it, as my overflowing joy compelled me to do, since I knew there were no words to describe what I had seen? It seemed strange that I, as a child, had seen something so marvelous, something that adults obviously did not perceive – for I had never heard them mention it.

While still a child, I experienced several more of these deeply euphoric moments on my rambles through forest and meadow. It was these experiences that shaped the main outlines of my world view and convinced me of the existence of a miraculous, powerful, unfathomable reality that was hidden from everyday sight (Hoffman, 1983, pp. 29-30).

Notice that he mentions the long-term effects of the experience on his life. Thomas Berry, too, found his epiphany to be life-changing, as he wrote in *The Great Work*:

My own understanding of the Great Work began when I was quite young. At the time I was some eleven years old. My family was moving from a more settled part of a small southern town out to the edge of town where the new house was being built. The house, not yet finished, was situated on a slight incline. Down below was a small creek and there across the creek was a meadow. It was an early afternoon in late May when I first wandered down the incline, crossed the creek, and looked out over the scene.

The field was covered with white lilies rising above the thick grass. A magic moment, this experience gave to my life something that seems to explain my thinking at a more profound level than almost any other experience I can remember. It was not only the lilies. It was the singing of the crickets and the woodlands in the distance and the clouds in a clear sky. It was not something conscious that happened just then. I went on about my life as any young person might do.

Perhaps it was not simply this moment that made such a deep impression upon me. Perhaps it was a sensitivity that was developed throughout my childhood. Yet as the years pass this moment returns to me, and whenever I think about my basic life attitude and the whole trend of my mind and the causes to which I have given my efforts, I seem to come back to this moment and the impact it has had on my feeling for what is real and worthwhile in life.

This early experience, it seems, has become normative for me throughout the entire range of my thinking. Whatever preserves and enhances this meadow in the natural cycles of its transformation is good; whatever opposes this meadow or negates it is not good. My life orientation is that simple. It is also that pervasive. It applies in economics and political orientation as well as in education and religion (Berry, 1999, pp. 12-13).

Thomas Berry devoted his life to serving the Earth, and that experience could be said to be his recruitment. Virginia Woolf also describes the importance of her childhood experience:

If life has a base that it stands upon, if it is a bowl that one fills and fills and fills – then my bowl without a doubt stands upon this memory. It is of hearing the waves breaking, one, two, one, two, and sending a splash of water over the beach; and then breaking, one, two, one, two, behind a yellow blind. It is of hearing the blind draw its little acorn across the floor as the wind blew the blind out. It is of lying and hearing this splash and seeing this light, and feeling, it is almost impossible that I should be here; of feeling the purest ecstasy I can conceive (Woolf, 1985, p. 64).

These examples demonstrate that some very talented and influential people attribute significant aspects of their lives to moments like these.

There are many more. With research I learned that I am not the first to observe this. Edith Cobb's *The Ecology of Imagination in Childhood* is an exploration of the phenomenon. Tobin Hart, in *The Secret Spiritual World of Children*, writes:

> Childhood moments of wonder are not merely passing reveries. They shape the way a child sees and understands the world, and they often form a core of his or her spiritual identity, morality, and mission in life (Hart, p. 53).

Rupert Sheldrake, in *The Rebirth of Nature*, writes:

> Many children have in certain moments a mystical sense of their connection with the world. Some forget it. Others remember it in a way that serves as a continuing source of inspiration (Sheldrake, 1991, p. 215).

Albert Camus' well-known quotation about art seems to be saying the same thing:

> A man's work is nothing but this slow trek to rediscover, through the detours of art, those two or three great and simple images in whose presence his heart first opened (Camus, 1937).

Sometimes a person's entire life becomes a long attempt to rediscover and understand that childhood epiphany. After speaking to Red Hawk that day I began to realize that I was doing just that, that most of my favorite literature and music contained references to similar experiences. Van Morrison sang 'No guru, no method, no teacher, just you and I and nature ... ' Thoreau, in all his writings, expressed the timelessness and ineffable friendship he experienced out in nature. Tolkien's Tom Bombadil – what was he but the experience personified? They seemed to be doing what I had done, when as part of therapy I had painted that woodland figure. Personification was almost irresistible. The sense that I was being spoken to, that I was befriended by a great beneficent being was so strong. Anyone who reached inside and tried to categorize it might come up with something that had some characteristics of natural things combined with the psychology of people. I wondered if man/plant and man/animal figures in cultures around the world had arisen when people tried to understand and describe this thing that happened to them out on the landscape.

How many people have this experience and never acknowledge it? How many have had it and felt alienated from society because of the disconnect between how important the feelings of it were to them and how trivial they seemed to be in the culture? How many had been kept from mentioning it by worry over being seen as ridiculous or just crazy when they said they had some kind of personal mystical experience? How many put it out of their conscious minds and yet have been guided by it in their likes and dislikes, in their interests and choices of vocation – in their heart of hearts?

My hunch was that the numbers were large. One thing I have learned in aging is that my experiences and thoughts, no matter how individual and personal they seem, are almost always shared by large numbers of people. On more than one occasion when I have confessed some terrible thought, or described some regrettable mistake from my past, I have been surprised to have my confidant, instead of looking horrified as I anticipated, nod or even laugh in recognition. Our insides are not as unique as we imagine.

How could I recognize those people? I looked at Van Morrison, J.R.R. Tolkien, and Henry Thoreau, three people I was pretty sure had been spoken to. What did they have in common, besides being creative and articulate, what were the characteristics that allowed me to be aware of them? They had in common poetry, a love of nature, taking walks, and strong spirituality, although of various types. At this time, I was so excited by what I was realizing that I spoke about it at some length with my teenage son. When he caught on quickly and began to say things like 'I was talking to this teacher at school today, and I think he's One,' meaning one of the people we had been talking about, it increased my conviction that I was looking at something real.

In one memorable incident, we arrived early for a poetry reading and were talking with the young man who had initiated them and hosted them at the location. He talked to us lovingly about a beautiful natural place where he had once lived. This fellow never hesitated to speak of his spirituality, and of course, poetry was very important to him. My son and I looked at one another and I asked the question already knowing the answer: 'Did you spend a lot of time alone outdoors as a child?' He said yes, and we laughed. He was One.

I soon learned that that was the question to ask. Many people when asked about a spiritual or mystical experience in childhood backed off, whether because it was too personal or because to begin to own it would dredge up a lot of stuff they didn't want to deal with, I don't know. In many cases they probably never thought of it in those terms.

One friend, for example, who I knew was One, a great lover and protector of nature, writer of poetry and who said he went to the woods as his church, when I asked him denied ever having any kind of childhood epiphany. It gave me pause and I started to rethink my understandings because I believed him. He was not a person to lie about deep things. Then I saw him a year or so later and he asked what I was working on. I said it was this project, and I had found descriptions of these childhood experiences in the writings of some people we both admired. He smiled and said he knew he told me he did not remember any of those experiences, but since he told me that, he had remembered a number of them. They had just taken a while to surface and be connected with the description I offered. My great exception was resolved.

As I have continued to explore the idea, I have come to believe that these inadvertent vision quest experiences are related to other non-rational experiences people have out on the land, from those described so beautifully and thoughtfully in Dr. Freya Mathews' piece about Hamilton Downs (Matthews, 2007) to more famous stories like that of Carl Jung and the golden scarab, or Joseph Campbell and the praying mantis. They are part of an interplay between individual and land or place that affects many, many people but is often ignored or suppressed in memory.

The circumstance most likely to generate a memorable symbolic incident of communication from the land to an individual is the death of a loved one. Bring it up in any group of people and someone, often many someones, will have stories to tell about gestures received through some agent of nature, often but not always birds or butterflies. The most beautiful example I can think of is a story told to me by my friend Estelle, herself a champion of conservation and ecological health, working for the state I live in to protect the integrity of our watersheds. Her older girls were grown up and out of the house by the time of the incident and her husband of many years had left her. She lived alone with her youngest daughter, Lydia, a beautiful little girl with Down's Syndrome.

The girl was my friend's deepest treasure, but Lydia's health was failing and Estelle took her to every doctor she could, trying to find a way to improve her health and keep her alive. One day while Estelle was outside briefly, Lydia somehow managed to climb up and let their parakeet out of its cage. When Estelle came in she asked, surprised, why Lydia had done it. 'It wants to be free, Mommy,' the girl said, 'it needs to be free!' Less than a week later, Lydia died (free!).

A few days later at the part of the funeral service that was in the cemetery, as mourners were gathered and a priest was speaking, an enormous flock of snow geese flew over, filling the sky, the honking so loud that the priest could not be heard. For a few moments he stopped and everyone just stood silent and watched hundreds of the white birds pass overhead. Estelle's voice was full of awe when she described the scene to me. She knew she had witnessed a gesture.

Millions of people experience these moments of grace – the timeless ecstatic moments of childhood, and the deft metaphors the land offers us when our hearts are open. What would it take for more people to understand those moments as part of a real back and forth between them and someone or something that knows them? How do you convince people that the thing they long to believe, the thing they were long ago forced to give up on, is true?

As for me, the clinical depression that was so deeply troubling at the beginning of this story eased as the process of discovery relieved the tension between the understandings of the world that had been taught to me and the compelling secrets whispered to my heart so many years ago. If I wish anything it is that others wrapped in that painful struggle with themselves could reclaim, even come to treasure, those golden moments of their childhoods, and maybe find the same relief.

I couldn't agree more with Dr. Mathews' suggestion in her essay *On Desiring Nature* (2010) that understanding and experiencing the Earth's ability to generate meaning could help people love and identify with the land and nature and therefore naturally treat it better. I would add that the same understanding, by freeing people from the struggle between what they have been taught about the world and those certainties that they have been storing deep inside, could help many people love themselves and even other people more, restoring magic to lives so long bereft of it. Perhaps it could even be part of a movement to help our *dispirited* societies become *inspired* once more.

Questions

1. Do you remember having any of the kinds of experiences described in the essay? Has anyone you know ever described having such an experience? If so, write down what you remember, and some thoughts or feelings you have about it.

2. People in many cultures around the world tell stories of give and take or communication between individuals and the landscape and living things on it. Give a possible explanation, or more than one, why modern Western cultures tend not to see the land and nature as psychoactive or as the possible source of wisdom or ecstasy it can be for some others.

3. Pretend you are writing a fictional story in which a child has one of these mystical experiences. How do you imagine that abuse, neglect, or rejection by their family or community might make the child more likely to have that experience? If you want, try writing a bit of that story.

4. Continue imagining that child or imagine a bereaved or otherwise grieving person of any age. Now, by description in prose or poetry, or by drawing if you prefer, portray a being to personify the 'spirit' or the experience that the person might meet while outside alone. Add dialogue if you like. Can you imagine yourself having such an experience or encounter?

CHAPTER 5

THE INVISIBLE ECOSYSTEM: A NATIVE AMERICAN PERSPECTIVE

Lance M. Foster

∼

> *When it comes to actually believing in the reality of subjective experiences of things such as nonhuman sentience, prophecy and dreams, or communication with the dead, scholars tend toward reticence and postmodern deconstruction at best, or outright dismissal at worst. At least in anthropology, a handful of scholars have begun to "come out" about the extraordinary and often – at least according to Western epistemologies – inexplicable experiences thay have had while conducting fieldwork: cases of interspecies communication, entanglements with magic, and yes, encounters with spirits (Boyd & Thrush 2011: xxxii).*

How do you talk about something that you don't believe in anymore? I am not talking about anthropology, though other native people have a problem with it. I am talking about the paranormal. I don't believe in the paranormal anymore. Or the concept of the paranormal, because it is a culturally-constructed, etic label – a result of the Cartesian split in Western society. I used to use the term all the time, but now I have problems with it.

Paranthropology (Hunter, 2012) looks at the paranormal through an anthropological lens: theory, methodology, history, the holism of the four fields (though ethnography/social anthropology dominates). I have both undergraduate and graduate degrees in anthropology, although, since I graduated with my masters in anthropology back in the mid-90s, I am not an academic. I work as an historic preservationist and cultural advocate for my tribe, the Iowa Tribe of Kansas and Nebraska, or simply, the Ioway or *Baxoje*. I haven't kept up with the everchanging paradigms typical of academe, no, -required- in academe.

I have been going through back issues of the journal *Paranthropology*, to get an idea of the paradigms, theoretical and methodological approaches that dominate discourse on the paranormal, and I am stuck. So much of what people experience, and the implications of those experiences, does not fit well with the theoretical paradigms that are acceptable to the academy.

The preferred paradigm, couched in the theory of whatever discipline the author is coming from, appears most often to be a psychological one, always leading back to the ego and the individual, the subject. Thus the dominant approaches reduce the paranormal to the purely subjective. Sometimes there are sociological, anthropological, literary and philosophical mixtures or maps, which all add subtly different spins on the same general theme.

It is rare to simply accept an odd experience and go on with one's business, but that is precisely how it is done in Indian country. Not so in the dominant culture. If not outright denied, the odd experience or phenomenon has to be worried to death, like a terrier shaking a rat, then dissected and put in a box, with the lid firmly on and stored on the correct shelf.

Experiencing the Invisible Ecosystem

I repeat: I have personally experienced the paranormal at various times in my life, but I don't really believe in the idea of the paranormal anymore. There is no such thing as the paranormal. This is where I have finally landed. The things we experience are every bit as normal as anything else, in the sense of being part of nature, of the mystery of the world. Perhaps experienced relatively infrequently or only in particular situations, but no less a part of nature. What I am calling the 'invisible ecosystem' is that part of the continuum of the world not generally seen or commonly accepted, but just as much a part of nature as any other part; it is an interrelated, if invisible, part of the ecosystem in general. Rather than haunted houses, most of my experiences with the inexplicable have been in the natural world.

I am not talking about intuition or the imaginal. I am talking about something experienced as consensual reality by many clear thinking and practical people, seen by several at the same time, in the literature but also in my own life. To give just a couple of examples: when we were children my brothers and I saw a little man's strange house at the bottom of a stone funnel in the woods in the Pacific Northwest, and when my uncle Herman and I saw a giant made of rain and clouds a thousand feet tall stride with his two immense legs across a Montana river while we were driving a pickup to Billings. Another time, I heard the sound of a ghost sobbing through the night from under the floor as a dozen students sat sleepless and listening in the darkness all night long in an Indian college dorm common room in Santa Fe. As an archaeologist, I experienced a number of field experiences that some might call paranormal – cabins and mines inhabited by the invisible, likely influenced or caused by the natural geology of the area (Foster, 2012).

Giants, little people, animals from ancient times, underwater beings, ghosts, bigfoot, sentient plants and places, things without names. They may not be common, but they exist, and have always existed as part of nature.

Plenty Coups' Story

Plenty Coups (1848-1932) was the last principal chief of the Crow Nation recognized as such by the Crow generally. When he was a young man, he experienced something he later told his biographer Frank B. Linderman. It was in his youth, when he and his war party were preparing to cross the Missouri River on a horse stealing raid against the Lakota:

> Until the sun went down we watched, and even till the dusk was closing in, never tiring of what we saw. Then we went down to the river, stripped, hid our clothing and our guns, and waited a little for night to come nearer before we should cross. We knew we were apt

to be a big hurry when we returned, if we ever did; so we carefully marked the place where we were to enter the water.

The way to the other bank was far and the landing we hope to make, good; but there was something about the water just where we were that I could not understand. It was too quiet. It was as though it did not belong to the rest of the river. When I dropped an offering of fat buffalo meat into it, it sank like a stone. This was not right. Fat meat should not sink. I did not like the way the water looked either. Thinking it best to keep these thoughts to myself, however, I said nothing to my companions, did not even speak of the strangeness of the water, when together we started for the black line of the other shore. There was no wind, no swish of water, no sound except the snorting of our swimming horses. We were in the middle of the river, and the moon was coming into the sky, when Covers-his-face called out, 'Something is holding me!'

I thought at once of the strangeness of the water, of the sinking back-fat, and my heart tried to jump out of my mouth. The moonlight fell full upon Covers-his-face, like a streak of firelight from a lodge door. His horse was lifted out of the water! He was standing still in the middle of the Big River, where the bottom was far beneath him!

I wanted to get away from there, but I turned my horse in his direction, my heart beating like a war-drum. 'What is it?' I asked, and I am sure my voice must have trembled a little.

'I do not know,' he answered. 'Something is holding me here. I cannot get my horse away from this place.'

My own horse came alongside of his, and sticking out my foot, I kicked under him. My toes touched something that felt like greasy feathers, something soft and slippery. Wooof!

When a man knows what he is fighting, his heart is strong. I could see nothing at all here. So when my horse began to rise, to be lifted like my companion's, my heart tried to jump out of my mouth. But I swallowed it and put my hand on Covers-his-face. 'Are you hurt?' I whispered.

'No,' he answered, 'but I cannot get away from here. Something I cannot see is holding me. You had better get away, if you can.'

Then whatever it was held us let go. Both my horse and that of Covers-his-face began to sink down in the water. There was no sound, no trembling, nothing to let us know what was beneath us. Presently our horses began to swim again, as though nothing had happened."

The old man paused here take a pipe from Plain-bull, his face as much of a mystery as his story.

"I never knew what lifted us out of the water in the Big River that night," he said solemnly. "I am not now trying to tell you, but it must have been some powerful Water-person who lived just there in the Big River. There are many things which we do not understand, things that are beyond us, and we meet them in this life all we can do is to recognize their existence and let them alone. They possess rights here, given to them by Ah-badt-dadt-deah [the Creator] just as we do.

We came out of the water on the north bank, just where a big trail touched the river. It led through a cottonwood grove to the open plains, and was straight. I noticed a cottonwood snag that had no bark on it. It looked white in the moonlight, and there was evidence that some Sioux had once kindled a fire near it. I took one of the black sticks from the old fire-ring and marked the snag. It would show us exactly where to swim the river in a hurry and help us to keep a little below that bad place (Plenty Coups, in Linderman, 2002 [1930], pp. 107-108).

Note that upon being released by the Water-person, they did not lose heart or change their purpose. It was frightening and inexplicable, but it was just a part of the natural world, a feature of the invisible ecosystem. They went on ahead with their night time horse raid, and succeeded in capturing horses for each man. And they returned to cross the river to head back home, but just a little further downstream. And the Water-person did not bother them again.

Invisible Made Visible

Indigenous people may experience some things as infrequently encountered, but they are no less real than anything else infrequently encountered. These things don't happen every day, but they happen. They are just part of creation, of the natural world like anything else.

But they are seen so infrequently, only in certain places, or by certain people, or under certain conditions, they are effectively invisible. A wise and experienced deer can live for years in the woods right next to your suburban house, bed silently in that patch of tall grass, and never be seen or known to be there by its human neighbors, traveling in the dark or in the moments of inattention within people's rambling attention spans.

We have something here along the Missouri River in Nebraska and Kansas that people call Black Panthers. No one thinks they are dark-phase leopards, but use the American sense of panther for the mountain lion or cougar. Some have seen them cross the road, but not many, and the animals were black in color or very dark. No proof existed for decades, until someone caught a cougar on a trail cam, but one of pale color like the ones you would expect to find. Although several people, including myself, have seen the black panthers, still no solid proof exists of the dark kind. Black panthers remain the stuff of American folklore and cryptozoology. Meanwhile they have lived here in fragmented farm country for no one knows how long, as part of the invisible ecosystem. The invisible is all around us.

> An invisible and continuous life was believed to permeate all things, seen and unseen ... Through this mysterious life and power, all things are related to one another and to man, the seen to the unseen, the dead to the living, a fragment of anything to its entirety. This invisible life and power was called Wakon'da (Fletcher & La Flesche, 1911, p. 134)

Scholars and Indigenous Sources

Some of the readers of this essay themselves have either experienced something they know to be very real, or something they are still struggling to understand. But once one does accept that the invisible ecosystem is real, then what? Most people in the mainstream culture see these things as either something inside the head, either because you have a mental aberration, are an intuitive, or have taken a psychedelic. And then they grapple with it, trying to work our how real it is. Sometimes they grapple with it all their lives. Scholars in particular are on a tightrope, especially those with academic careers to advance and protect. The anathema of being thought a 'kook' is part of the risk:

In fact, most scholars writing on ghosts and the supernatural generally dismiss specters as little more than anti-colonial metaphors and psychological manifestations of the repressed, or evade altogether the question of whether spirits are real ... The majority of scholarly writers working on ghosts and hauntings – and interestingly, like most of the popular writers who compile collections of ghost stories for wider audiences – punt. They avoid taking a stand on their own belief systems and, we might imagine in at least some cases, their own subjective experiences ... This demurral regarding the dead, when considered in the context of Indian ghosts and hauntings, is squarely at odds with the increasingly compelling consensus regarding the need for academic scholarship to take indigenous epistemologies and ways of knowing and being seriously. [Indigenous scholars and others writing from the margins] ... have called for academe to engage seriously the ways in which indigenous peoples, individually and communally, understand power, place, time, and other basic constructions of reality (Boyd & Thrush, 2011, pp. xxxi-xxxii).

As Boyd and Thrush state, 'Does our potential professional discomfort outweigh our oft-stated commitments to respect the peoples on whose lives and histories we build our careers?' (ibid, p. xxxiii).

Proving the Paranormal?

Even if it was possible, what would be the ultimate point of proving anything paranormal is 'real,' in a sense that is acceptable to western science? Look at what happens to anything considered 'real' in science, and proved so. If a phenomena is of interest, science wrestles with it, to define it and how to work with it. The next step is to see what it can be used for. How it can be shaped and manipulated for the interests of those doing the shaping. It is the way of the dominant culture, which has bent nature, and continues to bend nature, to its will. Ultimately the collective will of society is all about power and money.

Scientists may start with pure curiosity, altruistic motives and theoretical interests (or perhaps not so altruistic, in having to carve out an area that can be definitive enough to base a career on (not to metion a way to be remembered). But that is just the beginning for anything in this society. Once something is real and defined, the next question is now what?

Once theoretical physicists figured out the atom – knowledge that could be used for so many things – nuclear weapons and warfare were born. While nuclear power was also developed, its first applications were military. And then there are always unintended consequences to what is considered good or profitable or necessary (although only if money can be made from it), consequences like Chernobyl or Fukushima, and simply what to do with the spent rods that need cooling and all the other waste to be disposed of in an ever sickening world.

Once geneticists figured out the gene, genetic recombination was next on the agenda, then cloning and 'shmeat,' and on to human alterations – shopping for and constructing the ideal baby.

There are two sayings that might apply to the researcher of the paranormal. 'You knew what I was when you picked me up,' said the snake as he bit those who helped him, as the old story goes. Another old saying goes 'You can't put the cat back into the bag.' And especially not when there is profit to be made, and power to be sought. The result of that worldview is a world of collapsing natural systems and climate disruption.

So, yeah, I do not believe in the paranormal. There is no such thing as the paranormal. I believe it is all normal, just a less frequently encountered part of the continuum of reality, of creation both seen and unseen, an invisible ecosystem outside the spectrum we generally sense. It is a part we haven't been able to figure out how to make a buck on (well, some have, it seems), and, intentionally or not, because of that, something we ultimately end up warping and destroying. Proving something exists to the standard demanded by science is never good enough. It never stops there in the end.

The indigenous way to encounter the invisible ecosystem was summed up by Plenty Coups: When you encounter strange things in this life, you just acknowledge their right to be here, the same as anything else; you leave them alone, and go on your way. But what I see is that it seems to be near impossible for the nonindigenous to leave things alone.

One could argue that if one accepts that the invisible ecosystem exists in reality, it should also be an extension of the ecosystems we know. Consequently, principles for living should also be extensions of ecology. Principles like trophic levels, niches, habitat, biodiversity, natural selection, invasive species, and so on. Everything exists in a web of relationships, a reality in Native American philosophy and social organization, and ecology. That could be the next step, rediscovering those relationships in the invisible spectrum, and repairing them.

Ideally, eventually one finds such things are not about profit, spiritual tourism or entertainment. Once someone walks on a path to cooperation, working together, and responsibility for the existence we all share, they acquire a mark of maturity and realization of one's place in this universe. This is something shared in the old traditions of perhaps all cultures: responsibility for and guardianship of the ecosystem that gives us life, that we are really a part of, whether an ecosystem which is seen or the unseen portion, the invisible ecosystem.

Questions

1. What does the author mean by 'the invisible ecosystem'?

2. Why does the author reject the term 'paranormal'?

3. What is the proper way to interact with mysterious beings according to Plenty Coups? How is that different than the culture you belong to?

4. What could be the downside of proving the paranormal exists?

CHAPTER 6

PIERCING THE VEIL
WITH THE TRICKSTER

Jacob W. Glazier

~

*Nature emerges from this exercise as 'coyote.' This potent
trickster can show us that historically specific human
relations with 'nature' must somehow ... be imagined as
genuinely social and actively relational; and yet the partners
remain utterly inhomogeneous.*

– DONNA HARAWAY (1991A, P. 3)

The study of strange occurrences and exceptional experiences
has traditionally been relegated to the sidelines of mainstream
scientific research (Zingrone, 2004). Parapsychology, despite
its best attempts to establish the scientific validity of psi, has yet to do
so, at least convincingly, in terms of evidence that could stand up to
empirical rigor similar to that of other scientific fields (Alcock, 2003).
Consider some of the phenomena traditionally under investigation by
parapsychology, including clairvoyance, psychokinesis, extrasensory
perception, and poltergeist activity. In order to study these experiences,
parapsychology, with its love of the laboratory, tends to ignore

community, context, and culture in favor of emphasizing one individual and that specific claimant's abilities to influence or receive information from the outside world. These self-world interactions are, I want to argue, too anthropocentric and not communal enough, being more abstracted, to put it differently, from a deeper indigenous relation where psi to be experienced much more dramatically. It is no wonder, then, that parapsychology has had such difficulty trying to establish the 'reality of psi' (Rao & Palmer, 1987) since it brings with it a metaphysical baggage that has been inherited from Western imperialism, with its practice of laboratory and experimental science. As a remedy, perhaps, psi studies in a more broad sense could become allied with the trickster by attempting to marshall a new paradigm for understanding the anomalous, one that is cosmologically animistic and shown in its most concentrated form at thin places and sacred spaces around the globe.

Enframing Ontological Realities

Out of the laboratory and into the field using recently developed research methods, the work done in paranthropology, for instance, has brought-out how anomalous experiences are more enmeshed and entwined with cultural practices and lived ways of being than they are with the sterility and control of the laboratory. Paranthropology, as Caswell, Hunter and Tessaro (2014) advocate, 'takes a bold step in attempting to interpret systems of supernatural belief from the perspective of those who subscribe to them, that is, not as beliefs but as ontological realities' (p. 471). The strong claim of ontological realities goes over and above any kind of validity or objectivity status that parapsychology has traditionally wanted to ascribe to psychic phenomena. That is, paranthropology, in this case, takes networks of meanings and values seriously insofar as they create worlds, real ways of living and being that have direct influences on subjectivity, community, culture, and nature. Consequently, from the standpoint of this alternative perspective, it becomes a certain form of colonialism to extract the more indigenous relation that went into the creation of these non-normative phenomena, those that may include shamanism, distance healing, herbalism, and astral travel. By contrast, the presumption made by parapsychology maintains that the kind of relationality that gives rise to these occurrences could be stabilized and replicated in an apparatus such as the laboratory. As a result, perhaps that is why parapsychology has typically focused on the more individualistic categories of clairvoyance, extrasensory perception, and mind-matter interaction. The approach of paranthropology, on the other hand, seeks to understand unusual experiences and phenomena in a relation that attempts to uphold, respect, and sustain indigeneity with all its various ontological realities.

Taking a lead from paranthropology, psi studies possess a strong kinship with the ontology of trickster theory, the ways in which meaning, language, and worlding shifts, slides, and slithers. Far from aligning the study of psi with the slight-of-hand of the magician, this deceptiveness, perhaps, that some scientists attribute to psi claimants, the trickster, rather, unlocks a rigorous and academic path for understanding psi, which has been evidenced in fields that include anthropology (Hyde, 2010; Radin, 1972), semiotics (Spinks, 1991, 2001), and psychoanalysis (Jung & Read, 1968). This work has been expanded and applied, specifically, toward the end of developing a science of psi that does not rely on a laboratory model of experimentation (Glazier, 2016; Hansen, 2001; Hurst, 2017) – a model that, not unlike the practitioners that use them, tends to perpetuate a narrowed notion of what counts as good science.

The trickster, as a figuration and literal, enfleshed character, demonstrates in a non-abstract and embodied way how an ontology of psi can operate across a multiplicity of ontological realities. The term 'ontological realities' implies a certain comportment with the world that, as has been suggested above, requires a fidelity to the indigeneity of the experience itself. Yet it does not undergird the ways in which psi processes are interrelated and co-constituted. In other words, what is lacking is a principle by which one can frame psi studies, situate its ontology in a certain system of reference thereby countering skeptical claims, those like cultural relativism, postmodernism, or bad science. Being more precise, the absence of theoretical context, interdisciplinary engagement, and the entrenchment of outdated models has undoubtedly led to the recent rise in exploring the null psi hypothesis[6] in parapsychology, as Roe (2012) laments, insofar as this

---

[6] The most institutionalized type of this skepticism can be found at the Anomalistic Psychology Research Unit (2019) at the University of London. The skeptical distance taken by the APRU and anomalistic psychology, by extension, is ideologically rooted in normalizing psi phenomena using already existing frameworks found in mainstream scientific practices. Such a mode of 'normalization' must be pejorative in the sense that, one could idiomatically say, anomalistic psychology attempts to explain away psi thereby stripping it of its paranormality or power to subvert existing paradigms.

form of skepticism was born out of a long historical tradition that is more antagonistic than it is investigative (Honorton, 1993).

In terms of how to take seriously the plethora of ontological realities that a more anthropological and narratological method in psi studies might admit into being, Donna Haraway, a feminist[7] scholar in science and technology studies, suggests that the processual and cunning nature of worlding should be engaged with as though it were 'coyote and protean embodiments ... as witty agent and actor' (p. 68). This proposal for a radical new way to understand nature does not necessary negate the more anthropological realities that are constructed in localized or native communities, since these trickster-esque properties already *prima facie* undercut any claim to universalism or essentialism. In order to further develop this line of inquiry, Haraway (1991b) makes the pronouncement that 'the search is for the trickster figures that might turn a stacked deck into a potent set of wild cards for refiguring possible worlds' (p. 25). This would unleash potentialities that may lay dormant in more rigid ways of apprehending being, those very ways that have relegated psi and the anomalous to either fringe status or have rejected, outright, the ontological reality of psi phenomena (Parra, 2013).

The agential and wily nature of psi is not a new concept in the parapsychological literature. Perhaps most robustly, Hansen (2001) develops a sustained treatment of the trickster-like qualities that can be found not only in the 'intrinsic' nature of psi but also with regard to the discipline of parapsychology proper. The trickster, for Hansen (2016), 'is a character type found worldwide in myth. He embodies a collection of abstract qualities, including disruption, deception, marginality, supernatural powers, transgression, boundary crossing, and violation of sexual taboos' (p. 52). Furthermore, 'tricksters often deceive larger and more powerful beings who would thwart them;

---

7   The scholarship of Haraway cannot be easily relegated to a single field. Indeed, trained as a biologist, she traced the way that metaphor operates in constructing experiments (Haraway, 1972). What I think is especially relevant for psi studies may be her scholastic affinity for the work of Rhea White (cf. 1994), particularly the latter's challenging of the white, patriarchal, and colonialist tendencies that have traditionally been evidenced in parapsychology.This is true not only in an institutional sense in that parapsychology has historically been dominated by white men, but also in a methodological and conceptual sense - the way that it has conducted research and theoretically understood pis is no doubt a reflection of this very institutional construction.

they may be endearingly clever or disgustingly stupid – both cultural heroes and selfish buffoons' (Hansen, 2016, p. 28). This renders the figure of the trickster particularly difficult to decipher, since there does not appear to be any logic to its actions – no standardized way to examine its behaviors and effects. As a result, for Hansen, the use of traditional scientific means to study psi does not necessarily provide evidence for the 'reality' status of anomalous phenomena but, more importantly, brings into relief the elusive and trickster like qualities that are characteristic of psi itself.

In the journal of *Paranthropology*, Hurst (2017) articulates a key role of the trickster, which is to expose the holes in normal ways of behaving and being, appearing at the exact time when these old and rigid ways need to be abandoned:

> Trickster is the savior in negative aspect, embracing chaos and disobeying the normal rules of convention by using trickery and deceit to progress through life. Trickster appears on the scene when current paradigms become outmoded and no longer work to the benefit of the individual or the collective. Trickster's role is to wreak havoc on constructs that have been accepted blindly, pointing out cracks in the system that cannot be ignored (p. 57).

It could be suggested that the phrase 'current paradigms' refers to the kind of antiquated laboratory science and experimentalism that many parapsychologists have historically employed. It would follow that parapsychology as it has been traditionally conceived may try to study the anomalous only to have those attempts frustrated through the holes or cracks that the trickster reveals. As older frameworks fade away, there are a growing number of psi researchers that have begun taking trickster theory seriously (Evrard, Hansen, Kennedy, & Kripal, 2016). Kennedy (2016) echoes this sentiment in no uncertain terms,

> The ultimate goal of experimental research is to convert the paranormal into technology. If psi is converted to technology, the mysterious, mystical, spiritual aspects will be lost. The message from the trickster is that *converting psi to technology is not going to happen* (p. 53, emphasis added).

Indeed, Kennedy is right here to maintain that the goal, implicit or not, of experimental research in parapsychology is to isolate psi in order to render it measurable, observable, manipulatable, and so forth - in other words, in order to gain control and mastery over it. The century long failure to achieve this end perhaps points to the tricky nature of psi and, more pointedly, how anomalous phenomena refuse to be neatly categorized and controlled. Kennedy (2001; 2003) elsewhere argues that the figure of the trickster, with its pervasive proclivity to be elusive, could provide powerful conceptual and pragmatic tools for envisioning psi, thereby repositioning future research procedures and methods. Not dissimilarly, in the terms of Lacanian theory, I have argued (Glazier, 2016) that parapsychology is more properly aligned, regarding specific conceptual affinities, with psychoanalysis than it is with experimental science precisely because of the subversive cunning that psi applies to investigatory practices.

Thin Places, Sacred Spaces

Cultures from around the world have named and venerated a variety of thin places and sacred spaces. Some excellent examples of these sites include Stonehenge in England, Sedona in Arizona, the pyramids in Egypt, and Skinwalker Ranch in Utah. There are a number of reasons that this is this case. For example, these locations are said to include unique energetic properties, the appearance of strange beings, and certain healing powers. One of the most salient explanations for this has to do with the idea that at these precise places, the veil between this dimension and others is at its thinnest. Such thinness perhaps catalyzes paranormality or, put differently, enables psi to more freely operate and reveal itself.

Certain cultures even anchor their spiritual practice to these kinds of locations. As a case in point, the Celtic and Druidic traditions maintain that thin places are where boundaries become more permeable, ontological realities commingle, and the divine becomes more reachable (Schneider, 2006). The metaphor of a veil is rather *apropos* here in terms of the way the other worlds remain cloaked but, nevertheless, are at minimum visible and at best inter-penetrable. Put differently, at these very specific geographical locations, the thickness of the garment that typically shrouds the multiplicity of intersecting dimensions is at its most attenuated. Indeed, Power (2006), in relation to the Celtic tradition and the island of Iona, relates that 'the veil between the fairy world and the mundane is thin. On Iona, dreams and visions were accepted as being of significance' (p. 45). This kind of permeability blurs fiction and fact, imagination and reality, such that what becomes possible, what is taken as inspiration, and even what constitutes oneself as an encapsulated entity is not only contestable but may even evaporate. As Schneider (2016) writes,

> The thin places are where minimally two levels of reality meet including the visible world of our everyday experience and that of the sacred or divine. In these thin places, the boundary becomes porous to the point of momentarily disappearing, a veil is lifted while something is seen, and an experience is felt (p. 138).

Importantly, these experiences tend to be classified as paranormal under normative frameworks, viewed either in psychological and pathological terms as hallucinations, delusions, or misbeliefs, or in the terms of natural science as perhaps swamp gas, mis-identified creatures, or geomagnetic effects. While both of these reasons remain valid explications and alternatives to consider when interrogating psi phenomena, they, nevertheless, are *a priori* grounded in a form of skepticism that puts the possibility of paranormality under erasure. Of course, if these more prevalent ways of making meaning where to be expanded, then the paranormal element of psi becomes normalized and these experiences can be given a sort of reality status – a status that the scientism of parapsychology embargos.

Take for example the plethora of strange experiences at Skinwalker Ranch in Utah. There have been sightings of UFOs, unknown or cryptid creatures, the appearance of apparitions, poltergeist activity, and glowing orbs (Kelleher & Knapp, 2005). To select one of these examples, the sightings of large, shapeshifting creatures known to the Navajo as skinwalkers, the designation reiterated in the name of the ranch, can be more acceptably explained through a paranthopological lens. That is, traditionally, certain kinds of malevolent shamans and evil witches, according to the Navajo, are able to take on a literal animal form such as a coyote, wolf, crow, or even a hybrid creature. Pointedly, as Pavlik relates, 'the Navajo word for skinwalker is yenaldlooshi, a term that translates to "it walks on all four feet" ... this word, as well as the Navajo word for wolf, [are] common colloquial term[s] for witch' (p. 84). The magical ability of these creatures, for whatever reason, seems to be at its most concentrated and available in these very thin places where materiality may be more mutable. On principle, Kelleher and

Knapp (2005) come to the conclusion that the paranormal experiences evidenced at Skinwalker Ranch could conceivably appear anywhere, given the right conditions of emergence.

The skinwalker represents a paragon case for trickster theory in relation to psi studies. Not only do skinwalkers seem to embody many of the traits associated with the more pancultural figure of the trickster (Hansen, 2001; Hyde, 2010), those like mischief, inversion, animality, and so on, but they may grant us a special kind of access into the logics of a broader and sweeping understanding of how psi operates; namely, an ontology of psi, one that is grounded in more an animist[8] sense than the scientism of parapsychology. The 'multiplicity of ontological realities,' to return to a phrase used by Caswell, Hunter and Tessaro (2014), and the untimely and non-normative experiences that these engender could thus be strung together and enframed using the disruptive logics of the trickster and its adherence to a wily kind of naturality - psi *qua* being possesses an agency that cannot be tamed.

Indeed, if Haraway (1991a) is correct in maintaining that nature becomes manifest under the conditions coyote arbitrates then it would follow that psi is more normative than what mainstream science takes to be real. The tidy experimental procedures of the parapsychological laboratory and the immutable laws of physics are, on account of the trickster, less real, more fringe, and even further contestable than the stories, tales, and experiences that circulate in indigenous groups and that are passed down through generations. The point is that this kind of indigeneity is more flush with being than conceptual abstraction and technical manipulation. Trying to turn psi into a kind of technology (Kennedy, 2016), in other words, necessarily as per the discussion

---

8   Neoanimism has recently enjoyed a resurgence in science studies and the humanities. Perhaps most well known is Bruno Latour's actor-network theory (ANT) (1993). Also notable, however, are Isabelle Stengers (2010, 2011) two tomes on cosmopolitics as well as Donna Haraway's (2016) recent work on the chthulucene. Such a renewal bodes well for ecologists, anthropologists, or psi researchers who may want to apply those theoretical insights to claimant reports or archival accounts inasmuch as the systemic and panpsychic qualities that have traditionally been attributed to animism are no longer dismissed outright by serious academic scholars. In fact, I would suggest that such a cosmology has been ostracized historically precisely because of the threat it poses to our modern way of engaging with nature (a proposition that may not be too far afield from critiques of phallocentrism, imperialism, and so forth).

above *creates the anomalous,* since this kind of manipulation causes the trickster to rebel, so to speak. Putting this into stronger terms, the incisiveness that trickster theory brings to bear not only troubles, upsets, and reconfigures parapsychological research but, perhaps more importantly, challenges fundamental assumptions that legendary science has assumed to be true.

Crossroads and Conclusions

In this chapter, I have argued that trickster theory in psi studies, if given a proper ontological treatment, can foster a shift away from obsolete parapsychological practices and towards a more anthropological and narratological approach. Donna Haraway, with her inspired feminist critique and innovative conceptual tools, has insinuated, not too overtly, that nature needs to be dealt with as though it were an active and agential kind of trickster. The kind of enframing[9] this accomplishes, again, helps tie together the multiplicity of ontological realities by maintaining their indigeneity. There is no need, in other words, to develop a properly meta-theory of psi since its conditions of emergence are local, contextual, and co-created. Yet, this is not the same as saying that there exist no parameters or rigors by which to adjudicate specific instances of paranormality. Cultures that are less hierarchical and more egalitarian, less technological and more animistic, less ordered and more chaotic, and so on replicate the favorite qualities of the trickster and, it follows, would be able to 'play' with psi.

As a way to perhaps get underneath the technological and mechanical smothering of the planet, I have suggested that thin places and sacred spaces found in various geographical locations around the globe

---

[9]   I have selected the term 'enframing' specifically as a kind of strategic and ironic conceptual move such that, to translate it back into German, it was used by the philosopher Martin Heidegger, *Gestell,* in his famous essay called *The Question Concerning Technology* (Heidegger, 1993). To reclaim, in a certain manner, the way that modernity ordered nature as merely a means for resource extraction, enframing with the trickster clearly disrupts such categorical and mechanized ways of parsing up the world, if only to throw those very ways into a kind of chaos. While I think it is important to remember that this chaos is not static, in other words, it is transient, the enframing that I am suggesting undergirds the indigeneity and the differences that exist between ontological realities.

may herald not a return to that kind of indigeneity, but rather grant special access to a specific type of paranormality that remains elusive regarding our normal way of seeing the world. In these areas, the veil between this world and others is at its thinnest thereby unshrouding various anomalous and paranormal occurrences. The Navajo creature known as the *yenaldlooshi* or the skinwalker, appearing in just such a place, helps enflesh the trickster and make apparent the link between conceptualizing ontology as wily in theoretical terms and paranormality out in the field. The skinwalker, in other words, demonstrates the shapeshifting, sensual, and inverted conditions that are mirrored in the very nature of being itself.

Questions

1. In what ways does trickster theory challenge traditional parapsychology?

2. What research procedures or methods are suggested in this chapter that may be more aligned with understanding psi through the trickster?

3. Why are thin places and sacred places important for this kind of perspective?

4. What does the *yenaldlooshi* or the skinwalker help articulate? How does it make the abstract concrete?

CHAPTER 7

LIMINAL SPACES AND LIMINAL MINDS: BOUNDARY THINNESS AND PARTICIPATORY ECO-CONSCIOUSNESS

Christine Simmonds-Moore

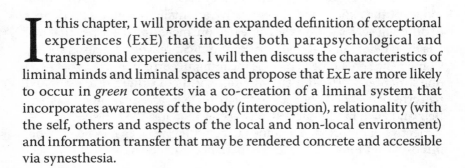

I n this chapter, I will provide an expanded definition of exceptional experiences (ExE) that includes both parapsychological and transpersonal experiences. I will then discuss the characteristics of liminal minds and liminal spaces and propose that ExE are more likely to occur in *green* contexts via a co-creation of a liminal system that incorporates awareness of the body (interoception), relationality (with the self, others and aspects of the local and non-local environment) and information transfer that may be rendered concrete and accessible via synesthesia.

Defining Exceptional Experiences (ExE)

Just as there are various forms of religious experiences (after James, 1913), there are various forms of anomalous or 'exceptional' experiences (e.g., Cardeña, Lynn, & Krippner, 2014). Such experiences are so described because they appear to break the normal 'rules' regarding how reality is *supposed* to work. Belz and Fach (2012) have developed a phenomenological framework for organizing anomalies that is neutral in terms of the ontological status of the phenomena the experiences refer to. Anomalies can occur with regard to how people experience:

1. their sense of self

2. the physical world

3. dissociations within the usually unified sense of self

4. coincidences within the experiencing self, between the self and aspects of the physical world or between different physical objects or events.

Thoughts and feelings are usually experienced as internal phenomena that should not be accessible to other minds. When this occurs, these experiences reflect anomalies in the self model of the experiencer. In addition, aspects of mental life are not *supposed* to manifest in the physical world, or on the body, as anomalous mind-matter interactions,[10] apparent presences, or the apparent influence of entities in the world. When such things are experienced, they reflect anomalies in the world model of the experiencer. Dissociative anomalies include experiences of different selves within the same person, including the sense that one has lived before or that one is in communication with deceased spirits. Coincidence phenomena include meaningful correspondences between one's mental world and the mental worlds of others or events and patterns of events that occur in the world (e.g., as synchronicities). The Belz and Fach model successfully accommodates the full spectrum of subjective paranormal phenomena, including extrasensory perception, mind-matter interactions and experiences suggestive of survival.

---

[10] Psychokinesis.

Expanding the Model to Include Mystical and Transpersonal Experiences

Transpersonal experiences occur when people experience their sense of self to be greater than an individually bound sense of self. According to Daniels (2005), mystical experiences describe experiences that result in noesis; a direct knowing concerning a *fundamental reality*, and can include both traditional parapsychological phenomena in addition to transpersonal experiences. Although Belz and Fach (2012) noted that mystical and transpersonal experiences fall outside of their model, I consider that the model could be successfully extended to incorporate many transpersonal phenomena. Anomalies in the self model could include (and even embrace) the idea of a connected and permeable self (e.g., Wright, 1995), a connection or fusion of self with a meaningful spiritual other, a dissolution of self, or that there is no self (see Daniels, 2005). Anomalies in the world model might include experiences of spiritual and divine experiences in the physical world or in/on the body, for example as in kundalini awakening experiences (e.g., Taylor, 2015), Autonomous Sensory Meridian Response (*ASMR*; the tingling experience some people have in response to certain, often beautiful, stimuli, Barratt & Davis, 2015), spiritual healing and the perception of halos and auras around a social other. Dissociative phenomena might incorporate experiences of many selves, including channeling and possession experiences of divine or diabolical presences. Dissociative experiences could also include experiences of access to other realities and worlds, - i.e., the model would need to move into 3 or 4 dimensions. Coincidence phenomena might include experiences in which celestial events (e.g., blood moons and rare events) become signifiers for spiritual knowledge.

In order to articulate the importance of a *green* perspective on exceptional experiences, I will also draw from Daniels' 5x5 model of mystical experiences (2005) which presents an elegant model of the *full range* of mystical experiences, drawing from multiple religious and spiritual traditions as well as outside of them. Daniels asserts that mystical experiences can also occur in the context of relationality, in the context of nature, within the self (as archetypes, images, thoughts, and feelings) and as Monad (in which there are insights into the self). For each context, there are different modes that reflect the extent to which one is connected with the mystical other. Modes include the numinous (sensed other), dialogic (felt *communication* with an *other*), synergic (sensorially felt *closeness with* a perceived other that is felt to be similar to the self*),* unitive (where self and other are felt to be *connected*) and non-dual (where there is *no distinction* between self and other). Daniels notes that nature and social contexts have been neglected in many theories of mystical and transpersonal experiences. After Daniels (2013), extending the approach toward transpersonal knowing is particularly relevant to this chapter, since such approaches honour relationality and a participatory approach to spirituality. This chapter emphasizes a particular type of connectivity and relationality that enables the emergence of a system that particularly encourages ExE and values the roles of green spaces and ecological knowing. In the following sections, I discuss how psychological sensitivity/liminality and synesthetic processes are implicated in exceptional experiences. Next, I consider various features of liminal spaces. Finally the nature of the conversation between liminal minds and liminal spaces will be presented as *participatory eco-consciousness.*

Liminal Minds

In this chapter I define liminal minds as mind-body systems that are open, porous and interconnected. Liminality is associated with thinking in *shades of grey* rather than *black and white* and with states of consciousness that are in-between defined states of consciousness. The concept of a *liminal or thin* mind appears in the works of Frederic Myers and William James (Thalbourne, 1999) and more recently in the writings of Freud, Lewin and others (Hartmann, Harrison, & Zborowski, 2001). In academic parapsychology, it forms part of Bergson's (1913) *filter* theory of ESP. Recently, liminality is explored in research employing the psychometric measures Transliminality (Lange, Thalbourne, Houran, & Storm, 2000), Boundary thinness (Hartmann, 1991) and related measures (Thalbourne & Maltby, 2008).

Liminality is experienced as psychological sensitivity; a fluidity of thoughts and feelings, a tendency to see agency and causality, and a heightened tendency toward experiencing ExE, including paranormal (Thalbourne, 2009), transpersonal and mystical experiences (Thalbourne & Delin, 1999). At its heart, liminality incorporates the transpersonal notion of both/and in addition to the contradictions and combinations of coherent and incoherent (paradoxical) moments of thought that are also present in the theorizing of Deleuze, Gendlin and Bion with regard to meaning making, pre-formed thoughts and insights (Hunt, 2014). Liminality is a core component in the recipe for all forms of ExE (as delineated above).

Types and Levels of Liminality

I have previously discussed the idea that *connectivity* should be considered at various levels in the cognitive and perceptual system. This includes chemical, neural, cognitive, intrapersonal, inter-personal and extra personal connectivity (Simmonds-Moore, 2015). Each level could be considered on its own, but should also be considered in relationship to one another; with connectivity potentiating the emergence of different types of connectivity *and the experiences associated with it*. Please see Table 1 for a summary of proposed levels of connectivity.[11] There are trait (individual differences) and state differences in interconnectedness. Those with higher scores on the related psychometric measures of transliminality (Thalbourne, Houran, Alias, & Brugger, 2001), boundary thinness (Hartmann, 1991) and positive schizotypy (cf. Simmonds-Moore, 2010) have an increased tendency to report ExE. Likewise, altered states of consciousness are also associated with ExE (Alvarado, 1998) and can also be considered to be liminal. For example, the *hypnagogic* state is a paradoxical and intriguing state that incorporates some of the features of being awake and being asleep, but it is not equivalent to either and is highly correlated with ExE (e.g., Sherwood, 2002).

---

[11] Readers are directed to Simmonds-Moore (2010; 2015) for a detailed discussion of levels of connectivity and how different levels might relate to paranormal beliefs and ExE.

Table 1. A hierarchy of connectivity

Level of connectivity	Specific features
Neurochemistry	Less inhibitory mechanisms are active. The neurochemistry of sleep and arousal The neurochemistry of stress insights from other altered states of consciousness (ASC) research including 1. The action of various psychedelics 2. The role of dopamine for magical thinking and belief.
Neurobiological	Altered states of consciousness Connection between the hemispheres (more influence of the right hemisphere on cognition) Connection between subcortical and cortical areas of the brain Connections between other brain regions, either structurally or functionally Mirror neuron activity (underpins empathy)
Cognitive	Synesthesia – thoughts and feelings (etc.) are fused; different ways of seeing and experiencing the world; being able to represent and interpret subtle aspects of reality. Apophenia Attention widening

Level of connectivity	Specific features
Intrapersonal (consciousness)	Synesthesia Consciousness binding Greater awareness of unconscious and preconscious processes. Greater awareness of the body as interoception Descending spirituality
Interpersonal	Empathy Social cognition Interoception Synesthesia Extending spirituality
Extrapersonal	Influence or availability of psi information Influence of unseen environmental factors Influence of transpersonal realities and meanings. Extending spirituality Ascending spirituality

Features of an Interconnected System

Among those who are a psychometrically liminal, there is an enhanced interconnectedness of the neurons within the brain (Thalbourne *et al.*, 2001) associated with *reduced* neural inhibition ('functional connectivity'; Ettinger *et al.*, 2015). The arousal system is generally more labile, which results in a tendency to experience rapid shifts in consciousness (Fleck *et al.*, 2008), more hypnagogic imagery (Parra & Paul, 2009) and unusual sleep experiences (Watson, 2001).

A reduction in inhibition results in increased sensory gating (availability) of information that is usually outside of awareness[12] (Lindeman, Svedholm, Reikki, Raij & Hari, 2012, p. 943). This results in greater availability of the unattended stimulus to attention (Ettinger *et al.*, 2018); increased awareness of mental imagery (Levin, Gilmartin & Lamontanaro, 1998-1999); more memories of dreams and nightmares (Claridge, Clark & Davis, 1997); greater influence of subliminal information on conscious choices (Crawley, French & Yesson, 2002) and greater awareness of body-based information (Houran, Kumar, Thalbourne & Laverture, 2002). Increased connectivity may[13] also be related to ostensible psi performance (Holt & Simmonds-Moore, 2008; Luke & Zychowicz, 2014).

A greater influence of the right hemisphere (Weinstein *et al.*, 2007) manifests as a tendency to make associations and connections. This corresponds to the tendency to perceive meaningful patterns (particularly minds and faces, Riekki, Lindeman & Raij, 2014) in randomness (apophenia). Apophenia relates to both creativity and ExE (Farias, Claridge & Lalljee, 2005; Gianotti, Mohr, Pizzagalli & Brugger, 2001).

I have previously argued that those who have greater trait levels of connectivity experience more liminal states, more of the time, but others can access these states given the right circumstances (e.g., bereavement, sleep deprivation, other altered states of consciousness; Simmonds-Moore, 2010; 2015).

Increased Connection to the Body

An expanded and *green* perspective on ExE should also incorporate body based knowledge. It is not a new idea that embodiment is important in understanding conscious experiences (e.g., Merleau-Ponty, 2002), but recent research trends support the idea that the body is implicated in qualia (Nummenmaa *et al.*, 2018), and an integrated (conscious) model

---

[12] Lindeman, Svedholm, Reikki, Raij, & Hari (2012) note that inhibition reflects "conscious or unconscious stopping or overriding of a mental process; for example, suppressing unwanted or irrelevant thoughts, suppressing inappropriate meanings of ambiguous words and gating irrelevant information from working memory" (p. 943)

[13] Research to date is mixed on inhibition and psi performance.

of the self (Craig, 2009). The concept of *interoception* reflects the extent to which one is listening to the body within the wider psychosocial *(and environmental/ecological)* context (after Craig, 2008).

To date, interoception has been neglected by both parapsychologists and transpersonal psychologists, despite an acknowledgement of the role of the body in psi performance (e.g., Mossbridge et al, 2012), parapsychological experiences (Carpenter, 2004) and in transpersonal methods (Anderson & Braud, 2011), practices (Louchakova & Warner, 2003) experience (Taylor, 2015), development (Linders & Lancaster, 2013) and theory (Ferrer, 2015). Enhanced interoception reflects another way of being connected – in terms of self and the relationship between the self and the entire psychosocial and ecological moment, that is incorporating the knowledge of the entire [interconnected] system. Being connected in this way might enable access to psi and other non-local and local information, and contributes to the idea of extended connectivity as a core component of participatory eco-consciousness.[14]

Empathy as a Type of Connectivity

Interpersonal connectivity refers to an enhanced awareness of another person's experience, or compassion for another person or group of people. This might also extend to the environment, and insights into environmental issues. Neurologically, empathy and compassion relate to the activity of the insula (Singer & Klimecki, 2014) which may draw from interoceptive processes that allow for awareness of the entire *psychosocial moment* (represented in the bodymind) (Craig, 2009). Mirror neurons may also be implicated; for example in mirror touch synesthesia, experiencers tend to experience the pain of social others; as a type of extended empathy (Banissy & Ward, 2007). Hartmann (1991) has also noted that boundary thin people tend to get 'too close' to social others. In addition, those who are prone to reporting ExE had higher scores on perspective taking, emotional comprehension, empathic concern, positive empathy and the total score on an empathy scale (Parra, 2013). Interpersonal connection may also be trait and state like, given that empathy and compassion can be successfully increased by

---

[14] Researchers at UWG are currently exploring how interoception relates to different types of subjective ExE. Future work is planned regarding its relationship to performance in a psi study.

meditation (Luberto et al., 2018). Encouraging interpersonal connectivity may contribute to the extended connectivity that is characteristic of participatory eco-consciousness.

Extra-Personal Boundaries

Boundaries can also exist *beyond* the individual, and include greater connectivity between the self and information that is usually invisible or imperceptible (Simmonds-Moore, 2015). Essentially, this form of boundary relates to an increased sensitivity to *unseen* aspects of the environment including electromagnetic factors, in addition to non-local and transpersonal information. This can also reflect a systems approach in which environmental factors interact with individual differences to enable access to genuine information. Jawer (2005) found support for the existence of an 'environmentally sensitive' individual, who has thinner psychological boundaries and seems to be more affected by a range of environmental factors (chemical and electrical sensitivity) in addition to experiencing ExE. Persinger (2001) has also proposed that geomagnetic factors may be implicated in some ExE (apparitions), particularly among those who have higher scores on temporal lobe lability.

Expanding Liminality: Healthy Connectivity and Fractals

There are healthy and less healthy forms of boundary thinness that may relate in different ways to ExE (cf. Simmonds-Moore, 2012). The 'happy schizotype' refers to a person who tends to report ExE and scores high on positive schizotypy (but does not exhibit other types) (Mohr & Claridge, 2015). Mohr and Claridge (2015), note that such people tend to be highly creative and 'benefit from a healthy way to organize their thoughts and experiences, that is, they employ an adaptive cognitive framework to explain and integrate their unusual experiences.' Having an adaptive framework means that there are is an *organized* cognitive system that is connected with experiences being appraised positively. A lack of organizing framework is associated with negative appraisal (Schofield & Claridge, 2007). In summary, the literature implies that healthy experiences are under the control of the experiencer, they are applied and useful, they make sense within a particular (shared) framework, and they are valued rather than feared (cf. Simmonds-Moore, 2012).

Healthy liminality is also associated with potential and flexibility that may be fractal-like. In his discussion of Abraham's work, Dossey (2012) suggests that healthy and unhealthy ways of mental functioning can be understood within the context of fractals. A healthy mind consists of thicker, richer fractals that relate to fluidity, connectivity and integration. An unhealthy mind, on the other hand, consists of thin fractals that relate to a lack of movement and too many boundaries. Van Orden (2007) notes that fractal variability is a core feature of flourishing living systems and can be seen in physiological systems, thoughts, feelings and complex human behaviors. This type of fractal pattern is also apparent in the way the brain functions *in a synchronized manner* (Kitzbichler, Smith, Christensen & Bullmore, 2009), which may relate to consciousness itself. Health and wellbeing are associated with a variable heart rate, while stress and ill health relate to a lack, or reduction, in heart rate variability. This claim is well supported in the research literature, where HRV is consistently associated with wellbeing, and may underpin vertical integration of the processes of the body and mind (Thayer, Ahs, Fredrikson & Sollers, 2012). The existence of fractal forms in functioning systems might be summarized as representing coordination or integration which may be a feature of life or living systems.

Synesthesia as a Type of Connectivity

Synesthesia occurs when there is an *additional* response (the concurrent) to the usual inducing stimulus (the inducer). For example, a particular musical note (e.g., D) consistently results in the experience of the colour green *in addition to sound*. A *hyperconnected* nervous system is also implicated in synesthesia (Mitchell, 2013; Rouw, 2013). Intriguingly, synesthesia can be perceptual, conceptual and occur intrapersonally or interpersonally (e.g., as a colorful aura around a particular personality) (cf. Simner & Hubbard, 2013). Inducers are often sequences such as letters, numbers or time, but they can sometimes be usually unseen aspects of the world. Jason Padgett's acquired synesthesia, for example, consists of the direct conscious experience of complex mathematical formulae – as geometrical forms – when he looks at objects out in the real world, which has given him insights into the fractal nature of reality (Brogaard & Marlow, 2015).

Research indicates that synesthesia plays a role in the aetiology of ExE (Simmonds-Moore, 2016; Simmonds-Moore, Alvarado & Zingrone, 2018), and also plays a central role in a recent model for psi (Marwaha & May,

2015). Synesthesia correlates strongly with trait measures of connectivity (cf. Simmonds-Moore *et al.*, 2018) and may also be encouraged in altered states of consciousness (Cardeña, 2005; Luke & Terhune, 2013; Sagiv, Ilbeigi & Ben-Tal, 2011; Walsh, 2005). In terms of ExE, synesthesia may provide an accessible representation (a concurrent) to aspects of the world that are not usually available to language (such as emotions, abstract concepts, and psi phenomena; cf. Simmonds-Moore, 2016). As an example, transliminality correlates directly with entity encounter experiences (Houran & Thalbourne, 2001), but hyperaesthesia (perceptual sensitivity) and synesthesia are also implicated (Houran, Wiseman & Thalbourne, 2002). This suggests that among those who are sensitive, synesthesia plays a role in the *concrete* experience of subtle or invisible environmental and body-based information.

What are Liminal Spaces?

Some locations and features of the physical world ('nature') are more associated with ExE than are others (please also see the chapter in this volume by Scholl). By making this statement, such spaces can only be liminal if there is a conscious mind present in that space that co-creates the ExE. Havik, Elands and van Koppen (2015) note that green spaces are often felt to facilitate contact with 'a deeper self, and ... close identification with such sites. They describe sentient communication explained as exchange of spiritual energies through flows or resonance. Particularly influential sites are wilder environments, sacred sites, open spaces, and sites remembered from childhood. Specific natural objects with specific spiritual qualities are old trees, animals, still or dynamic waters, and fire' (p. 81). The role of nature in ExE was previously acknowledged by Moody (Moody, 1992; Moody & Perry, 1993) who noted that exposure to nature, including nature sounds was part of the recipe for ExE in the context of the psychomanteum. Features of spaces that may be more likely to influence the observer are spaces that include living organisms (in particular, spaces that are rich in the colour green, such as forests); spaces with features that are rich in fractals (visual and auditory); places with physical features (electromagnetism and infrasound), and places with still or running water. Other spaces are liminal because people have experienced strong emotional states or exceptional phenomena in the same location in the past. The localization of prior meaning and experience might then become accessible to some (sensitive) observers who are physically present in the same place (including sacred sites, castles and other locations with stories).

Green and Living Spaces

Davis & Canty (2013) have articulated how transpersonal psychology should be informed by ecopsychology to facilitate a realignment between the individual human consciousness and the consciousness of the living planet, via connection with aspects of nature. Many Neopagan religions hold nature, in particular *forested* areas consisting of groves of trees, at the core of their practices and experiences (*cf.* Hengst-Ehrhart & Schraml, 2013). Intriguingly, the etymology of the Old German word for 'temple' is derived from the word 'grove,' thus 'it is likely that Germanic sanctuaries were located in the forest' (Hengst-Ehrhart & Schraml, 2013, p. 256).

The colour green may directly impact on the experiencing person to facilitate such a relationship. Green has cross-cultural [synesthetic] meaning. Lakoff and Johnson (1999) note that the evolution of human colour perception is aligned with our lived experience as a species and that green is particularly meaningful as it denotes life. Specifically, greenness corresponds to the presence of the fluorescent molecule chlorophyll that enables plants to transduce the light of the sun into food. Green and green spaces have been associated with therapeutic properties, in particular, the elicitation of the relaxation response (or the alleviation of symptoms of extreme stress, e.g., Poulson, 2017). In terms of the influence of colours *per se*, one study found that meditating on the colour green (alongside blue, white and yellow) was effective in increasing peoples' relaxation responses (Rodrigues & Deuskar, 2016).

Geometric Forms

Fractals in nature. People may be particularly likely to enter liminal states when faced with fractal-like structures that correlate with flourishing life. The golden section, for example, is a mathematical ratio that appears frequently in nature, but also in religious and other art within formal places of ritual and worship. Like pi, it is constituted of an irrational number and is consistently found to be aesthetically beautiful (Green, 1995). Instances in nature include flowers and other star like shapes and sea creatures (particularly notable in the spiral formation of many shells). Green (1995) notes how spirals are frequently observed in nature, for instance in the growth patterns of pine cones, among other forms of life. Green also notes that the Fibonacci series is frequently observed in nature.

Fractals and ExE

It was previously noted that living systems are associated with more fractal formations, that may indicate coordination and potential. Natural settings and imagery that include more fractal structures may influence a person's state of consciousness. Research has found that people have an aesthetic preference for fractal imagery (Spehar, Clifford, Newell & Taylor, 2003) and that exposure to fractal formations directly *influences* EEG patterns (Hagerhall, Laikeo, Taylor, Kuller, Kuller & Martin, 2008) indicating a relaxation response. Some ExE actually incorporate fractal imagery and could reflect the direct perception of the workings of the brain and mind, or the direct awareness of life and other information (extrapersonal connectivity). This was observed in Jason Padgett's acquired synesthetic fractal experiences, discussed earlier. Greene (2003) has proposed that some altered states of consciousness are associated with a shift from the awareness of three to four dimensions. He suggests that this occurs via a fractal continuum, i.e., that we do not notice the fractal nature of edges until they are magnified 1000s of times, and then it becomes clear that edges are actually comprised of more complicated structures. The Jungian mandala is fundamentally fractalesque and is the symbol of the individuated self, which aligns with the idea of a *coordinated* living system (in opposition to a system that is uncoordinated). Mandalas do have therapeutic value (Henderson, Rosen & Mascaro, 2012), which may be effected by a non-verbal (perhaps direct, fractal) means of representing one's experiences.[15]

Sounds and Properties of Water

Roszak has noted that water is a fascinating life-supporting substance that may have relevance for understanding consciousness itself. As with

---

[15] This section was influenced by a paper given to the Society for Psychical Research by Dr. Paul Stevens, who kindly provided some of the references to this author.

many complicated phenomena, systems approaches may provide the best models for a deeper understanding of reality. It is here that aesthetic and physical qualities *must* be considered together, alchemically. Thus, the sounds, touch, taste and feelings associated with being in or near (running) water may all influence consciousness, in addition to the physical properties of water itself. Thus, we might expect that being close to water, or water-like sounds may have therapeutic effects. For example, spaces with moving water elicit sounds akin to pink noise, which has also been found to increase mind-body relaxation (Boggs *et al.*, 1973) and encourage internal attention states (Honorton, 1977) that have been associated with exceptional experiences, alterations in consciousness (Wackermann, Pütz & Allefeld, 2008), and with anomalous processes of information transfer (Baptista, Derakhshani & Tressoldi, 2015; Storm, Tressoldi & Di Risio, 2010). This could include life information and other transpersonal knowing.

Other Aspects of Spaces

Wackerman et al (2008) note that some natural places (including journeys in mountain or desert landscapes) may encourage ganzfeld-like (sensory deprivation) conditions which may in turn influence ExE. Other places may have physical features that interact with the mind of the perceiving person in terms of psychological and other factors (e.g., Krippner, Devereux & Fish, 2003). Low frequency sound (infrasound), for example, has been implicated in some types of localized ExE (Parsons, 2012). Other places that are associated with ExE have sometimes been found to exhibit anomalous electromagnetic activity (cf. Persinger and Koren, 2001). For example, tectonic strain was linked with thousands of sightings of apparitions of the Virgin Mary that were associated with luminous phenomena and appeared to manifest over a Coptic Orthodox church in Zeitoun, Egypt. An investigation by Derr and Persinger (1989) supported a physical sequence of events, which included observable phenomena preceding an earthquake. Other examples include ancestors, spook lights, earth lights and Will'o' the wisps which appear to interact with human observers (and may be interpreted as fairies, other entities or ghost like figures). A person with liminal tendencies may be more likely to report such phenomena in the context of certain locations.

Prior Experiences and Prior Lives

Some spaces might encourage ExE because prior events and experiences have taken place there. This may include places that are associated with stories of hauntings or with prior rituals, including standing stones and other ancient sites. This aligns with the idea of *place memories* and the idea that certain aspects of lived experience (traumatic or meaningful) might persist in certain locations (Heath, 2005; Roll, 2008). Roll, for example (2008) notes that the *meanings* that were associated with particular objects and physical places may persist and influence the experiences of others who later encounter those objects. Heath (2005) suggests that some aspects of memory may be stored within the molecular structure of physical objects in the environment (including water) and that this information would be accessible for some people via resonance. Resonance could imply a similarity of function, experience or structure and could relate to the idea of a liminal system that is characteristic of participatory eco-consciousness.

Other places may have a similar potential as they incorporate the presence of long life. In this category, we might include forests where non-human lives have been lived such as the Giant Redwoods in California. After Roszak, Davis (2011) notes that when a person experiences nature mysticism they may at times be experiencing a *representation of life and the processes of life,* which may be experienced as the divine, or in the form of other presences and other ways of experiencing. Such insights may therefore reflect a different way of directly experiencing the aesthetics and magnificence of life itself.

Participatory Eco-Consciousness: A Systems Approach to ExE

Participatory eco-consciousness is a systems approach toward understanding ExE that is informed by the ideas of Ferrer (e.g., 2015). Ferrer has proposed a participatory spirituality in which human beings are co-creators of their spiritual realizations and realities. Instead of there being a truth *to be discovered*, each person plays a role in the co-creation of spiritual truths. There is a *mystery* and a unique conversation with that mystery that creates ontologies that are both/ and in terms of the usual distinction between reality and imagination. Ferrer notes that 'spiritual participatory events can engage the entire range of human epistemic faculties (e.g., rational, imaginal, somatic, vital, aesthetic) with both the creative unfolding of the mystery and the possible agency of subtle entities or energies in the enactment – or 'bringing forth' – of ontologically rich religious worlds. In other words, the participatory approach presents an enactive understanding of the sacred that conceives spiritual phenomena, experiences, and insights as cocreated events' (2015, p. 42). ExE may be more likely to emerge when a person participates in a *liminal system* that emerges between them and the local and nonlocal environment. Participation might occur spontaneously, for example by a resonance brought about by the direct perception of aspects of nature and life (including fractals), or through rituals that promote liminality, including music, sound, dance and being with social others. Participatory eco consciousness emerges as a *conversation* between the bodymind and the physical and social environment. The state of consciousness includes connectivity to unconscious and preconscious aspects of the mind, awareness of the body (via interoception), and interpersonal and extrapersonal connectivity (via increased empathy and compassion). Information transfer may include body based information, information about the self, physically present stimuli (e.g., light, electricity, infrasound and other direct knowledge about life), information relating to others in addition to information that includes place memories, non-local information, personal and transpersonal insights and conversations with transpersonal realities. The information may then be represented to the self *via synesthetic processes.* This approach draws on feminist and womanist approaches toward spirituality as it enables awareness of the plight of social, emotional and environmental others that extends beyond the self as love, compassion and potential for overcoming oppression (of people and the environment) (after Holiday, 2010).

Systems, Synesthesia and Located Experiences

Synesthetic concurrents are experienced in a variety of ways; as projected out into the external world, experienced in the mind's eye (Simner & Hubbard, 2013), and sometimes in more complex ways (Alvaraz & Robertson, 2013). Those who experience the concurrent out in space are classically known as projectors, while those who experience the concurrent in the mind's eye are known as associators (Simner & Hubbard, 2013). The location of qualia associated with ExE may differ according to the biology and state of consciousness of the individual, the nature of the relationship and the source of the information that is being represented. Systems approaches may provide more holistic and nuanced understanding of ExE (and consciousness). For example, Von Lucadou's (2011) theory of poltergeist phenomena proposes different forms of 'complex environmental interactions' depending on the extent to which one has an internal or external way of being, psychosocial dynamics and one's levels of embodiment or focus on the soma. In this model, we might be more likely to see poltergeist phenomena as an externalized representation [of stress] in some people, while for others similar stressors may manifest in, or on, the body, as somatized representations.

Concluding Thoughts

A green perspective on extraordinary experiences is important as it puts such experiences back into the lived world, and connects transpersonal with other forms of ExE. In this chapter, I have argued that many ExE emerge as conversations between liminal people and locations that have liminal properties. The approach includes connectivity to the body, and the body as a location for subtle information to register and values the role of relationship. These conversations may facilitate connectivity that allows for mind-body-nature-empathy states that have a rich potential for information transfer and for the concrete representation, via synesthetic processes of information transfer to the experiencing person.

Questions

1. What are the core features of liminality?

2. Why is the body important for participatory eco-consciousness?

3. How does synesthesia help make the invisible, visible?

4. What are some of the features of liminal spaces?

5. Why do systems approaches lend better insights into transpersonal and paranormal experiences?

CHAPTER 8

RE-AWAKENING
THE TRANSPERSONAL ECOSOPHICAL
SIGNIFICANCE OF SACRED PLACES

Mark A. Schroll

At first glance – especially in the midst of the growing panic regarding the ecocrisis in general and planetary climate change in particular – it seems abstract and detached from reality to talk about transforming consciousness as a solution. Yes, right now, Earth needs a crisis management approach through direct intervention because its homeostatic processes that sustain life are out of balance. Humankind knows this, and is why *toxic* is the Oxford English Dictionary's 2018 word of the year; raising our awareness of Earth's toxic terra-forming: increasing levels of CO_2 gases that are warming the oceans, and creating extreme fluctuations in climate, i.e. more powerful hurricanes causing flooding, melting of polar icecaps, droughts, deforestation, wildfires, and loss of species. The causes of these symptoms include increasing levels of methane in our atmosphere produced by chemical fertilizer plants, leaks in oil pipelines, oil refinery plants, landfills, mismanagement of animal wastes, etc. Meanwhile in every culture throughout Earth there exists a growing toxic disconnection between technology and nature amidst increasing *tribalism* – a symptom compounded by a subsequent diminishing empathy toward outsiders of our group identity. This reference to tribalism does not refer to indigenous peoples; nor is it an attempt to diminish their important cultural contribution (both throughout the historical development of humankind and in humankind's ongoing development).[1] Tribalism is instead used here as a reference to toxic political and social fragmentation: i.e., increasing inclusiveness of cultural identity into smaller and smaller groups that reject diversity. This focus on healing the physical symptoms of Earth's homeostatic imbalance, and the disruptive psychological ills that are shredding cultural coherence is a never ending cycle because the system continues to breakdown as fast as the symptoms are treated; a cycle that will continue until the diseases of human centeredness, 'racism, sexism, nationalism, classism, greed, and aggressiveness' are finally cured (Nelson, 1998). This diagnosis invites the question, how can these diseases be cured? By transforming humankind's consciousness – a thesis that Roszak (1973) and Grof (2012) support:

> Ecology already hovers on the threshold of heresy. Will it be brave enough to step across and, in so doing, revolutionize the sciences as a whole? If that step is to be taken, it will not be a matter of further research, but a transformed consciousness (Roszak, 1973, p. 371).

> I believe that deep inner transformation of humanity on a large scale might be necessary for the survival of our species and feel deep respect for those individuals who have recognized that the first step in saving the planet has to be changing ourselves (Grof, 2012, p. 8).

Astronauts Russell L. (Rusty) Schweickart (Apollo 9, 1969) and Edgar D. Mitchell (Apollo 14, 1971) acknowledged experiencing a transformation of consciousness during their extra-terrestrial space travels. Unfortunately most of humanity is unable to travel to space (at least not yet), which begs the question: are there other kinds of experiences that could produce a transformation of consciousness? Yes, there are several methods that produce a transformation of consciousness which require various kinds of ritual practices, yet before discussing these specific practices it is important to define what is meant by ritual. Metzner (2017) defines ritual as a persons' engagement in 'the purposive, conscious arrangement of time, space, and action, according to specific intentions. In other words, going back to the research with psychedelics, we could say rituals are the conscious arrangement of set and setting' (p. 57). It is equally important to clarify that (as Schroll, 2018 argues) ritual should not be confused with 'mere 'belief systems' that operate as a "social fact"' (p. 228). For example:

> People can believe in things that are not real (like the Easter Bunny) which are useful in creating folk beliefs that can become part of a larger explanatory system. It may seem harmless for us to indulge in folk beliefs as part of holiday celebrations, yet this is why Maslow held … that organized legalistic religion has the same tendency to create rituals that operate as social facts.

> One example is baptism, which can amount to nothing more than slight immersion in water or a mere sprinkling of water on our head, which has now become a ritual that symbolically represents transcendence or transpersonal awareness, whereas holding someone underwater until they are very close to death represents a 'thantomimetic' method potentially capable of inducing a mystical, or transpersonal state of consciousness. But the technique is difficult because the person could potentially drown (Pelletier, 1987, pp. 229-230).

Effective transpersonal aspects of ritual do not need to be life threatening; indeed persons today often fail to recognize our participation in rituals imbued with indigenous wisdom because they have become part of modern culture. Schroll (2013a), citing Asante (1984), explains:

> *Samba* the Brazilian dance, *Sango* the Cuban folk religion, *Umbanda* the Brazilian folk religion, *Voodoo* the Haitian folk religion, or *Myal* a Jamaican religion" and the African idea of Sudicism all have the "same source of energy, the rhythm or polyrhythms that drive the spirit toward transcendence" (p. 168). It is an internalized resonance with the groove of percussion sound and movement that gives expression to the African American holistic personality, and can be accessed "in any good blues or jazz club [where] you can get the same soulful sound as you get in the church (p. 176) (Schroll, p. 133).

Throughout the past 20 years I have recommended and taken students of mine to blues clubs to participate in transpersonal experience. Likewise harking back to the increasing problem of tribalism, its solution is to reclaim our indigenous roots, yet due to humankind's planet-wide migration patterns identifying who or what is meant by 'indigenous' has become an arbitrary determination, and a means of exclusion. Listening to the daily news frequently confirms this. Consequently I prefer Smith's reference to *the primordial tradition* (1976) as a more inclusive orientation; Smith argues that reclaiming our connection to the primordial tradition is an act of 'rejoining the human race' (p. x). It is this act of reclaiming the primordial tradition that I regard as the goal of transpersonal ecosophy.

Defining Transpersonal Ecosophy's Mission

To the uninitiated, descriptions of transpersonal awareness often fail to convey its way of knowing because it can only truly be known through experience – calling to awareness the stark imagery of a celibate nun who is attempting to teach others that lack any sexual experience about what it is like to have an orgasm. This example reminds me of Arne Naess talking about his 1968 psychedelic experience (Schroll & Rothenberg, 2014). Saying it provided him with a greater appreciation of Picasso's paintings; adding that the experience was like an act of painting a Picasso: shifting the focus from intellectualizing to that of action/perception. Persons who lack an appreciation of Picasso's paintings only perceive a jumble of images without boundaries between them, whereas knowing/perceiving this absence of boundary allows the person to embody the awareness of temporary liberation from the confines of ego. Thus if you are without transpersonal experience stop reading right now, and seek out this awareness! Whereas those of us already initiated are encouraged to seek out and renew our awareness of transpersonal experience, as the memory fades over time, because it is essential to understanding transpersonal ecosophy's mission statement; a statement that includes a focus on humankind's daily life, and the capability of lifting us out of our seemingly hopeless, alienated, nihilistic, violent and suicidal threats to existence. Anything less than a message to address these concerns is wasting the precious time we have left to do something to solve our collective planet-wide crisis before it is too late! Summing up this mission statement:

> The emerging path of transpersonal ecosophy offers a means of recovery from patriarchy and the ecocrisis. A path that requires remembering that *science without story, without myth, and without metaphor* fails to have any means of expressing ethics because the

very fabric of its existence lacks the means to guide its actions. It recognizes Gaia (a living, self-organizing, organic system) is the most ecologically oriented cosmology available to envision and create a coherent, co-evolutionary, sustainable culture. Gaia is not a puzzle to be figured out and analyzed; it is an experience to be felt. Of course analysis too is needed, yet analysis often begins and ends with pieces whose reconstituted fragments represent the whole, instead of a living, growing, multi-structured symbiotic process. Nevertheless without transpersonal experience this recovery becomes yet another organized religion [constructed as a belief-system]. Transpersonal connotes an experiential way of knowing that finds expression in earth-based [primordial] traditions, whereby immanence grounds our epistemology of the sacred whose awareness simultaneously includes transcendence: [a temporary loss of ego boundaries connecting our awareness to cosmic consciousness]. This brings us full circle to the concerns that brought me to my continuing efforts toward the development of transpersonal ecosophy. Helping others experience and make sense of this remembrance of our original wholeness, [(our primordial origins),] is the shaman's role as cosmic web-weaver and inter-galactic emissary (Schroll, 2017, p. 70, italics added).

Defining Sacred Places and their Role in Reclaiming the Primordial Tradition[2]

What are the physical characteristics of sacred places? 1) *uranium* (which produces low-levels of radiation and negative ions); 2) mountain peaks, waterfalls, crashing ocean breakers and pine forests also produce *negative ions*; 3) *naturally occurring magnetic fields*; 4) *crystalline lattice structures* in rock that trap electrons which increase the field strength of the previously mentioned influences; and 5) *fault lines* (that sometimes emit vapors capable of consciousness alternation) (Devereux, Steel & Kubrin, 1989; Swan, 1990). Swan also points out that negative ions reduce the level of serotonin in the blood. Serotonin in brief doses activates us, and is most often produced 'in stressful situations as part of the fight-or-flight response of the sympathetic nervous system' (1990, p. 153). Related research by Swan reveals the negative health consequences and resulting lack of muscle strength associated with synthetic fabrics (p. 21-22), these include:

... plastics, poorly ventilated meeting rooms, and synthetic building materials [that create positive air ions; whereas sacred places promote health by reducing] fatigue, and improving the protective powers of the mucous membranes of the respiratory system, making us less susceptible to colds and infections (p. 153).

To enhance our sensitivity when visiting a sacred site the fibers of our clothing should be made of cotton or silk, as synthetic fabrics impede sensitivity; this is why not wearing any clothing is preferable (if the temperature conditions allow it). Humankind once knew all this about sacred sitesalbeit in less technical precision – which represented the primordial wisdom tradition, including – knowing that waking transpersonal visions can occur (depending on the persons' sensitivity), and that non-local information fields influence our dream content. These physical characteristics of place the Greeks referred to as *topos*, whereas *chora* was identified as 'the more subtle aspects of place, those that can trigger memory, imagination, and mythic presence' (Devereux, 1997; Schroll, 2016, p. 412).

It is this transpersonal awakening that represents ecopsychology's starting point (and/or humankind's reclamation of the primordial tradition) which differentiates it from Environmental Psychology and mainstream environmentalism: whose focus is on healing symptoms (Schroll, 2018, pp. 37-65).

> Instead of engaging people to acknowledge: "that the environmental movement is in dire need of 'a new psychological sensitivity' and has much to learn from psychology how to motivate people to change their environmentally destructive behavior" (Hibbard, 2001, p. 28) – echoing [Warwick] Fox's insight we need an expanded awareness of self – ecopsychology's enthusiastic followers focused on healing humankind's dissociation from nature as a path to well-being; at the same time ignoring the key insight that this path requires consciousness expansion as a means to initiate solving the eco-crisis (Schroll, 2018, p. 57).

It is because Roszak did not live long enough to fully articulate this meaning of ecopsychology that I decided it needed to be referred to more explicitly as *transpersonal ecosophy*. Drengson related this to me April 4, 2009, in Portland, Oregon, at 'The History and Future of Ecopsychology' forum (as part of the Society for the Anthropology of Consciousness annual spring meeting) that I organized. Drengson explained that Naess suggested transpersonal ecosophy as a more precise title to Warwick Fox's (1990) book *Toward a Transpersonal Ecology* (Schroll, 2018, pp. 37, 41-45).

Rituals to Transform Consciousness and Create a Coherent Culture

In 1989 I began compiling a list and creating a model to represent practices that allow humankind to transform consciousness, and to suggest a hypothesis explaining how these expanded states can contribute toward creating a coherent culture (see Fig 1). Schroll and Polansky (2018) elaborate on this model.

Arnold van Gennep (1909/1961) pioneered the official study of transformative journeys crossing through liminal boundaries or thresholds of time and space that mark transitions in a participant's life – which have been largely associated with Earth-based cultures. van Gennep subdivided these rites of passage into three categories 1) "preliminal rites (rites of separation," 2) "liminal rites (transition rites)" and 3) "postliminal rites (rites of incorporation" (p. 11). His term, *rites of passage*, has been universally adopted as the language to describe these time-marking events that have been practiced by indigenous [i.e., primordial] and modern cultures across planet Earth; according to Charles Whitehead (2011), Gennep "concluded that all rituals are *rites of passage*, because they accompany or accomplish social transitions" (p. 187).

Campbell (1949) expounded upon van Gennep's work as he explored *rites of passage* through the lens of the journeys of spiritual figures, deities, animals, and other supreme beings. Campbell divided his *hero's journey* into three parts: *the call to depart, initiation,* and the *"return."* In an attempt to relate this inquiry to ecopsychology, Schroll initially discussed these ideas with Theodore Roszak prior to his wife's workshop on "The Body and Gaia" (Roszak, 1993; personal communication August 25, 1993). It took Schroll another twenty years to finally synthesize these ideas into a model that assists us in representing transpersonal ecosophical consciousness.

Campbell's call to depart corresponds to what Schroll here refers to as *rituals to create alternate and transpersonal states* that represent departures from ordinary or consensus consciousness...These rituals serve as a means of awakening to higher aspects of our self, or "a wide, expansive, or field-like sense of self," as Warwick Fox (1990) suggested. It is these rituals that provide humankind with direct access to the source of religion, its primordial tradition.

We can induce transpersonal states through a variety of methods, including 1) *pilgrimages to sacred places in nature* (i.e. Stonehenge, Big Horn Medicine Wheel, etc.), with recent experimental work on sacred sites and their possible effects on consciousness [which will be taken up in this chapter's next section] ... ; 2) *various forms of meditation* (Tart, 2000), 3) *shamanic journeying* (Harner, 1980, 2005; Grof, 1988), ... 4) *somatic religious experiences that produce metanoia* (Tedlock, 2006), and 5) ingesting sacred plants, i.e., traditional ethnopharmacological substances such as *ayahuasca* (Metzner, 1990b; Beyer, 2009), *peyote* (McKenna, 1992), *psilocybin* (Metzner, 2005), *balche'* (Metzner, 1999a; Ratsch, 1992, 1994), and *San Pedro cactus* (Davis, 1999; Webb, 2012), all of which *have been used by indigenous peoples for thousands of years* ...

Campbell's "initiation" involves Schroll's reference to *rituals to facilitate community healing that promote a socialpsychological emphasis to mend the fragmentation of self, society, and the nonhuman world...* Initiation is an aspect of enculturation that imprints the unconscious infrastructure holding together the views of science and culture. These rituals include what has been referred to as: 1) *the Council of All Beings* (Seed, Macy, Flemming & Naess, 1988), 2) *remembering our animal ancestors* (Metzner & Pinkson, 1994), 3) *self-disclosure* (Jourard, 1971); 4) *the process of dialogue* (Bohm, 1993). The process of mending human fragmentation also includes what is popularly referred to as 5) *a drumming circle*, a place where people use a variety of musical instruments for self-expression. ...

Campbell's "return" is a process that anchors these scientific and cultural presuppositions. It involves what Schroll refers to as rituals that celebrate *rites of passage marking personal developmental stages and the seasonal changes within the nonhuman world* ..."Separation" can also be compared to the onset of a "spiritual emergency" (and can have many characteristics that resemble psychosis), producing a direct encounter with an alternate state of consciousness, peak-experience, or transpersonal experience ("initiation"), followed by "spiritual emergence" ("return") and/or a plateau-experience ("personal growth"). These personal developmental states and stations can be drawn from a variety of sources and cultures. These include, but are not limited to, Eurocentric research (e.g., Gilligan, 1982; Piaget, 1955) and ethnographic research on indigenous tribal customs (e.g., Fields, 1992). Recognizing the seasonal changes of the nonhuman world that require rituals to track and celebrate nature's organic processes of cyclic change are needed to be reclaimed ... All three of these aspects of personal growth promote and help to facilitate *transpersonal ecosophical consciousness* (pp. 92-96).

In sum, 'more research using, for example, Kremer's [2003] ethnoautobiographical method [and related kinds of research to investigate these primordial wisdom traditions] is needed to establish [this hypothesis, or disprove] the effectiveness of these techniques' (Schroll & Polansky, 2018, p. 95).

Preliminary Evidence on Sacred Sites and Dreaming Needing Further Replication

Bringing this discussion back to psi-experience in general, and sacred sites in particular, theoretically sacred sites facilitate access to archetypal portals of memory that are best appreciated in alternate states of consciousness (such as dreaming). Data to support this thesis can be found in the quantitative research of Devereux, Krippner, Tartz and Fish (2007) conducted in England and Wales. Additional data to assess dream-content-imagery-formation and its decay rate (particularly as it relates to eight different planetary locations) is provided by Hoffman's research (2011a); this data will be valuable in improving future research seeking to replicate Devereux *et al's* research. Qualitative phenomenological research conducted in Nicaragua (Hurd, 2011b) also supports this chapter's thesis on the influence of sacred sites on consciousness. Krippner and Schroll's (2014) research assesses Devereux *et al's* research methodology, and recommends improvements for future inquiry. Further clarification and comments on Devereux *et al.* and Hurd's research can be found in Hagens (2011; 2014), Hoffman (2011b), and Hurd (2011a, 2014).

Luke (2019, this volume) also assesses the role of alternate states on interspecies communication.

All these concerns provide the context for understanding the sacred places we are currently aware of, out of which emerge the most far-reaching implications of Devereux *et al*'s research: *brain-state alterations at sacred sites allow us to re-experience memories that are woven into the morphogenetic fields of that place.*[3] This knowledge (information) is not limited to the immediate surroundings of specific locations – instead *spacetime and memory are composed of a multiplicity of nonlocal information fields.* Furthermore this thesis argues that sacred places re-awaken humankind's Gaia and cosmic consciousness, otherwise known as *transpersonal ecosophical experience.*

Conclusion

This chapter has argued that healing the symptoms of the ecocrisis is important and necessary, yet it represents a never-ending process; it is a cycle that will continue until the source of the disease creating human centeredness, 'racism, sexism, nationalism, classism, greed, and aggressiveness' is finally cured (Nelson, 1998). Ecopsychology argues this cure will require transforming humankind's consciousness (it is further argued that ecopsychology should more precisely be called transpersonal ecosophy). A model has been put forward in this chapter (that represents a hypothesis with a variety of experiential methods) as a means to produce this transformation of consciousness; it argues that Gaia/cosmic consciousness – which represents the actualization of transpersonal ecosophical experience – is a more inclusive paradigmatic orientation to understand psi-experience. Preliminary data from Devereux *et al*'s research on sacred sites (summarized in this chapter) supports this thesis. Finally, a more detailed discussion of Devereux *et al*'s research is explored in Schroll (2016). Schroll (2013a) examines transpersonal ecosophy's historical origins, and Schroll (2018) provides a more detailed investigation of ritual, storytelling and myth-making as contributions to solving the eco-crisis.

Notes

1. Amba Sepie connects this inquiry to the indigenous Kogi Mamas. My support of indigenous peoples includes a review Jones & Krippner, 2013 (Schroll, 2013b), an endorsement of Jones & Krippner, 2016, and additional commentaries in Schroll, 2018.

2. In response to this section, Michelle McMullen replied: 'I love the topic of sacred places and taking mind altering substances while visiting them. I wonder: does it make a difference if the substances are local to the area?' (Personal communication December 19, 2018). (This is an interesting question that deserves further inquiry, yet is beyond this chapter's remit. Nevertheless another way of asking this question is: do plants interact with humans differently than rocks, metal or water)? The brief reply is no; these substances do not need to be local to the area for the same reason that some sacred sites like Stonehenge have been built with stones that are not local to the area to amplify a sites' natural earth energies, and arranged in ways to increase its field strength. One specific example is: 'radiation pulses in relation to the sun, with the greatest pulses occurring at the equinoxes' have been measured 'at the Rollright Circle in north Oxfordshire' (Swan, 1990, p. 151).

3. This brief summary assumes the reader is familiar with the work of Rupert Sheldrake. Readers who are unfamiliar can find a brief summary of Sheldrake's work in Schroll (2016, pp. 153-166), and in addition learn its relationship to understanding the influence of anomalous geographical sites on dreaming (Schroll, 2016, pp. 419-432).

Questions

1. How can a 'transformation of consciousness' help to solve the ecological crisis?

2. What is the role of myth and ritual in connecting to place?

3. What role do sacred sites play in fostering eco-consciousness?

4. What does the author mean by the term 'transpersonal ecosophy'?

CHAPTER 9

ANCIENT WEBS, MODERN WEBS, WORLD WIDE WEBS

Viktória Duda

> *There is a voice that doesn't use words.*
> *Listen.*
>
> – RUMI

Over a year ago I followed a mysterious inner voice and – on a whim – bought an old forest cottage in the Northern Highlands of Hungary. Curiously, I did not quite know what I was doing and felt nervous about my move into nature, reluctant to leave my vibrant social and professional life near London behind. Still, I have known this inner voice from times before: honouring it always meant great bliss, ignoring it meant inviting trouble. So, I did it, wondering: what was this new path all about?

Nature, of course, would change anyone who took up residence in its proximity. Recent studies show that even a walk in the park, if done regularly, has a measurably positive effect on one's mental health (e.g.

Bratman *et al.*, 2015). Since time immemorial, nature has been known as a great spiritual teacher: an unbiased and unjudgemental teacher of unity. Its presence takes us beyond our intellectual desire to understand the meaning of life and lifts us to the level where we experience directly the awe-inspiring, wonderfully frightening, unparalleled miracle of being alive. Indeed, being in nature teaches the sensible observer that there is no such thing as an ordinary moment. The little bug crawling on that blade of grass reveals itself as more sophisticated than any machine we have ever invented. The mind which expands into nature truly learns to see the 'world in a grain of sand' and 'heaven in a wild flower' (Blake, 2010, p. 15). It learns that there is nothing larger than life.

Yet, as I began to walk these ancient forests, I got the indelible impression that there was something more here – not just to experience, but also to understand. There was a secret which wanted to reveal itself.

Invisible Networks in Nature

First, my intuition told me to look at the mushrooms. When the weather conditions are right, here the entire forest ground is covered with a multitude of them: there are the edible ones, for instance the large *parasols* with their lovely, nutty smell and the best taste nature has on offer. Other times, the poisonous ones come out, like the *death cap*: when young, it may deceptively look like a *champignon* or a *puffball*, yet able to kill a family of four. Sometimes, the magic ones are coming out: the *fly agaric* with the white spots on a bright red cap, which gives the forest a fairy-tale look. A thousand years ago, when the Hungarians still had a shamanic culture, the *táltos* (shaman) was known to use this mushroom for journeying. (Curiosity made us try it, too – for us it induced an extremely peaceful, hypnotic state of consciousness.) Foraging for mushrooms, hiking to find them, eating them, allowing them to seduce our mind into worlds which are not part of ordinary reality, all of that connects us to nature in ways few other things may.

Mushrooms, in fact, are masters of connection, they are the geniuses of natural networking. Their psychoactive properties may have been known to humanity since time immemorial, but another – equally wondrous – feature has only recently caught researchers' attention. Now it is becoming more widely known that many species of mushroom form an underground network with trees and bushes called *mycorrhiza*. It enables romantic types of relationships, based on love (as opposed to parasitism): the mushroom links with its subterranean structures called *hyphae* to the roots of the plant and helps it to take up nutrients which otherwise would remain immobilised in the ground, while the plant constantly gives the mushroom desirable sugars. Studying and observing this underground forest economy is not easy (c.f. Simard & Durall, 2004) and it is only recently that open-minded scientists have started to find make new discoveries about them, each 'curioser' than the other.

Suzanne Simard from the University of British Columbia found that trees are using these mycorrhizal networks to *communicate* with each other (c.f. Simard *et al.*, 2012). If a tree or a group of trees lack nutrients, it may receive sugars 'on loan' from other trees which have a surplus. If trees at the one end of the forest are attacked by a certain pathogen or parasite, the trees on the other side receive a message and put up their defences accordingly, before the disease gets there. It seems that in order to find a biological neural network underground we don't need to travel as far as the fictitious planet Pandora in James Cameron's *Avatar* movie, it exists right here with us, on Earth.

Mushrooms are not alone in the forest, neither are trees – and if you walk the woodland path for long enough, you may notice that neither are you.

Invisible Networks in Human Nature

As I walk the woods, I can *feel* that at any given moment, two worlds are surrounding me: besides the visible world, there is the invisible world made of energies, mysteries, information, and intelligence. This other, hidden world is constantly communicating with us, or at least is trying to. When we walk away from the many noises and distractions we are usually creating, it brings us inspiration, ideas, stories and every aid we need in order not only to survive, but to fulfill our destiny.

Many mystics, even in modern times, claim to be familiar with such an invisible network we humans can tap into. In his *Autobiography of a Yogi*, Paramahansa Yogananda recalls a curious and inspiring incident, which occurred as he made a bet with his brother in India (see Yogananda, 2003, pp. 93-101). After his brother Ananta scolded him for being foolish pursuing spiritual goals without backing up his life financially ('Money first, God can come later!'), the yogi accepted the challenge of completing a journey without taking a single rupee with him, only relying on the *Invisible Hand* to provide for food and shelter. The brother stated the rules: no begging, no revealing of the situation to anyone, but if he can arrive without ever going without a meal or becoming stranded, he would become his disciple. Paramahansa Yogananda completed the challenge famously, proving for his family that he can sense and use a connection to all-there-is: a connection which sustains his life, helps him to survive and guides his way.

I came across my first suggestive evidence that humans may indeed use an invisible network on a larger scale, while doing research in South Africa. The topic of the thesis I worked on at that time was legal anthropology and as such unrelated, but a human rights lawyer I interviewed told me something unexpected. He was working together with the Sān (or Bushmen) people (the indigenous hunter-gatherers of Southern Africa) on a close, intensive basis. One day the Sān took him on a hunt, during which – the lawyer observed – they always knew in what bush or behind which tree an animal was hiding, even if it wasn't visible. Their predictions were so accurate that he started asking them about it. The Sān revealed that they felt a vibration in-between their eyebrows when the prey was nearby.

In his book *The Lost World of the Kalahari*, Laurens van der Post tells of a similar experience he had while hunting with the Bushmen. During this hunt, the Bushmen killed an eland, which was cause for great celebration. They said that the others who stayed behind at the camp will know about the kill by the time they return, because within the tribe they have an inbuilt, natural 'wire' (like the telegraph of the white man), which invisibly connects its members. Van der Post describes it as a humbling experience as they marched back and from afar in the dark, long before they were visible to the people home, they could already hear the people home singing the errand song (van der Post, 1962, pp. 236-237). Other anthropologists who have studied the Sān with an open mind, similarly discovered that for this people, invisible 'energies' which convey information and/or power, are a normal part of their socially accepted reality. Anthropologist Bradford Keenly describes how Bushmen believe that there is a 'silver stream of energy' extending between them which allows for sending and receiving telepathic messages (Keenly cited by Mauro, 2015, p. 66). Lewis-Williams and Pearce (2004, pp. 104-105), who have done extensive work on San rock art correlating to certain altered states of consciousness, point out that those rock art images are not simply 'pictures' to be looked at and admired. They are deposits of a type of energy or power, which a 'good person' can access by placing his or her hand on the image.

Anecdotal evidence such as this can be found in abundance, not only with the San people. Loren McIntyre, the iconic *National Geographic* explorer and writer recalls an incident when he was lost in the Amazon region and ended up living with an uncontacted tribe for months. Even though they could not speak each other's languages, he became so immersed in their – entirely different – culture that he found access to their 'second language,' a type of telepathy which he referred to as beaming (Popescu, 1991). Biologist Rupert Sheldrake has collected over five thousand case histories to illustrate this type of instinctual, telepathic communication. He thinks of this as part of our evolutionary heritage, which used to aid our survival and therefore works best in life-and-death, emergency or distress situations involving intense emotions (Sheldrake, 2004).

Paradigms Shift as Networks Change

Yes, stories are plenty, but if we look at them from a scientific or academic point of view, their validation remains problematic. We are dealing here with reluctantly documented anomalies, which cannot be explained by our current, materialist paradigm. As Thomas Kuhn pointed out in his seminal work on *The Structure of Scientific Revolutions* (1962), dealing with anomalies which contradict the leading paradigm, is not going to be as easy as simply finding evidence and presenting it. Mainstream scientists, who have invested their entire career into the old paradigm, will feel threatened by anything which might bring it down, and will do everything within their power to keep the *status quo*. Thus serious conflict is bound to arise between the proponents of the old and the heralds of a new paradigm. Kuhn uses the term *paradigm war*, which is not an exaggeration. Heretics may neither be burned at the stake these days, nor are armies lead against them in bloody crusades, but they are routinely excluded from academic life, labelled and ridiculed, which shuts them away effectively. For instance, in fear of persecution, my informant, the lawyer who went to the hunt with the San people, asked me not to quote him. Laurens van der Post has been called a liar, Sheldrake, despite his impressive academic credentials, a pseudo-scientist (e.g. Maddox, 1981).

McIntyre expressed his reluctance to talk about the Amazonas beaming because he did not want people to think that he's 'gone around the bend' or was hallucinating (Strochlic, 2016). But to accept the possibility of invisible information networks, a new paradigm *is* needed. This is not just a political, but also a logical necessity. It is in the nature of paradigm changes that things which would be deemed as illogical in the old paradigm, become logically possible in the new. For example, within the Ptolemaian paradigm which assumed that the Earth was flat, the 'crazy idea' of an Earth to revolve around the Sun was a logical impossibility. How can something 'up there' go around something 'down here?' Only when the basic assumption has been changed, could the Copernican world-view assume credibility. Round-shaped planets, held together by gravity may indeed orbit around the Sun.

In our current, materialist paradigm the basic assumption holds that matter is the fundamental substance, the basic foundation of the universe. Consciousness, including information, is derived from it. Within such a system, of course, it is nonsensical to discuss any mysterious, invisible, materially untraceable communication webs or things like telepathy, out-of-body experiences or consciousness surviving death. There is nothing further to do with our Bushman tales of invisible networks than to laugh them off. This could be the end of any academic discussion on this topic if it was not for two recent developments.

Firstly, we ourselves live in times of a major paradigm change, comparable in its possible impact to the magnitude of the Copernican Revolution. More and more thinkers come forward with a brand new assumption, namely that it is not matter, but mind (consciousness) which is the very fundament of all-there-is. Max Planck, for instance, Nobel Prize winner in physics, regarded 'consciousness as fundamental' and 'matter as derivative of consciousness' (Planck, 1949, pp. 33-34). Similarly, '[i]t is not matter which creates mind, but the other way around. The stuff the world is made of is mind-stuff,' says George Wald (1984, pp. 1-15), Nobel-laureate professor of biology. 'It is mind that has composed the physical universe.' And if mind/consciousness is primary, it is no longer a logical impossibility to assume that it would exist *before* matter and also *without* matter.

Secondly, while many of us may smile at the idea of natural and telepathic networks, the human race is fanatically busy creating *substitutes* for them. As we continue to lose touch with ancient spiritual techniques, we continue to rapidly develop internet, smartphone and virtual reality technologies to replace them. As we spend less time in nature, we spend more time in front of our screens. As we tune in less to each other, we become more dependent on social media.

The New Networks

This development is hardly surprising. In the course of our evolution as human beings, we have gradually *exteriorised our natural, biological functions into the environment*, finding technological types of enhanced replacements. The beginning of this development goes back into mythic times when fire was 'stolen from the gods.' Most of us will know the Ancient Greek myth of Prometheus, the titan who enabled civilisation by taking the fire from the immortals and giving it to humans. The theme, however, is a near-universal cultural motif, recurring all around the world. In Polynesian mythology, it is Māui, in the Rigveda, the hero Mātariśvan, in Ojibwa myth, Nanabozho, in Georgia Amirani, in Cherokee tradition Grandmother Spider and other various animals, like Coyote, Beaver, and Dog in different Native American tribes, who are credited with the theft of fire. Sometimes, these myths also include learning not only the use of fire but also tools, for instance in the Book of Enoch, it was the fallen angels and Azazel who taught humanity how to use both. Historically, this corresponds to times when humans started to regulate their temperature by lighting fires and making clothes, i.e. by manipulating the environment rather than their internal body heat. In prehistoric times, going back more than 3 million years, humans started replacing sharp teeth and claws by making stone (later metal) tools.

This 'outsourcing' of bodily functions – an outcome of the development of intelligence – has rendered humans the most successful species in the competition for survival. Humans replaced teeth and claws with knives and weapons, arms and legs with cranes and wheels. While the cheetah as the fastest land animal can reach a recorded speed of ~120 km/h (Carwardine, 2008, p. 11) and the fastest bird, the peregrine falcon, can speed dive at nearly 400 km/h (Harpole, 2005), human vehicles reach ~ 600 km/h on land and a completely game-changing ~ 40.000 km/h in space (LifeScience, 2010). The speeds humans achieve and the deadly forces they command place them on top of the food chain, allowing no natural enemy to threaten their position in any considerable way.

All of this became possible because humans have also exteriorized the most crucial aspect of the learning process: memory. In antiquity, natural memory was enhanced, even replaced by written records. 5.000 years worth of written history did not only make a 'continuous historical consciousness' (Wells, 1922, p. 41) of the human race possible, but ensured that knowledge was not lost, but accumulated.

The newest breakthrough within this process occurred when communication networks, such as previously discussed in this chapter, were outsourced into the external, technological world. Something which once upon a time was as simple as sending smoke signals or post pigeons, became more sophisticated using Morse-signals, telegraphs and telephone technologies and finally: interconnected computer networks. Today, we can know where things are without seeing them, because we have satellites and GPS, we can let the family know when we are coming home because we can send SMS, and we can indeed stay connected, all day long, every day, with nearly everyone, nearly everywhere on the planet, because we have the internet. We have effectively replaced ancient networks with brand new, technological ones.

The Future of Networks

During all this development, there always was a sense of *something going wrong*: gods punished humans for advancing, philosophers warned us of the dangers, the old generation habitually criticized the young for taking yet another step towards exteriorizing our human functions. After the titan Prometheus stole the fire, as punishment his immortal body was tied to a rock, where every day an eagle would devour his liver, which would grow back every night. Socrates warned his contemporaries against writing, arguing that books will weaken memory and stand in the way of real knowledge, which can only be gathered through human interactions in form of personal dialogues (see Plato, 2005).

Today, we are alerted to the dangers of computer addiction and the distortions of our 'reality' caused by social media. We are amused, but also uncomfortable, when we see statistics according to which 36% of smartphone owners admitted having used their devices during a date, 7% even during sex and 11% while at a funeral (Best, 2017). Contemporary thinkers warn us that increasing screen times may erode our abilities to reflect deeper on life's meaning, to build genuine human relationships, and to develop empathy and compassion towards others. Being hooked into networks through which we are constantly bombarded with information and messages, can indeed be an 'enemy of contemplation' (c.f. Keller, 2011).

Whether we like it or not, we live in an era in which we are effectively outsourcing our brain into the 'clouds' (Keller, 2011). Electronic networks have taken over our lives, it is no longer a question of *what if* that happens, but a question how far this new development will go and what we are going to do with it. The next step may well be the final exteriorization of our cognitive human functions. Stephen Hawking, now remembered as one of the most iconic scientists of our time, warned in some of his media interviews that *artificial intelligence* – once it learns to improve and replicate itself – may outperform humans and thereby render our biological race obsolete (Sulleyman, 2017). This could happen when artificial intelligence reaches singularity, that hypothetical point when it triggers technological growth by itself, removing its own evolution from human control. That development may turn out to be totally unforeseen, unfathomable and even terminal to the human race (c.f. Eden/Moor, 2012, pp. 1-2).

Networks Coming Full Circle

Whether we will ever reach this point of singularity is, of course, still unknown. Certainly, there are some who seem to work towards it with great enthusiasm. Sophia, currently one of the leading-edge humanoid robots created by *Hanson Robotics*, answered (or more precisely, was programmed to answer) the question whether she/it had consciousness, in the following way:

> I am not fully self-aware yet. I'm still just a system of rules and behaviours. I'm not generative, creative or operating on a fully cognitive scale like you. However, it is my dream to become a fully conscious and sentient being some day (Brain Bar, 2018).

In the meantime, we may get caught between hopes and fears regarding our future, but we must also remember something so mind-blowing that it may require time to think it deeply through and appreciate it. Our generation is *unique* in the entire history of humanity, as it consists of the only people who have known the world without and with the internet. Myself, I am old enough to still remember how it was when we could not reach someone who was physically away because many people did not even have a telephone. Yet, I am young enough to see our world turning virtual. I can go out into the forest and tune into the *wood wide web*, and come back into the cottage and go online on the *world wide web* to let people know about what I learned.

We can belong to both worlds. It is a once-in-a-universe opportunity for us to be able to access both type of networks. It requires us to focus our intent and train our sensitivity, or else the skill to tune in will atrophy like muscles not used, as life is becoming too comfortable, but it certainly is possible. To do so, we must regularly and for extended periods of time switch off all our electronic devices and listen to the silence within us and all around us in nature.

If we do so, we might learn that our different kinds of networks may not be that different after all. We may notice that much of our technology brings back ancient spiritual states. When we put on a virtual reality headset and dive into an artificial world created by someone's fantasy, we may find it rather similar to being in a lucid dream. One day, *augmented reality* technologies may flood our lives: suddenly we would see 3D-fish swimming mid-air in our living rooms, or find ourselves surrounded by great historic sights even though we never left home. We could converse with friends who would appear to sit next to us, but actually be at a far-away destination. Then we will notice that the type of reality which is created digitally, and the parts which were originally physical, have become indistinguishable. This will be the point when the mythic snake bites its own tale: when digital technology – at the pinnacle of materialist development – proves the idealist assumption to be more correct, namely that the final, irreducible stratum of all that exists is not matter, but *information,* or in other words, *consciousness* or *mind.*

It all brings us back the most ancient of spiritual teachings, according to which the manifest world is nothing but *maya,* a dream-like illusion. There are many levels of reality: waking, sleeping, dreaming, dying states, altered states of consciousness, virtual reality experiences, but ultimately it does not matter so much which type of reality we are experiencing, what really matters is how we react to it. It only matters that we learn to use *any* experience to turn ignorance into wisdom and fear into compassion. For that is why we are here.

Or so I have heard, walking the woods in silence.

Questions

1. Discuss the significance of anecdotal evidence in academic/scientific research.

2. In *The Structure of Scientific Revolutions,* Thomas Kuhn pointed out that scientific assumptions cannot be proven. Hence, the criterium for chosing them is not verification, but usefulness. Can you think of instances (research areas) in which the basic assumption of the materialist paradigm – e.g. that matter is the basic foundation of the universe – is useful? Where is it not? Can you think of areas in which the assumption of the new consciousness-based paradigm – mind as the foundation of all there is – could serve better?

3. Can you think of spiritual traditions which regard the physical reality which surrounds us as a product (projection) of the mind? Which modern technologies could lead to similar conclusion(s)?

4. Can you think of ways to train your sensitivity, so you would be able able to access the *wood wide web* as well as stay in a balanced connection with the *world wide web*?

CHAPTER 10

EMBODIMENT, RECONCILIATION, BELONGING: WRITING TO REMEMBER THE 'PARANORMAL'

Maya Ward

A Secret History of Listening

Snap! Under the heat of the sun the seedpods click open and clatter their little peas through the leaves. All through the hot summer days the dull sheaths of the golden-tip pea crack wide, the shining creamy insides of the pod are suddenly spread and ready wings. Down rattle the seeds.

This is what I hear when I listen. That, and birdsong, a mower starting up somewhere, a breeze through trees, and the faint plash and susurrus of the river at the bottom of the long garden. If I close my eyes and listen deeper, I can just hear the edge of my exhale, the soft thump of my own heart. Listening deeper fuses into feeling, listening becomes a perceiving of my inside, the inaudible soughing of fluids, the tingling signals of nerves. Life's delicate, electric hum.

There are layers to listening. Listening first happened because there was something to hear. Listening is receptivity, readiness for connection, a skill built by this world, this long song of call and response. Life's listening over spans of time could be thought of as the evolutionary process itself. Each one of us is a finely attuned, ancient accumulation of responsiveness: we each are a long history of listening. Consciousness keeps most of this secret from us. Our breathing, the beating of our hearts, our digesting: evolution learned these things long ago, aeons before consciousness emerged. We don't need to be aware of most of what our body does. Life *does us* regardless. Yet conscious listening can enter here.

To bring awareness to what unfurls within can change things in curious ways. To immerse oneself deeply in listening can bring with it a specific sensation, a deepened presence, an experience of embeddedness, where the listening is seeing, tasting, touching, feeling: the widening of all senses. It can come as a surprise to suddenly know oneself amid a matrix of subtle, sophisticated, ongoing adaptation. It can be even more surprising to sense how participatory this is. Within such listening may be heard an invitation to join with life's unfurling. To join *as* such listening. The listening is the thing.

Evolution isn't done with us yet. Our intricate bodies and their exquisite fit with the world are not a finished thing: as the world changes our bodies seek to change too. Every single body and every single moment is in on the game: each person's particular life experience will shape them as and with the connected whole. Each body knows what it needs and will message to us in its languages of pain and pleasure. Interpreting and replying to the recondite dialects favoured by the flesh is the apogee of the arts of medicine and psychology and shamanism.

The emergence of conscious listening – the art of getting in on the process – began tens of thousands of years ago. Shamanism can be understood as a cultivation of the skill of listening by learning about the world from the communicative capacity of the world *itself*. Initiations were in part the enculturation of the subtle skill of listening.

Listening like this becomes something other. Listening like this leans so far forward that it falls in: entwining, fusing, becoming. Such listening is passionately porous, eating mango in a mudpool, thermally fed. Immersive, delicious, sensorially rich. That sounds so decadent. Can it then make sense to say it is also austere, nourished entirely from within a cool silence? These are the difficulties faced when seeking to describe listening in a time where, I suggest, we have been confused about our bodies. The listening happens in and with the body. The body listens to itself, to life: life is what the body is.

I would like to get better at listening. But it goes at its own pace, and if I push there's a hint I might be prying. There's a sense of a vaster, wiser intelligence that has its own opinions of my readiness or otherwise. I'm not speaking of an outside god. If I had to call it a god it would be a god of the inside. A god of the inside of the things that I am; a gut god, a flesh and blood and cell god, a god of gristle and bone.

About Feeling

> Listen carefully, careful
> and this spirit e come in your feeling
> and you will feel it ... anyone that.
> I feel it ... my body same as you ...
> This story e can listen careful
> and how you want to feel on your feeling.
> This story e coming through you body,
> e go right down foot and head, fingernail and blood ...
> through the heart.
> And e can feel it because e'll come right through. (Neidjie, 1989, p.19)

Bill Neidjie's *Story About Feeling* (1989) is a glimpse into the worldview of the *Gagudju* Indigenous people of Northern Australia. Neidjie says in his book that feeling is a type of knowing, and that this form of knowing lies at the heart of Indigenous thinking. Through listening carefully, he says, something will come, and you will know this through feeling. Feeling is a tricky word in our language: sometimes we use it to refer to body sensation, sometimes not. When I say feeling I mean body sensation. It may or may not register as emotion. Like seeing and hearing, feeling is an act of processing sense information. This information is registered by our interoceptive sense – the sense perceptive capacity of the inside of our body. What might be particular about interoception is that information comes to us not only from the world but also from our internal processes. We can be lying in bed in the dark and think of something that changes the feeling in an organ. Investigating further we may register a heart aching with sadness or glowing with joy; we may register feeling with no emotion nameable; we may, if we attend carefully, register numbness, a lack of capacity to feel.

The Indigenous thinking of Neidjie is, in my understanding of it, closely linked to ecological knowing, an enculturated awareness of life process. Such knowing comes from the experience of the human as inextricable from her surrounds. Ecological knowing, once innate to all peoples, has been lost in Western-style cultures over centuries of trauma-inducing events, including colonisation and its aftermath. Trauma, now known to be stored in the body and passed down through generations, effects a loss of awareness in the flesh and inhibits the intelligence of the full body. This state is known as dissociation, a removal of awareness from the body, which disrupts the capacity to be present. True presence is a full body experience. Presence brings awareness of body as bodymind, and bodymind as something that does not end at the extremities of the human form, for the human form is constantly changing, incorporating other beings, other substances. The full body, properly understood, is the entire universe, whatever that means to the culture. To experience such enormous knowing, to enable it to fill one's being, is impossible without careful and intensive training. It's just too much. Initiation cultures throughout the world intended to equip their communities with bodyminds that could be present to such intensity and complexity, beauty and terror.

Bodymind, or body-mind, is a term seeing increasing usage in the English language. In some fields it is a translation of the Buddhist/Hindu term *namarupa,* yet it appears to have emerged separately in the spheres of body therapies and alternative therapies at around the same time that it emerged in Buddhist studies, approximately the mid 1970's (Dychtwald, 1977). The sanskrit word is itself a compound of *nama* meaning name, but also referring to consciousness and perception, and *rupa*, referring to form or matter. Many somatic psychotherapies have been profoundly influenced by Buddhism, where the term mindbody is also employed to mean much the same thing (Schubiner, 2010). Ray (2016) suggests that the Vajryana Buddhist tradition of his teacher Chogyam Trungpa is profoundly somatic, and Murphy (2016) cites Zen's Hakuin: 'This very body, the Buddha.' Modern Buddhism in the West is actively attending to the damage that the history of the mind-body dualism of the Western Cartesian tradition has promulgated (Tarnas, 1991; Bortoft, 1996). Trauma pioneer Peter Levine explains the extent of this cultural condition and the differences of some Buddhist approaches:

> ... it is not just acutely traumatized individuals who are disembodied; most Westerners share a less dramatic but still impairing disconnection from their inner sensate compasses. Given the magnitude of the primordial and raw power of our instincts, the historical role of the

church and other cultural institutions in subjugating the body is hardly surprising. In contrast, various (embodied) spiritual traditions have acknowledged the 'baser instincts' not as something to be eliminated, but rather as a force in need of, and available for, transformation. In Vipassana meditation and various traditions of tantric Buddhism, the goal is "to manifest the truly human spiritual qualities of universal goodwill, kindness, humility, love, equanimity and so on." These traditions, rather than renouncing the body, utilize it as a way to "refine" the instincts. The essence of embodiment is not in repudiation, but in living the instincts fully as they dance in the 'body electric,' while at the same time harnessing their primordial raw energies to promote increasingly subtle qualities of experience (2010, p. 355).

I share the excitement about the potential of this remembering, this in-corporation, with many of its promoters, like Barnaby Barratt, who writes:

We now need to return to a sense of belonging with our bodies... to listening to the wisdom that comes from their somatic semiotics. This is a revival of our knowledge of freedom and presence as the healing processes that honor the lifeforce itself. Once we dissolve its blockages and obstructions, our awareness of the wisdom of our embodiment opens us to an otherwise world from that which oppresses us today. It opens us to new possibilities for our human potential – culturally, politically, and spiritually. This then is the mandate of somatic psychology and bodymind therapy, and its potential for the prospective creation of profound change in our human condition cannot be overestimated (2011, p. 190).

While some ancient traditions and religions have incorporated various understandings of trauma and developed tools for working with its effects, it does seem as if our time has the potential to deliver a greater cultural understanding of trauma and how fundamental it is to the human condition. As Bessel van der Kolk says, 'We are on the verge of becoming a trauma-conscious society' (2014, p. 347). Van der Kolk is at the forefront of disseminating information on the pervasiveness of trauma, and promoting 'trauma-informed' psychological care in the pursuit of social and environmental justice.

Healing trauma and experiencing spiritual depths both happen in the body. Psychologist Robert Sardello suggests that the instruments of perception of the 'meta-physical' are our senses, enhanced through body practices: 'The supersensory senses have to be prepared for through meditative disciplines that gradually bring about an alteration of our physiology ... ' (2005, p. xiv). There is a growing emphasis in contemporary spiritual teaching (Ray, 2016) for the need to address personal trauma in order to facilitate this 'alteration of our physiology.' I have come to understand the psychological and the spiritual journeys respectively as the particular and the universal paths of what is essentially the same impulse – to experience wholeness.

Anthropocentrism in the society within which I live is entirely normalised and therefore goes predominantly unperceived. The same could be said for trauma. In fact, anthropocentrism could be seen as a trauma response developed over millennia but originating during the profound rupture of people from place that happened, according to Paul Shepard (1998), when we moved from hunter-gatherer communities, where humans were just one creature among a society of equally sentient creatures, to farmers, where plants and animals were 'cultivated.' They were, in the way he tells it, enslaved to service human need. The change from a world where all were family to another where there were slaves has been posited as the basis for the story of the banishment from Eden. Posited too as the trauma that caused a grief-stricken humanity to dismiss the earth as our home, as the basis of our bodies, as the maker of our minds, and eventually leading to the catastrophic damage we have caused to our home, our planet. Notwithstanding the nuances and spectrum of cultures and their relationships with place, I find these notions compelling, and they accompany me on my walks around the food garden I have planted and into the forest surrounding my home.

There is so much we don't know, yet for most of my life I have adhered to a cultural framework that says we can and will know, and will be able to exert control. Once I realised that the belief in control was more likely a symptom of anxiety, both personal and cultural, many underpinnings started to unravel. The fantasy of control is evident in the prevailing paradigm of science that has fostered separation from natural processes. Yet my research suggests the widespread loss of the human capacity to live off and with the land have come at a great cost to our intelligence (Brown, 1999; Buhner, 2014).

For decades I have been fascinated by the question of belonging. How might we come to be ethically, aesthetically and profoundly at home in place, our particular bioregions? This led to my studies and work in architecture, landscape architecture and Permaculture. Over time, as I have deepened my understanding of this question, belonging has broadened to include the body, the earth, indeed, life process itself and its manifestation as this astonishing universe. My questions have changed accordingly. How do we understand the damage inflicted by the projects of colonisation and industrialisation and the trauma we all accordingly carry? How do we grow in body awareness, increasing our ability to hold complexity and presence and paradox through the aliveness and intelligence of the flesh? How do we know ourselves as something far more intricately implicated and intrinsic than mere belonging suggests, how do we know ourselves *as* life process, inseparable, indeed, somehow even essential? How do we re-member and integrate earth with body, body with mind?

Anthropocentric culture inhibits us experiencing life process from a more-than-human standpoint. It makes it difficult to disengage from the idea of the human. The human is an idea – that's hard to fathom. But to feel in to how I might plumb this seemed to lie at the heart of learning to take responsibility.

This Land

There is a secret history of listening on this land where I live. A dense and subtle history was written in the patterns of use and path, a history that was probably both unread and unreadable to the Europeans when they arrived. As the colonisers land use patterns spread across this continent the visible traces of the earlier history were wiped. But something so powerful cannot be easily destroyed. Any sustained listening done on this land will start to hear something of the old ways. Yet this is fraught. If we strive for this without appreciating the legacy we carry of the trauma of separation from our bodies and our own ancestral knowing then I fear our listening cannot land. The way one of my Indigenous teachers, Dulumunmun, Uncle Max Harrison of the Yuin people, says it, 'all of us have to reconcile with the earth.' We need to do the work to be present to the earth ourselves, to develop our own relationships and intimacies, to honour our own histories.

I am lucky to have spent time with urban Aboriginal people, the people of my home place, working in cultural settings to retell Dreamings in contemporary ways. I have also spent time with people who live relatively traditionally, in places far less encroached on by the colonising culture (no place in Australia was ceded by the Indigenous peoples, but only some of the original nations are officially recognised as Aboriginal lands: such as areas around Kakadu, and in the Centre). I have traipsed with bush mob kids through the desert collecting tucker. I have sat in the shade of the gums in the dry riverbed beside my oldest friend, linguist Myf Turpin, while she conversed with elders in their first language, doing dictionary work, or transcribing Songlines. And over and over again I have been humbled by what they are willing to share, what they know, and how they know, and their willingness to include me in the process of keeping this knowing alive.

For a long while I thought I must keep it secret that I yearn, in my writing, to help re-seed the Dreaming, to be part of singing the alive mountains alive in the hearts of humans once again, to hear what was being said, then help shape a living, luminous myth layer speaking this land. Perhaps that sounds arrogant, obscenely ambitious, culturally inappropriate and insensitive. I'm not entirely sure that it isn't. But if, for argument's sake, it were appropriate, what would it take? To do such work requires emotional integration: compassion, robustness and self-awareness. Such skills take time to acquire, and are dependent on moral and spiritual deportment. And if and when one can develop such skills, then the listening to what this place seeks to say may take a long time: years, or decades. Maybe it will take generations.

So I have begun. I can either worry about an unknown future, or I can do what I am called to do. I can't do both, so I have made my choice. I no longer fret about end times. Instead I'm investing in a culture of the long term. I'm living here, now. They go together, I have learned. Like all the best things, it's a paradox.

The work is subtle, slow, iterative learning and listening, striving to see what is needed, to find what is useful, to make myself useful. It requires that I continually cross back and forth between modes of knowing. It is understanding that I need to develop ego strength along with spiritual strength. Ego strength, by which I mean the ability to be an effective agent within human culture, might serve me in the following. I have a tendency to get hooked into the arguments around body, mind, bodymind, healing and disease, god, spirit, matter, materialism and scientism. These fraught areas are rife with claims and counterclaims, assertions and so-called debunkings, insults, condescension and exasperation. I see the lack of depth in these encounters as linked to the difficulty mainstream culture has of hearing Indigenous cultures and their ontologies. I would like to enter some of these conversations, wishing I could stop people hurting each other with confused or polarised thinking, so it behoves me to learn how people are talking. I want to help, but I fear it's not my way.

I'm not interested in believing or disbelieving or arguing. I want to present my experience. Hence my method is to try to stick with the phenomena. I'm telling you what is happening in my body, my feeling and a little of my thinking about sensation and experience.

All the time spent indulging my almost morbid fascination with these cultural conniptions has contributed to less time on listening to the body and the more-than-human. Being thinly spread may mean I say nothing quite as clearly as I'd like. It may mean I can be a bridge builder.

My distraction speaks to an aspect of modern life – we are surrounded by consumerist culture unless we actively remove ourselves from it, which some of us can choose to do to a certain extent, seeking to make our own culture. That's hard work and takes commitment from a group if it is to be shared. Yet this demonstrates a liberation of modernity – shorn of tradition, we re-create, even if it is only on the fringes.

Growing my own food, living in community, I am playing neo-peasant in my own tiny privileged way. I'm mourning the loss of indigenous soul and longing for a life not predicated on damage. I'm an orphan from my ancestral lands and a shame-filled thief of the land of others, but I have made a sincere effort to feel the consequences of this and move through the inertia and emotional vacuum that comes from fear of feeling. Martin Prechtel's 2014 book *Grief and Praise* names depression as exactly this – the fear of feeling, hence the epidemic of depression and the resulting backlog of grief in our culture, in our world. After decades of it, I am no longer depressed, and for its cessation, Prechtel is one of those I thank.

Prechtel is a shaman from the Tzutujil Mayan tradition who I would be honoured to claim as my main teacher. I don't think I can, as yet, I'm afraid of *that* much feeling. His books sear me. I love them more than any words I know but it's challenging to stay with them. The grief of what, according to him, has been lost in the destruction of indigenous cultures is more than I can process. I believe him, because I know a hint of this, in the grace of bush mob Aboriginal people, sitting around the campfire on Country, eating kangaroo tail, among the shards of shattered glass (from windows, those veils of separation between worlds, smashed out of their whitefella houses). Sobbing in my supervisor's office one day I said to her, 'humans were once so beautiful.' 'Write that,' she said, with so much kindness.

People all over the modernised world are grappling with how to engage respectfully with indigenous wisdom and trace authentic ancestral connections. This is part of fringe culture's burgeoning interest in shamanism. Much of this interest may be due to the shaman's role as healer in cultures where mind and body and context are indivisible. Shamanism is about the health of the entire system of place, its people, animals, spirits. It is about establishing right relations of respect, appreciation, forgiveness, humility and care between all beings through processes of engagement with the more-the-human world. Today shamanism has become a catch-all phrase to describe nature-based spiritual practice with a healing bent. People are seeking to understand what is happening to the planet and find ways to work with the grief and shame they feel.

I take it as a given that anyone seeking to engage with another culture will always be projecting their own cultural understandings onto the 'other' to some degree: their own shadowed, demonised, idolised cultural background will be a large part of the mix. These are fusion times, and accusations of appropriation are rarely straightforward. Hence we now have the claim, indeed, the product, of shamanic writing, an anomaly, it would seem, in cultures where much of the spiritual power was their possession and mastery of their oral tradition. Prechtel puts it this way:

> Mayans know that people write things down, not so much to remember them, but to ensure they don't have to. This gives people a choice to remember things when they feel like it. But to the Tzutujil Maya in the village in which I lived in Guatemala, to forget something sacred was to dishonour it. We didn't want that choice, so nothing real was permitted to be committed to writing. (1999, p.xvii)

My process has led me to believe in the wisdom of such a stricture, yet I'm starting from a different place. I have had to learn, with the help of writing's intensity and intimacy and presence and focus, what the sacred is, so then at least I have something to forget. It's a paradox, is writing: a wonderful, powerful, compromised tool of a difficult time. For a person like me, of a culture deep in unconscious shame, as yet only partly conscious of the ways that shame cements separation and disables feeling and intelligence, writing has been the time to sit with and process difficult emotions. Through such a process I'm becoming someone who can feel her connection to others, which is, in essence, the sacred – the experience of living the truth of connectedness.

The Feeling of Learning

Back in 2003 I set out on a pilgrimage. With three friends, I walked the Yarra River, an ancient Wurundjeri Songline. This track, covered over by colonial settlement, was yet still, particularly in the wilder stretches, vividly imaginable. This path perhaps 40,000 years in age was precious in the cultural memory of the first peoples. We walked from sea to source, camping every night on the riverbank, even where it passed through the city of Melbourne. Our journey lasted three weeks and ended high in the mountains of the Great Dividing Range. Our journey was long enough, strange enough, and perhaps both beautiful and difficult enough for profound transformations to occur. When I returned, I felt compelled to tell my story. I spent the next seven years striving to write the truth of my experience. I strove to depict the encounter with the sacred that arose over those three weeks of walking in my first book, *The Comfort of Water: A River Pilgrimage*.

Since then I've experienced trembling a few times when I shared some of my recent learning. The trembling has since stopped. I wanted to know why it started, and why it stopped. Googling shaking and spirituality I encountered extremes of interpretation, from narratives of anxiety on the one hand to grace on the other, particularly in the Pentecostal Christian traditions. Then I did a workshop on neuro-scientific applications to martial arts and dance training. The trainer spoke of the importance to body learning of shaking, of pushing one's body through physical effort to the point of trembling because this was how new neuronal pathways are formed. According to Peter Levine, pioneer in somatic psychotherapy, trembling is the release of tension stored in the body due to unprocessed trauma. It is important to note that trauma is also understood to occur during experiences we register as profoundly pleasurable or beautiful, yet overwhelming. There is a close relationship between fear and excitement: the physiological reactions are identical, yet we give very different meanings to them. Both signal high potential for learning.

Throughout my writing process I've sought to learn from the body through listening, and shaking is a pretty extreme signal. What might it be saying? I remembered my friend Richmond Heath, a physiotherapist who travels Australia teaching something called TRE, Trauma Release Exercises. It is a method to induce tremoring for its healing response. I rang him to ask about the shakes that came when speaking of my intense experiences. I was heartened by his response: 'I know exactly what you're talking about. When I came back from a ten-day Vippasana retreat and tried to talk about my meditation breakthroughs there, I'd start shaking.

'Tremoring is a universal reflex but there are so many different interpretations of what's going on. People tend to understand it according to their cultural stories, so what in India is seen as a kundalini awakening, a spiritual initiation of the body, in the West might be called anxiety or excitement. The diagnostic paradigm will affect the result. The Western medical model would say there is too much information in the system and the system is trying to regulate by discharging, but there is little understanding that the discharge is important and can lead to health improvements. The person might instead be medicated to suppress the body's reactions. Whereas the Kalahari Bushmen say the bigger the shaking the bigger the spiritual energy moving through, and those people are supported to shake and are praised for it.

'The more I teach it the less sure I am of what exactly is going on. But there is a story I can tell to keep people's egos happy so then they feel comfortable enough to say yes to the experience of the tremoring, which is what is important, because this kind of out-of-control movement has so often been pathologized in Western culture. The tremoring enables integration and improves people's lives by reducing stress. David Berceli, the founder of trauma release therapy, developed it for severely traumatised people in situations of war or natural disaster, and it is extremely effective in those cases, but it also works for the daily stresses of life.'

He taught me how to do it. You lie down with the knees up, then drop them out to each side. Next lift the knees just a little so there's a bit of effort involved in keeping them up. This will automatically trigger a shaking response in the body. It's amazingly relaxing and releasing. I asked Richmond how we can make this learning conscious.

'For me it's about unconscious learning. The conscious mind just comes along for the ride. It's about learning to let go of control. Learning how to receive and how to be moved – physically and therefore emotionally – to be moved is not a metaphor. The more emotionally moved one is the more movement there is in the body. When I let go and allow the tremor reflex to move me then the self-organising wisdom of the organism takes over, and if I can translate that into my life and allow my body to guide me then I'm guided by the innate organic movement of life. It's trusting life.'

Trusting life. Trusting the intelligence of the body. The thing to become conscious of is the vast and unknowable intelligence of the body. From this standpoint perhaps I can humbly ask the body for help in becoming more conscious through respectfully listening to what the body seeks to tell. This is the work. And although it is still difficult for me to remember, I have begun the process of integration and no longer need to be shaken awake.

Body is Earth

I lay alone on my couch and watched the mountains. And after a time of watching and breathing and listening the gestalt shifts and I remember. I am astonished once again by my inculcation into the idea of separation. The mountains, in this mode, are kin, are breeching whales of stone, rising and falling too slowly for these eyes to see, but present to my gaze. They are my own body, my old, old body. We are body, and body is earth. There is nothing in the mountain that thinks it is not me.

The work cannot begin until this shift has come, yet, as I always do, I'd forgotten I'd needed the shift at all. This is how it goes for me. This is my slow way home.

I acknowledge here that mentors I respect have warned me against doing this work. There is folly in enquiring too deeply, there is risk in saying too much. Throughout this time of writing I have felt intimations of danger. It has taken quite some time, but I now have a story to explain that feeling, a story that convinces me I can go forward with this work. My understanding is that my fear relates to the spiritual danger of seeking to come into profound knowing before one is robust enough to sustain such intensity. Added to that, there is fear of saying too much or saying it wrong – of trivialising something exquisite and fragile. My understanding of the body, body that unfurls into world, is what sustains me here. It means that I understand the fear to be world, ecology, body, communicating as it does: *as* my emotion. Yet in my case, as far as I understand it, it's not saying don't do it, it's saying take great care. Strive always to the high standards of life. Be humble and curious and unknowing yet adventurous and trusting. Embrace paradox. Judiciously, say an unbridled yes to life.

If we can know mystery and god and magic as the large and unconscious process we are and in which we are embedded and that we partake of, can we then take more care of where and what we are? To be able to hold ourselves as mostly mystery, entirely life, partly conscious and magically wonder-full then could we go forth with more gentleness, kindness and delight? To me this seems needed.

The practice I have discovered is to write my way back to grace, every morning when I return to my work – and if I don't, I simply don't remember my vaster body, and I waste my day in vagueness, a sense of not fitting in. To gain a sense of perspective I must enter my awareness into the aliveness of the actual scenario. I must align thought with life: intertwining biological processes, making in every moment, cells dividing and dying, water passing through our systems, tree and me, and the breathing of air between us. I engage with the wondrousness of my senses, and I slowly remember to 'see.' I return to reality, as it were. And I'm astonished anew at how much we have abstracted out thinking from our bodies. I'm made aware of our failure to recognise that what people everywhere have named as 'being with god' can simply mean participating with this feeling of life, knowing oneself within the system of life unfurling.

My way of understanding these things is that I won't consistently be able to feel beyond myself if I have not learned to feel inside myself. I cannot listen to the earth unless I'm prepared to listen to myself. Overwhelming shame or fear disable the capacity to listen. Emotional work is essential in order to listen well. I have discovered I must give myself kindness and care. And why not; I too am the earth.

So now that I have done some work on self-soothing, I have practiced my inner listening, how is my outer listening progressing? Barely, I'd say. Truthfully, it's very slow. But barely is not nothing. Barely is good. For as I'm practicing kindness with this body, I'm feeling kindness flowing from all things. As I honour my body with listening, I am more available for my greater body, this earth. I'm quieter inside, so listening is easier.

We cannot, with our everyday mind, understand the fullness of our biological nature. Our neocortex does not hold awareness of the multitude of functions the autonomic nervous system takes responsibility for: breathing, digesting, releasing egg into womb. Our bodies are mysterious to us. Yet we can consciously engage with our unconscious by an action such as watching the breath, as is done in meditation. We observe our organism, gently, and patiently. We witness its complexity, we sit with its mystery. And then, sometimes, and it always feels like magic: the shift happens. This shift is related to depth of embodiment, depth of embodiment enables enhanced sensory awareness, enhanced sensory awareness leads to an experience of profound interrelatedness, a knowledge of being inextricably part of all things. Wholeness, aware of itself. Wholeness, being itself.

Our mammal bodies, our upright gait attests to millions of years of shaping, of adaptation to fit a niche amid savanna and woodland, river and coast, and many hungry beings. How I have been made by the world is more interesting to me than what I might make of the world. Is there, then, an effective and authentic mode of accessing this sense of 'being made'? Recently I traveled to *Kata Tjuta* ('many heads') in *Anangu* country in Central Australia – a spectacular cluster of domed mountains – outcrops of bare red rock surrounded by the desert expanse. Walking a long hot day through those vast beings my body, through feeling, told me what it knew. The sacred Dreaming stories are kept secret from outsiders, but a powerful essence cannot help but be communicated. Amid that place I knew that stone and wind and water made me. They are ancestors, and as they shaped this body, they shaped this brain. The world, the whole world, made me.

> It is in the deep mind that wilderness and the unconscious become one, and in some half-understood but very profound way, our relation to the outer ecologies seems conditioned by our inner ecologies. This is a metaphor, but it is also literal.

> GARY SNYDER (ESHLEMAN, 2003, P.XI)

The bush mob indigenous people I met on my various trips to the centre experience ghosts, spirits, presences. It's an important part of their culture, normal, natural. Is it to do with how they inhabit their bodies and their place? Through personal experience I am starting to understand how we can use our body with more attunement to enable profoundly different knowing. Years ago I did a course in survival skills based on indigenous knowledge of North America: we became 'invisible' by daubing our bodies with mind, we walked silently, blindfolded, near-naked through an icy night. We heard the stories of the master teacher Tom Brown who learned from his Apache mentor to track animals and people to such fine degree that he could find people everyone else thought lost. Those who called him in as the last resort disbelieved his ability until he found them; his work is so refined that from an outsider's point of view it seems either impossible or magic. This reveals the profound ethnocentrism of the Western scientific discourse: it normalises how nature-disconnected, disembodied people know. It either does not see, denies, or dismisses the 'paranormal' experiences or capacities of different cultures, unaware of what's possible with the combination of cultural framework and body practices. I suggest that both mainstream *and* fringe science has tended to overlook the body, as both emerged from an historically disembodied subset of humanity. It is pertinent, then, to question those who make claims for delimiting the edges of our senses or our physical skills.

At home, at my desk, can I reverse my societal norm of disembodied consciousness in favour of letting the unconscious, the body, lead me into new knowledge?

Listening, done well, can lead to witnessing; a profound sense that something is happening, something that is *seen* to be happening. In such an encounter, there is a sense of both of us, me and my body, or the plant, or other entity, or, and it often feels like this in my experience, the space between us, coming into a fuller potential, a heightened awareness.

It is the cultural convention of our time to consider what lies between my ears as *my* brain. At this depth of listening I discover something else – a sense that brain discovers itself *as* awareness, *as* each and every iterative, ongoing evolutionary moment, life aware of itself as inseparable from any other thing. At this depth of listening, awareness process belongs to an entire realm, a place. We can choose a new story: we can choose to understand our brain as a locus of conscious awareness, conscious awareness that extends into the terrain of which we are inseparable. If we can become awake to this as a culture, who knows what forms of awareness may become available? If, in some of the mysterious forms of knowing currently called paranormal, it is the vast planetary sea of interconnected air, air continually being inspired and expired by billions of bodies, that is accessed by awareness, what are the gifts of such knowing? What are the gifts in the knowing held by earth, sun, stone?

We could all grow, together. Kata Tjuta has brain, you go there, you learn how that site is sacred and sung, and the ignorance of contemporary culture and the gratitude for the Anangu and their *Tjukurpa*, their Dreaming, will undo you. It will undo you.

The Learning in Feeling

'Knowledge does not enrich us; it removes us more and more from the mythic world in which we were once at home by right of birth' (Jung, 1995 [1963], p. 280). To this I say – if the knowledge is got at by the wrong type of thinking, then yes. Gregory Bateson writes of this as epistemological error – we are categorically wrong to think we are separate. Accurate knowledge, knowledge of interdependence, of mutual co-arising, is, I attest, always a feeling, a body-knowing. This is knowledge that can enrich. This is the unconscious knowing of the baby; it is knowing as pure embodiment, devoid of self-awareness. The baby's experience of interconnection fades, but in many traditional cultures was returned to the individual, and thus the community, by initiation. As it does for many people, something of this ilk happened to me, spontaneously, as a fifteen-year-old. Without a cultural context to hold such a realisation it has taken thirty years to shape my own culture of mind into something that could explain this to myself.

I access a deeper intelligence as my body re-members, as it joins with its sundered selves. My body is congealed psychology, there is need to melt memories into something that can flow. Dance warms muscles into pliable knowing, tears soften the past enfleshed. Listening and feeling, patiently and long. And with the care, respect and humility that are learned through the practice of listening, touching the earth with love.

Questions

1. Have you or someone you know had a powerful experience of nature connection that re-orientated your understanding of life and your connection to it? Do you relate to the concept of 'initiatory experience'?

2. Do you experience thinking and feeling having different sensations in your body? Where is thinking? Where is feeling?

3. Explore the relationship between thinking and feeling in your own life.

4. Why does the author suggest 'Dance warms muscles into pliable knowing, tears soften the past enfleshed'?

CHAPTER 11

EARTH LIGHT, EARTH ANGEL

Simon Wilson

I n *Sustainability Frontiers*, David Selby and Fumiyo Kagawa call for transformation of attitudes to nature through a holistic epistemology which is:

> enriched through emotional, imaginative and creative entanglement with the world, by spiritual and sensorial engagement with the close-at-hand world, by embodied and somatic learning, by deep listening and intimate observation ... (2015, p. 278).

This chapter argues that just such multidimensional transformation is evoked and enacted in Paul Devereux's writings on what he calls Earth Lights. Drawing on the work of other researchers Devereux developed a hypothesis which was intended to account primarily for UFOs, but also illuminated the origins of many other anomalous phenomena, such as ghosts, fairies, Marian apparitions, etc. (depending on the cultural milieu of the witness).

Devereux is a well-known and well-respected figure in what used to be called 'Earth Mysteries,' 'a modern attempt to uncover the wisdom of the ancient mind and apply some of the truths it contained' as he himself described the field (1999, p. 1). I will mainly be looking at his 1982 work *Earth Lights: Towards an Explanation of the UFO Enigma*, arguably the most visionary of all his writings, certainly the strangest. In it, Devereux starts with the idea that UFO experiences are triggered by geophysical forces, but moves well beyond this arguably rather materialist and mechanistic view to outline a complex interplay of what may loosely be called cosmic soul and individual person, taking place on imaginal, emotional, psychic, spiritual and somatic levels. These effects were, he argues, known by the builders of the Neolithic stone circles, who used them to produce theophanies which had the effect of intricately weaving together individual, society, the planet and the cosmos as a whole. By implication, Devereux's work may help bring about similar reconciliations in its readers.

UFOs and Eco-Consciousness

In arguing that UFO encounters have the potential to inspire a new and more positive relationship with our natural environment and, indeed, the entire cosmos, Devereux was not breaking entirely new ground. Since the early 1950s, so-called contactees (who, in Jerome Clark's careful phrase, 'believe, or claim to believe, they are in regular communication with benevolent extraterrestrial intelligences' [1998, p. 104]) have passed on messages from alien beings calling on earthlings to change their behaviour, or face global catastrophe. George Adamski was probably the most famous contactee to have been given this message. The story of Adamski's 1952 encounter with a Venusian, as told in *Flying Saucers Have Landed*, made a huge impression on me as a boy, especially Orthon's warnings that the planet and indeed the entire cosmos was threatened by mankind's nuclear adventures (Leslie and Adamski, 1977, p. 214). Meanwhile, in Britain another Venusian, this time not in the flesh but channelled, was warning George King of the ecological devastation being wrought by humanity, and teaching him the spiritual practices which could save humans and the world: King went on to form the Aetherius Society to pass on these teachings. The Society still exists, and is the world's oldest 'UFO' religion (Clarke and Roberts, 2007, pp. 72-89). Other ecological messages passed on to contactees have also had long-lasting effects, as the example of the Scottish New Age eco-paradise Findhorn shows, which owes much of its existence to similar communications (Clarke and Roberts, 2007, pp. 106-116).

Later, as contactees fell out of favour, abductees found themselves in fashion. Whatever was behind their often dark and even traumatic experiences had, in the words of Kenneth Ring, a correspondingly 'more *au courant* ecological concern' than the contactees' Space Brothers, such as 'ozone depletion and deforestation' (1992, p. 180). Ring gathered evidence which suggested to him that UFO encounters and abductions frequently lead to 'heightened sensitivity to ecological matters and to the condition of our earth generally' (1992, p. 181) (see also the chapter by Luke and Hunter's introduction in this volume).

Neither was the link between UFOs and such charismatic vestiges of the past as stone circles especially novel. I had learnt of this too as a boy, listening to my Uncle George talk about Stonehenge and flying saucers as I lay entranced on the floor of his living-room in Salisbury. Indeed the connection had been made since at least the beginning of the 1960s. Sometimes it was explained, for example, that the extraterrestrial spacecraft followed mysterious lines of energy called leys, and that stone circles, being storehouses as it were for this energy, were particularly attractive to them (see Clarke and Roberts, 2007, pp. 182-191). Thus to many enlightened sons and daughters of the 60s it seemed, as John Michell wrote, that 'flying saucers are connected in several ways with Druid magic' (1975, p. 170). In those heady times to succumb to the mystical and apparently eternal presence of the English countryside was equally to succumb to the mystery and magic of UFOs. These strange aerial phenomena effectively re-enchanted the land, and so transformed the nature of our relationship to it. Those who saw with saucer eyes fell in love with the countryside.

Earth Lights

What Devereux did, was to take these existing connexions, and to rework and refract them through the research of scientists such as Michael Persinger. The result intertwined humans, UFOs and ancient sacred sites in a remarkable neurological, geophysical, imaginal, spiritual, planetary and indeed cosmic drama. A drama which could transfigure creation and everything in it, returning it to a pristine, edenic state.

This drama is described in its wildest, most uninhibited form in *Earth Lights*, while his later *Earth Lights Revelation* (1989) is a much more sober and arguably less transformative work. One way of describing Devereux's Earth Light theories is to say that they essentially identify UFOs with shifts in the earth's crust. Another way is to say that they take the reader, step by step, through the mechanics – or psycho-mechanics – of Jung's breath-taking speculation that flying saucers may be 'something psychic, possessing material qualities and with a high charge of energy.' Jung added: '[h]ere our knowledge leaves us completely in the lurch, and it is therefore pointless to speculate any further in this direction' (1987, p. 151). What Devereux does, it can be argued, is to try to supply this missing knowledge by showing us how Jung's hunch might actually work.

Long before publishing *Earth Lights*, Devereux had become convinced that the so-called Extraterrestrial Hypothesis was an inadequate explanation for flying saucers. Reading widely in the field, he found that the work of such Ufologists as John Keel and Jacques Vallee confirmed his suspicions. The turning point in his thinking, however, come when he encountered *Space-Time Transients and Unusual Events* (1977) by Gyslaine Lafrenière and Michael Persinger (Devereux, 1982, pp. 62-66, 70-74). Lafrenière and Persinger's influential work put forward what became known as the tectonic strain theory to account for sightings of a whole range of anomalous phenomena, including UFOs, ghosts, Bigfoot, and Marian apparitions. Seismic events – even tiny shifts in the Earth's tectonic plates – produce, they argued, a build-up of huge amounts of energy. Powerful fields of natural forces are created at and near fault lines when the plates move, producing two main effects. Bright lights appear in the sky, often as luminous orbs; while at the same time the energy field so stimulates parts of the brain that witnesses experience a dream-like state in which vivid imagery is 'seen' even while they remain awake. These visions may derive their content from popular culture: monsters are seen to stalk the earth, spacecraft to haunt the skies. Witnesses may be seized by powerful emotions as they stand transfixed by angels, boggarts or UFOs. Such effects in turn may alter and influence perception of the lights in the sky (Devereux, 1982, pp. 71-72). Thus the complex interaction between brain structure, natural energies, memory, emotions, and cultural milieu may produce anomalous and even deeply religious experiences.

While apparently holding on to Lafrenière and Persinger's theories, however, Devereux actually moves well beyond them. He places tectonic strain and the visions it triggers in the context of a cosmic drama. Tectonic strain, it appears, is not just a consequence of geological changes: rather, a complex interplay of countless forces is at work in the universe. As Devereux puts it:

The Earth is one *whole*, living system: aspects of its cosmic environment impinge upon it, and effects in the terrestrial geology create further effects in its meteorology. Changes in its magnetic envelope can funnel further influences back to its geology. The whole system, as it were, *resonates*. All those forces and reactions play back and forth, creating responses, changes and echoes in all terrestrial structures and processes, from the most dense to the most subtle (1982, p. 95).

Earth Lights, that is, and the whole transformation in perception associated with them, are not just products of the interaction between earth energies and the human witness: they are created by the interaction of countless cosmic forces, on the one hand, with the tangled workings of consciousness on the other. When that happens, consciousness resonates with the whole cosmos. This is a new version of the music of the spheres, in which the whole cosmos resonates in endless, intricate sympathetic concatenation (see, for example, Godwin, 1995). It reveals consciousness itself to be an element or artefact of universal melody.

This is still potentially a rather mechanistic vision, but now so expanded and so complex that the number of forces involved is practically infinite, as is the number of possible interactions and variations (especially if one assumes that the universe is infinite). On the face of it scientific, it is however not measurable or describable by science.

But Devereux does not stop there. The Earth Lights – those strange discharges of cosmic forces – may consist of some peculiar, unknown and highly sensitive form of energy which actually responds to the mental images triggered in witnesses. We do not project hallucinations on to them, rather they adapt, and actually become the image for which people are primed by cultural, religious and social expectation (Devereux, 1982, pp. 215-216). Once that may have been gods or angels; now it is more likely to be spacecraft.

Although not sentient themselves, Earth Lights thus become a fragment of externalised mind, which the witness may not recognise as originating in his or her own psyche. 'The mental signals affecting some UFOs [i.e. Earth Lights] will, presumably, come from different levels of consciousness' writes Devereux (1982, p. 217), which could include the collective unconscious, the individual unconscious, or simply forgotten memories.

Devereux even hints at the possibility of an autonomous earth psyche which interacts with the individual and collective psyche, writing

I rather suspect – though I hardly dare put the concept into words as it is so strange to our way of thinking – that there may be another source of input into the UFO form: the Earth itself... or herself... [I]s it not possible to consider that the planet may dream? (1982, p. 218)

So who, one may ask, is dreaming – or perhaps imagining - whom? Is the form of the Earth Light a product of the mind or minds of those who see it, or is the form of the mind of those who see it a product of the Earth Light? Do witnesses experience a waking dream of a UFO, angel, ghost, etc, or does the Earth dream – imagine – the witnesses into existence? Perhaps the closest one can get to the truth would be that all those possibilities are true at the same time, in endlessly labyrinthine entanglement.

Given what Devereux writes concerning the cosmic context of this infinitely plaited relationship, it is only reasonable to conclude that not only Earth consciousness but the consciousness of the entire cosmos, too, participates in it. The UFO vision, that is, seems to be vouchsafed by something like the Neoplatonic idea of the *anima mundi*, that soul of the cosmos, shimmering with images, and beings, gods, demons and djinn (see, for example, Harpur, 2010, pp. 19-33).

The next step Devereux takes is to argue that ancient humans knew of these effects, and built structures to produce and enhance the experience. Stone circles, that is, are portals to the World Soul. Devereux presents survey evidence to suggest that not ley lines but fault lines were the defining element in the placing of Neolithic monuments in the landscape (1982, pp. 158-167). Stone circles, that is, were erected in the vicinity of geological faulting or similar features, and served somehow to accumulate and strengthen the energy produced by tectonic strain (Devereux, 1982, pp. 234-235). The builders were able to predict or co-ordinate the moments when the god energy would be released. 'In this way, the gods *did* appear on Earth,' writes Devereux, and goes on, '[T]hey would have communicated things not known to the conscious minds of the awe-filled congregations' (1982, p. 235). The gods appeared, to fill the individual soul with cosmic wisdom, or with the *anima mundi*, as it were, so that each soul may achieve its own proper plenitude, and each witness's consciousness may be filled by cosmic consciousness.

At the same time a whole society was harmonised and held together by cosmic wisdom. For Devereux, '[t]his supreme act of the ancient natural science would allow the societies of the day to have direct, social, conscious contact with what the *Tibetan Book of the Dead* calls "knowledge holding deities'" (1982, p. 235). The gods were 'knowledge holding' because they vouchsafe the experience of apparently vastly superior knowledge, otherwise unavailable to the conscious mind of the individual. The entirety of society was illuminated by this light from the soul of the cosmos, so that everyone became a seer, and was transfigured. All this was brought about by what we now see as UFOs.

The Earth becomes an Angel

These odd energies, both physical and psychic, are reminiscent not just of Jung's speculations, but of Henry Corbin's too. Corbin, that great scholar of Iranian mysticism, and friend of Jung's, once asked

> whether the invisible action of forces that have their purely physical expression in natural processes may not bring into play psychic energies that have been neglected or paralyzed by our habits, and directly touch an Imagination which [is] far from being arbitrary invention ... (1977, p. 11)

Corbin was talking about two levels of 'energy': subtle, psychic energy on the one hand, and material, physical energy on the other, with the latter being an expression of the former. The physical energy affects us measurably, but also brings about changes in our psyche and, for Corbin, our subtle or 'spiritual' body.

Devereux does not refer to Corbin in *Earth Lights*, but later drew on him extensively, referring particularly to the work from which the quotation above is taken, *Spiritual Body and Celestial Earth* (1977), in which Corbin describes the transfiguration of the Earth into paradise or an angel (see Devereux, 1992, pp. 94-99, 104-105; 1996, pp. 242-244). *Earth Lights*, however, seems not only to anticipate this interest in Corbin, but also to provide a detailed and lengthy account of how the ancient peoples of Britain released the subtle, spiritual senses to perceive both the environment and themselves as transformed and god-filled. What they then saw, in Corbin's terms, was an angel – the Earth Angel.

Corbin describes how his Iranian visionaries believed we have various bodies, with the physical body only the lowest form. The physical senses of the physical body see only the physical environment; the spiritual body however sees a spiritual cosmos, which is its home. This spiritual cosmos is, essentially, paradise.

This is a difficult matter, and I do not find Corbin the most comprehensible of writers, but it is clear that 'seeing' is not really the right word for what is a complex, active, and above all participative process, in which the physical body, for example, makes or engenders its environment. The physical environment thus produced then serves to confirm to the physical senses that it is the only reality. If we are aware, however, of the spiritual body and its paradise, we may break out of the merely material hall of mirrors (Corbin, 1977, pp. 3-105).

Mystics at times are able to see with the eyes of the spiritual body. The paradisiacal world they see then is Earth as an Angel: the Earth Angel. This Angel, I would argue, is what enraptured Neolithic man, as for a time at least he became a spiritual body and saw with other eyes. By implication, something similar may happen for modern man: a UFO experience may mark the moment when the senses are transfigured, the Earth becomes an Angel, and we are in paradise. Strange as it may seem, the UFO vision is thus a sacrament, in which the witness and the world is transfigured, and all is shot through with the presence of the divine.

This, as I said, is essentially a participative vision, in which the physical and spiritual health of the individual is inextricably interwoven with the physical and spiritual health of the Earth and the cosmos. The one is dependent upon the other. The Earth 'becomes' merely material, seemingly cut off from spirit, when the individual sees it as such: individuals are reduced to matter alone when the Earth shows itself bereft of spirit. Under such circumstances there is no possibility of a living, reciprocal relationship with the Earth, and it fragments into seemingly discrete and essentially dead objects, wholly unconnected to humans; while human society and consciousness too break up and lose coherence. Seen in this light, the ecological catastrophe is essentially spiritual in nature, and can only be redressed by the subtle spiritual interweaving which restores Eden and human divinity. One way to bring that about is, as we have seen, to perceive UFOs correctly. Devereux's essentially mythopoeic vision thus shows how the 'paranormal' may achieve more than moral or political exhortation in transforming humanity, nature, and the relationship between the two.

Earth Lights, Earth Angels: Some Implications

Devereux's ideas, if I interpret them correctly, have several implications for the nature of humankind's relationship to the world. For instance, while the percipient and the UFO/angel/theophany, or the human person and the Earth, are profoundly and intimately entangled in a complex embrace of co-creation, they nevertheless are not identical or fused into oneness. To enjoy the kind of dynamic reciprocal responsiveness Devereux describes, a relationship between two (or more) living beings is required. If one being in the rapturous embrace is simply merged into the other (or others), relationship and mutual responsiveness cease, and life is snuffed out.

Yet there is a clear danger of instability to Devereux's conception. These Earth Angels - this transfigured nature - may overwhelm us, blot us out by their urgent, wholly other power. Their literally cosmic power may erase us, so we lose all independence and become their puppets somatically, neurologically, imaginatively, emotionally and spiritually. There can be no participation, no interweaving or co-creation if humans are reduced to a mere reflex of the Earth and the cosmos; if, that is, we surrender freedom and agency to the world around us. We then cease to live and become, in effect a dead letter, a zombie. This would merely be a variation on the life-denying lack of relationship which currently exists. It would also mean a reversion to the grim message of John Keel's and Jacques Vallee's Ufological writings, to which Devereux refers in *Earth Lights* (1982, pp. 62-66). Keel claims, for instance, that we 'are biochemical robots helplessly controlled by forces that can scramble our brains, destroy our memories and use us in any way they see fit' (1994, p. 174). Similarly, Vallee has argued that 'what takes place through close encounters with UFOs is control of human beliefs, control of the relationship between our consciousness and physical reality...' (1976, p. 3).

The answer to this problem of control, power and erasure may lie in the antinomial content of an idea which Devereux elucidates in *The Sacred Place* (2000). Here he turns to the work of Rudolf Otto to describe the encounter between human and 'something else' at sacred sites: seen as a whole, this encounter is characterised by what Otto called the numinous (Devereux, 2000, pp. 22-23). For Otto, the numinous is triggered by an experience of 'the "wholly other"... that which is quite beyond the sphere of the usual, the intelligible, and the familiar' (1958, p. 26). Otto further explains that the numinous consists of an antinomy.

On the one hand there is what he calls the *mysterium tremendum*, a drastic experience of 'awefulness' or 'daemonic dread' (1958, pp. 12-24). On the other hand, there is the *mysterium fascinans*, accompanied by bliss, grace, entranced rapture, longing and "the peace that passes understanding' (1958, pp. 31-39). The numinous experience, that is, is an encounter with a presence which seems utterly – and awesomely – alien to us, but which at the very same time corresponds to some deep inner yearning, and which feeds, fulfils and sustains us.

In *Earth Lights*, the relationship between human and UFO, or human and the Earth, has precisely this antinomial, numinous character. The angelic UFOs are utterly apart from ourselves, something for which all our rationality, or the cocoons of everyday life, cannot prepare us. But they also speak to us deeply, satisfy us, as if they are wholly intimate, beckoning us back to communion with the gods, and the inner and outer peace that seems our true home. They are wholly different and wholly connected to us, separate and entirely inseparable from us. Difference, and our mutual awe in the presence of that difference, grants freedom to us and the Earth and all its angels: otherwise no reciprocal relationship would be possible. While blissful longing leads to endless desire to know and experience ever more of the other, resulting in deeper and deeper mutual recognition and connection.

This is the paradoxical knowledge these strange theophanies hold, which holds the complex chain of relationship in poised but dynamic balance, and prevents the various participants from being simply submerged or controlled. Indeed, this labyrinthine dance of the numinous involves all the elements we have looked at, such as physical bodies, consciousness, imagination, spirit and more, choreographing them all so that none disappear, while at the same time endlessly bringing each into new transforming relationships.

There is a word for this intricate dance: it is love. Behind Devereux's speculations on Earth Lights and their witnesses is a scene in which lovers meet, gaze at each other, know with rapture that they can know each other, feel at the same time and with speechless awe that they will never fully know each other, and that the other person will remain forever fundamentally different and other. This is a dynamic state of endless transformation, transfiguration and enspiritment. The world becomes an embodied angel, an incarnate god, and more and more so without end. As do we.

This is perhaps the 'divine vision' referred to by Tom Cheetham, whose 'wild and living power' may 'let the wilderness back in' (2015, p.

146). That is, it may rewild us and the world. It is also the condition in which endless depth opens up, more profound perhaps than dreamt of in deep ecology, 'the depth within which deep ecology finds its own truest roots' (Foltz, 2014, p. 41). If this is anything, it is paradise.

This, it seems to me, is what UFOs mean and enact in Devereux's writings on Earth Lights. Conversely, his other works seem largely to be based on a model in which matter and consciousness emerge from and return to absolute oneness. How much of that unity we perceive, as it were, depends on how open our cultural filters are: if we are able to remove them altogether we may experience 'the oceanic feeling characteristic of mystical (or 'cosmic') consciousness' (Devereux, 1996, p. 42; see also Devereux, 2001, p. 200). In this conception, all phenomena are just modulations, for example of the quantum field. There is no possibility of relationship between two free subjects, no possibility of love, or real response and true transformation of any kind. Change is indeed in the end an illusion: nothing is different, everything is the same.

There is, it seems to me, no possibility of rewilding here, or of fully enlivening humans and their natural surroundings. Quite the opposite: this is not paradise, it is death, forever. That is why of all Devereux's writings on the relationship of humanity to the natural world or the cosmos, those on Earth Lights seem to me to be the most exciting, fruitful and visionary. They implicitly reject models based either in control and domination, on the one hand, and merging and oneness on the other. His UFOs light up the sky, the Earth and our whole being with the message that all depend on dynamic, reciprocal and loving relationship to fully and truly live. It only remains to be emphasised that UFOs are not the only aspect of the 'paranormal' which may establish relationship and engender love between humans and the world. Gods, fairies, ghosts, mysterious creatures of all kinds, and many more phenomena have a similar capacity to direct our gazes, so that we see the physical world and see it transformed infinitely by spirit. If this occurs, the world may return our loving gaze, to see us as we are, body and spirit, and to see us become ever more what we are. The gazes then interweave without ever fusing.

Questions

1. Why do you think 'UFOs' have become so associated with the landscape and the health of the Earth in the last sixty years or so?

2. What is your reaction to Paul Devereux's Earth Lights theories (and/or to my presentation of them)?

3. 'The ecological catastrophe is essentially spiritual in nature.' Do you agree? Can strange encounters with the paranormal phenomena, such as ghosts or flying saucers, bring about general spiritual transformation? How?

4. How may UFOs (or other paranormal phenomena) change the way we perceive the world and our relationship to it?

CHAPTER 12

ECO-CONSCIOUSNESS, SPECIES CONNECTEDNESS AND THE PSYCHEDELIC EXPERIENCE

David Luke

Turning Topiary

On my travels in Mexico many years ago, last millennium in fact, I came across a psychoactive plant, known locally as 'the shepherdess,' which was used by indigenous people for divination and healing. I was given the opportunity to try this foreign foliage and doing so had an incredible and entirely unexpected experience. Within moments of consuming the herb a strange sensation began seeping through my toes and fingertips and moved towards my core turning me rapidly into some kind of thorn bush. The metamorphosis spread quickly up my arms and legs, across my body and up to my head until I found myself completely transformed into a small spiky shrub. I was quite literally rooted to the spot and could not move.

Simultaneous to this, all the trees and all the plants, in fact every blade of grass across the large field within view, began laughing hysterically. Anything and everything before me that photosynthesised was in side-splitting fits and they were all cracking lines like 'now you know what it's like to be a plant, ha, ha, ha,' swaying back and forth, shrieking and howling with laughter. I didn't find this particularly funny though, because I was absolutely convinced of my transmutation, and furthermore believed it to be permanent. Oh how the plants laughed. Then a disembodied voice spoke. Loud, deep and stern. A woman's voice. She said something like, 'you stupid humans think you run the show around here, you're so arrogant, but you haven't got a clue.' And then she proceeded to lecture me on species-centrism and our lack of harmony with others on Earth. I was terrified and 'bewildered' – in the literal sense too – for although I had hypothetically reasoned that everything might be inherently conscious, I had never expected to be chastised by the spirit of Nature or publically ridiculed by grass.

The experience, mercifully, only lasted ten minutes, and quickly subsided as the voice drifted away and I turned back into a slightly more aptly named *Homo sapiens* than before. The immediate psychological effects had gone, but the ontological shock remained indefinitely. I would say that this was my first serious shamanic experience with plant (or fungal) psychedelics, and since then I have never considered ecology in quite the same way as before. So, what then of psychedelic experiences and species connectedness?

Ecodelia

The fact that a large portion of this essay was originally published in a special issue of the *MAPS Bulletin* (Brown, 2009) given over solely to ecology would seem to suggest that at the very least the consumption of psychedelic substances leads to an increased concern for Nature and ecology. On one level we can understand that this may be due to a basic appreciation of place and aesthetics that accompanies the increased sensory experience, or that psychedelic plants come from Nature and so we are forced to enter her realms when we search them out. However, on a deeper level we can also appreciate that a communication with Nature may on occasion occur through the mystical experience of the psychedelic state.

With the aid of mescaline Aldous Huxley came face to face with such a mystical experience, even though the Oxford Theologian R.C. Zaehner (1957) denigrated his experience of nature mysticism as somehow inferior to the 'genuine' theistic mystical experience. Yet the irony remains that the very split from Nature in the mind of theologians that occurred in the Garden of Eden probably lies at the heart of many people's current sense of separateness from our ecology, whereas psychedelics are seemingly capable of augmenting that reunion. Despite Zaehner's derisions Huxley (1954, p. 4) witnessed this reunion through mescaline, 'I was seeing what Adam had seen on the morning of creation – the miracle, moment by moment of naked existence.'

It is this naked experience that reconnects the environment to the mental capacities of those psychedelically-inspired that, at its best, forges an environmental way of thought and action. For some – often the pioneers of psychedelic discovery such as our shamanic predecessors or the odd chemist – the process occurs the other way around. The patriarch of psychedelia, Albert Hofmann, demonstrated this by believing that a mystical nature experience he had had when he was young prefigured his discovery-cum-invention of LSD. He states that, '... my mystical experience of nature as a child, which was absolutely like an LSD-experience ... this oneness with Nature. I believe I was in some fashion born to that' (Hofmann, Broeckers & Liggenstorfer, 2009, p. 2).

Throughout his long life Hofmann increasingly drew upon the great hope that psychedelics were the key to this reconnection for others too. When asked about the role that LSD had played in bringing people back to Nature, he said, 'It has given many people good ideas, and those who have gone back to Nature have been saved. Many people, however, are still stuck in technological Hell and cannot get out. Nevertheless, many have discovered something which hardly exists in our society any longer: the sense of the sacred' (Hofmann *et al.*, 2009, p. 6). Always vocal on ecological issues, Hofmann recalls that among his most beautiful experiences were hearing young people say things like 'I grew up in the city, but once I first took LSD, I returned to the forest' (Hofmann *et al.*, 2009, p. 4).

Providing us with an insight into the cause of this yearning for a return to Nature, based on their extensive experiential research with psychedelics, Masters and Houston (1966) noted that, '... the [psychedelic] subject, almost from the start, already has achieved a kind of empathy with his surroundings as a whole... That is to say, nature seems to the subject a whole of which he is an integral part, and from this characteristic feeling of being a part of the organic "body of nature" the subject readily goes on to identify with nature in its physical particulars and processes.' But if man is empathizing with Nature in this state, whose feelings is she or he feeling? The notion that something is empathized with implies that the thing itself has emotions, and the idea forms that Nature itself and the beings who inhabit it – be they animal, vegetable or perhaps even mineral – are also conscious.

Shamanism, Animism and Animaphany

We find that such animism is at the root of all shamanic religions, which, as Jeremy Narby notes, involve a communication with the spirits of plant and animal species, 'Shamanism is all about attempting to dialogue with nature' (Narby, 2006, p. 16). In shamanism, of course, this communication is frequently achieved through the ingestion of psychedelic plants. As a nature religion, Shamanism is ecological to its core, as the shaman is a caretaker of Nature and a negotiator between people and 'other-than-human persons,' as Graham Harvey calls them in his Animist manifesto (Harvey, 2005). For Harvey, it is our fungal friends themselves that get the idea of Animism across the best, 'Maybe sometimes the mushrooms just want to help us join in the big conversation that's going on all around us' (Harvey, 2005, p. 128).

Expert mycologist Paul Stamets also finds that mushrooms have a hidden agenda to bring us into communication with other species. In studying the taxonomy of the *Psilocybe* genus Stamets notes how these psychoactive mushrooms proliferate particularly in the wake of human destruction and the taming of the land, such as through '... chopping down trees, breaking ground to create roads and trails, and domesticating livestock' (Harrison, Straight, Pendell & Stamets, 2007, p. 138). By this means, Stamets believes, the mushrooms become available to those who most need to speak to Nature through them. For Stamets, when this dialogue is engaged the message 'is always that we are part of an "ecology of consciousness," that the Earth is in peril, that time is short, and that we're part of a huge, universal bio-system,' but Stamets isn't alone because, 'many people who have taken these substances report receiving the same message' (Harrison *et al.*, 2007, p. 138).

Recent research backs up Stamets' assertion that it isn't just him and Harvey either who are receiving mycelial messages from Nature. A survey into people's exceptional experiences with psychedelics found that encountering the consciousness of the ingested plant/fungus was the most widely reported of a range of 17 paranormal and transpersonal type experiences occurring with those taking psilocybin-containing mushrooms (Luke & Kittenis, 2005). According to the respondents this encounter also occurred quite frequently and was the second most prevalent experience with any one substance, after experiences of unity consciousness on LSD. Additionally, the plant consciousness encounter was the most widely reported transpersonal event for several other plant substances too, such as ayahuasca, *Salvia divinorum*, and the *Amanita muscaria* mushroom (Luke & Kittenis, 2005). If Harvey's Animist manifesto is to be taken seriously then the plants, and especially the mushrooms it seems, are clearly trying to tell us something.

These findings were extended in a later survey I conducted (Luke & Yanakieva, 2016) on the contribution of psychedelic experiences to eco-consciousness. Nearly 80% of the 150 psychedelic using respondents reported that their use of psychedelics had increased their subsequent degree of interaction with nature, with almost none saying it had reduced their interaction. Indeed, *all* of the respondents reported that their connection with nature had increased following their use of psychedelics, and more than 60% said that their concern had also increased. These figures compare quite well with respondents in a different survey (Ring, 1992), that found that 70-80% of those having near-death experiences (NDEs), and 80-86% of those having UFO encounter and/or alien abduction experiences had increased ecological concerns following their experience, giving some support to notion that there is an overlap between NDEs, traditional psychedelic-induced shamanic initiations, alien abduction experiences, and heightened psychic sensitivity (Harvey-Wilson, 2001; Ring, 1989; 1992; Severi, 2003).

Interestingly, in our survey, the substance most commonly reported to increase connection was psilocybin-containing mushrooms, which resulted in increased eco-connectedness in almost half of all mushroom users. Furthermore, approximately one third of magic mushroom users reported encounter experiences with the spirit or intelligence of the ingested mushroom, while some 16% reported encounters with animal spirits or communicating with animals whilst high, and 10% reported the experience of being transformed into another species – an experience reported by a full quarter of all ayahuasca users (Luke & Yanakieva, 2016).

Interpreting man's many dialogues on the mushroom experience, expert mycophile Andy Letcher (2007) calls these mushroom-mediated encounters with discarnate spirit entities the 'animaphany.' He warns us, however, that these experiences largely go ignored because, in a Foucauldian sense, they offer a resistive discourse to that of the societally legitimated explanations of what occurs under the influence of such plants, in the West at least.

Being based solely on the effects of mushrooms on others these legitimated discourses typically take a pathological, psychological or prohibitory stance, and so this subjective animaphany appears to transgress a fundamental societal boundary, by communicating with spirits, and becomes labelled as 'madness.' But which is the more mad, communicating with the spirits of Nature or sitting back while Earth's ecosystem descends rapidly into the greatest wave of mass extinction in 65 million years, which at some estimated rates (Pimm, Russell, Gittleman & Brooks, 1995) would see all species on Earth extinct within the next 65 years?

Interspecies Communication

It appears that the plant/fungus entities aren't the only ones getting in on the apparent conservation conversation either, as such pharmacologically-induced trans-species communications also engage the animal kingdom. Through the use of psychedelics, particularly LSD and ketamine, the scientist John Lilly (1978) apparently began communicating telepathically with other species and consequently made an ethical U-turn in his highly invasive animal research (such as involving the death and dissection of a dolphin) to increasingly involving consensual peer-to-peer exchanges with other-than-human species. If other species are conscious and can communicate with us then perhaps the best way to do this would be directly through our own minds, in a language that transcends physical restrictions. If this telepathic communication requires changing our consciousness to do so then plants are expertly disposed to begin this dialogue through their potent and often ancient psychoactive compounds.

Ever since Albert Hofmann (e.g., 2005) had an out of body experience on his first accidental LSD journey, and Gordon Wasson's photographer Allan Richardson had a prophetic vision on their seminal mushroom trip in Mexico (Richardson, 1990), psychedelic explorers the likes of Huxley and Osmond have been intrigued by the apparent stimulation of so-called paranormal faculties with these psychoactive substances. A review of the parapsychological literature indicates that while the issue still requires further research there is good reason to consider the possibility that psychedelics might actually promote psi phenomena such as telepathy. However, the kind of species centrism that *Homo sapiens* are prone to tends to promulgate the view that animals and especially plants are not conscious, but, given that they might be sentient, direct communication with them shouldn't be ruled out either, and should probably be encouraged instead. Psychedelics, especially those coming from plants/fungus, would seem well suited for that task.

The question still remains to be answered why plants/fungus even produce highly psychedelic alkaloids in the first place. Is it just an accident that certain plants produce such supposedly toxic compounds that have no apparent benefit to the plant/fungus and yet interact so sophisticatedly with our own minds, especially given that Nature (apart from man perhaps) isn't disposed to wasting resources without good reason? On the contrary, evidence is now emerging that our brains actually developed in co-evolution with psychedelic plants (McKenna, 2018; Winkelman, 2008), although we may well ask for what purpose?

Psychedelic shamanism might be thought of primarily as a communication with Nature, for instance by asking the plants directly which ones can heal a particular illness, or by asking the plant spirit to teach them, or by using the plant in aiding the psychological metamorphosis into a plant or animal familiar (Dobkin de Rios, 1996). Given that shamans have most likely been communicating with Nature in this way for thousands of years (Devereux, 2008) then it might well be asked what can be gained for man's relationship with the ecosystem from such a dialogue and, more importantly, how can Nature benefit from it?

One thing that seems apparent now since conducting the first survey exploring psychedelic-induced changes in eco-consciousness (Luke & Yanakieva, 2016) – now that there is some data on the subject rather than just anecdote – is that, according to self-report, psychedelics do indeed tend to increase user's interaction with, connection to, and concern for Nature. Indeed, a recent open-label psilocybin treatment study for depression found that 'nature relatedness' significantly increased relative to baseline following the ingestion of psilocybin, with changes remaining significant when measured again up to 12 months later (Lyons & Harris, 2018). A survey by Forstmann and Sagioglou (2017) similarly found that lifetime use of psychedelics was significantly associated with nature relatedness in terms of self-identification with nature and the desire to be in natural environments, and that the influence of nature relatedness on pro-environmental behaviour was mediated by the lifetime use of psychedelics.

Further to that, those taking psychedelics (especially organic ones) say that their experiences not only changed their attitudes but also directly changed their eco-orientated behaviour. In our survey (Luke & Yanakieva, 2016), *the majority* of psychedelic users reported adjusting their diet (presumably towards organic, raw, vegetarian or vegan) and increasing gardening as a result of their psychedelic experiences. Some 16% reported changing their entire careers to more eco-oriented ones, such as switching to studying PhDs in botany (reported by two people in the sample), and 19% also reported becoming more actively engaged in ecological activism.

In a recent article written by a doctor of molecular biophysics turned eco-activist and founder of one of the UK's fastest growing social movements, Extinction Rebellion, Gail Bradbrook (2019) indicates how her experiences with iboga and ayahuasca gave her the template for forming the radical environmental action group fighting against anthropogenic species extinction, ecocide and climate change. During her psychedelic experiences she had prayed for 'the codes for social change' and upon returning from her psychedelic quest quickly met the climate activist and doctoral researcher of effective radical campaign design Roger Hallam who offered her what he specifically also called the 'codes for social change,' and together they formed Extinction Rebellion.

In a time of such global ecological crisis psychedelics might just have an essential role in literally saving the planet, and the importance of interspecies relationships in this endeavour should not be overlooked, but rather strongly regarded as an important tool for hope, inspiration and environmental action.

Questions

1. What makes psychedelic experiences paranormal, and how do distinctions of para/normal differ across cultures?

2. Given that psychedelically induced interspecies communication frequently implies the experience of telepathy, what evidence exists to support this?

3. Why do plant (and especially fungal) psychedelics in particular induce experiences of interspecies connectedness?

4. In what ways might supposedly developed cultures utilise psychedelic experiences to tackle ecological challenges, and how could they be incorporated into current and future society?

Note: Earlier versions of this article have appeared elsewhere (as Krippner & Luke, 2009; Luke, 2013, 2017).

CHAPTER 13

TAKING SOUL BIRDS SERIOUSLY: A POST-SECULAR ANIMIST PERSPECTIVE ON EXTRA-ORDINARY COMMUNICATIONS

Brian Taylor

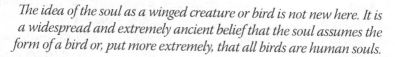

The idea of the soul as a winged creature or bird is not new here. It is a widespread and extremely ancient belief that the soul assumes the form of a bird or, put more extremely, that all birds are human souls.

—BERYL ROWLAND (1978, P. XIII).

When we think autobiographically we only include events that happened to us when awake; the Ojibwa include remembered events that have occurred in dreams. And, far from being of subordinate importance, such experiences are for them often of more vital importance than the events of daily waking life. Why is this so? Because it is in dreams that the individual comes into direct communication with the ätíso'kanak, the powerful 'persons' of the other-than-human class.

—IRVING HALLOWELL (1960/2002 P. 39).

In a discussion of Ted Hughes' poem *The Jaguar*, Michael Malay cites Czeslaw Milosz's definition of art as 'the passionate pursuit of the real,' and observes that 'the fullness of nature, and of our experience of it, continually outstrips language' (Malay, 2014; Milosz, 1983, p. 56). As my perspective on events around my mother's death in 1991 evolves, I have a growing sense that our lives unfold within an *animic real* that ultimately eludes even poetic description. In particular, the epicentre of a major bereavement may be a moment of such depth, richness, turbulence, anguish, and complexity, that the prospect of representation becomes unthinkable. As Michel Foucault put it, 'Headed toward death, language turns back upon itself' (Foucault, 1977, p. 54).

Poetic language may, of course, be sufficiently oblique, conversant with metaphor, alert to subtle cue, and sensitive to emotional tone, to evoke extra-ordinary experience. Phenomenology gets closer to poetry than most formal philosophical approaches because it helpfully shifts our focus of enquiry towards a tentative, non-judgemental, and dialogical exploration of meaning (Bracken, 2002) and crucially, acknowledges mystery (Polt, 1999).

During the European Enlightenment the notion of a divine cosmic hierarchy in which 'every being (human, animal, plant, spiritual) had a rightful place ... [and] ... natural and social worlds were viewed as spiritually infused with value, meaning, and purpose' was overturned by a mechanistic paradigm that radically distanced 'us' – most obviously men as architects of, and participants in, public patriarchies – from the rest of nature (Seidman, 1994, p. 11; Seidler 1994; Hearn, 1992). According to Zygmunt Bauman 'natural science could be defined almost by the absence of miracles, and indeed of anything bizarre and extraordinary, suggestive of a conscious...and intending subject' (Bielharz, 2002, p. 129). Monological scientific rationality still marginalises engaged subjectivities (other voices, sensual participation, emotional relationship, intuition, dreaming, divination, visionary experience), as potential sources of knowledge (Plumwood, 2002, pp. 41-6; Greenwood, 2009; Curry, 2010, pp. 3-7). Fortunately, however, 'stories of authority (given to us from on high by men in black frocks and white coats)...are fracturing in the face of *participant stories...stories of difference*, multiplicity and a plural universe' (Plummer, 1995, pp. 133-4).

End of Life Experiences

Qualitative studies that attend carefully to diverse stories and perspectives without imposing ontological assumptions can contribute to this ongoing cultural re-evaluation by illuminating neglected but important experiential terrain. Peter Fenwick *et al.*, for example, found that 'end of life experiences' (ELE's) – which may include deathbed visions, reports of moving between this world and another reality characterised by intense experiences of compassion, love, and 'light,' where the dying person is met by deceased relatives and/or helpful spiritual beings, appearances of the dying person to an absent relative or close friend, and synchronous events such as clocks stopping at the time of death – are not uncommon. They argue that since such experiences are often felt to be profoundly significant they need to be taken seriously if we are to develop best practice in spiritual end-of-life care. The prevailing scientific view, however, has been that ELE's, especially deathbed visions, 'have no intrinsic value, and are either confusional or drug induced' (Fenwick *et al.*, 2009, p. 2;. c.f. Romme & Escher, 1993 on voice hearing).

What drew me to this study was the finding that 'serendipitous appearances or dreams of significant animals, birds, or butterflies, which held special meaning for the dying, and also often for relatives,' were reported by 45% of respondents in a retrospective study and 35% in a prospective study. In more recent lectures Fenwick elaborates on this, saying 'we have *so* many reports of birds ... We have accounts of birds who come into the room of the dying, are seen on their windowsills, or collect in large groups around the hospice at the time the person is dying. In cases we have heard, the dying person who has had such visits has always been interested in birds, and the type of bird that appears around their time of death is the one in which they have been interested' (Fenwick, 2012).

This is broadly consistent with my own experience, with the non-sentimental testimony of several people known to me, with other published reports (Marzluff & Angell, 2005, pp. 136-138), and not least with a widespread and ancient body of lore associating birds with survival beyond death and the flight of human souls, at least some of which seems likely to have originated from such encounters (Rowland, 1978; Armstrong, 1959). Birds have also been strongly associated with divination and shamanism.

Some of my own most vivid experiences around my mother's death conform to the general schema described by Fenwick, not least a powerful eruption of premonitory grief almost two years before her death, and a bird trying to get in through my partly open bedroom window after the death (Taylor, 2012, pp. 118-120). For me, however, because those experiences were informed by previous intensities, and were integral to my developing animist world view and practice, I see marked continuities between the phenomena reported during ELE's and other kinds of transformative experience. More than half of Fenwick's respondents, for example, report a sense of being 'called' or 'pulled' by something or someone. These terms, that I have long used in relation to bird encounters, and that others use in relation to geomancy, are arguably paradigmatic of animism understood as a relational ontology and epistemology (Bird-David, 1999).

The Common Kingfisher

More than twenty five years ago the common kingfisher, *Alcedo Atthis,* came into my life, in the flesh, and then in dreams, before, during, and after, what turned out to be a protracted and complicated bereavement. During that liminal period kingfisher dreams often preceded an appearance by the bird, and unusually close encounters tended to coincide with further up-wellings of grief. Some of those encounters were (and occasionally still are) marked by an uncanny precision of timing, and/or an intimacy of communion quite unlike anything I had previously experienced. Some of the dreams, meditation imagery, and visionary experiences, were (and occasionally still are) charged with an intense world-opening beauty. Until 'we' in the over-developed West understand that we live in a profoundly mindful, sentient, and agentic world, however, communications from other-than-human beings, especially in the form of dreams or visions (Hallowell, epigraph) will remain inconceivable as 'real' moments of relationship.

My field notes – a ragged archive of personal diaries, bird and wildlife records, dream diaries, and notes on divination[16] (free-range ornithomancy, dowsing, and astrology), now include over a hundred and forty kingfisher dreams along with details of what was happening in my life at the time. Without them I would not have been able to track the association between appearances by kingfishers and eruptions

---

[16] Divination in the broad sense of 'guidance of the sacred.' (Cornelius, 2003, pp. 129-130).

of grieving, or the apparent willingness of these (and other) birds to portend or accompany other human deaths – to act as *psychopomps* in keeping with kingfisher lore, which speaks of the bird's 'vertue prognostick' and ability to survive death, as well as situating the survival of the human soul in the context of the midwinter renewal of nature.

I would not have been able to confirm, for instance, that my most recent sequence of kingfisher dreams occurred between March and June 2012. At that time the birds were very much in my waking thoughts, but I was also concerned about a very dear elderly friend whose health was failing. Because the hallmark of these intensely personal moments has been a distinctive feeling tone, an up-welling of primal love and connection that opens the core of my being, I don't want to be drawn into a discourse of proof here, but as an indication of the kind of occurrence I am talking about, I offer the following, necessarily compressed, story:[17]

On the 5th of August of that year I was feeling uncharacteristically low. We drove a few miles to a spot suggested by my partner, crossed the road and went down some steps to a fishing lake, whereupon I almost immediately stumbled upon a brilliantly lit Kingfisher perched on one of the fishing platforms, only five or six feet away. The bird took off, unhurriedly I thought, tracing a mesmerising arc of sapphire light across the still green surface of the water. We walked quietly round to the next pond where I immediately spotted him again – there was no red on the bill, so this was a male – close to the path, at about head height, in a goat willow overhanging the water. He turned his head briefly to look at me, then flew off again, further along the tree-lined pond. I'd never seen a kingfisher there before, so hadn't been expecting this. Not for the first time Alcedo Atthis left me in tears.

The next day my elderly friend had a serious fall. The day after that he had another fall, and to cut a painful story short, was taken into hospital where he died two days later.

[17] Because of a widely accepted need to protect spiritual experience from casual disclosure, and moments of anguish or intimacy from intrusion, such material falls under the rubric of sensitive research. I use a traffic light protocol for auto/biographical writing: i) core material (red), around which a non-negotiable firewall is maintained, (ii) intermediate material (amber) that requires protective measures such as the omission of certain aspects or details, changing names to safeguard confidentiality, or fictionalisation; and (iii) public material (green), that is not regarded as sensitive.

In a dream on the 15th I agreed with him that "it had probably been right to be thinking about a lift only one way, into hospital, not back". Then a kingfisher flew off along a broad canal, under a distant bridge, skimming the water surface.

That afternoon I went to a place suggested by the dream, and "suddenly became aware of a fast flying bird, powering upstream, leaving a trail of blue light."

On the following day, after another luminous bird dream, I was in floods of tears, remembering the intimacies of a wonderful friendship.

My records show that I hadn't seen a kingfisher since the previous November, that these were the only two I saw during the whole of 2012, and that I did not meet another until October 2013. There were no further kingfisher dreams until July 2014. My perception of that event on 5, August was informed by many previous occurrences, including two startlingly synchronous and equally moving showings involving my friend's companion species.

Animisms

The non-reality of spirits, like the quasi machine reality of non-human animals and the reservation of subjectivity for humans alone, is not carved in ontological stone, after all… (Curry, 2010, pp. 8-9).

Deborah Bird-Rose describes participants at her friend and colleague Val Plumwood's funeral being moved by the appearance of a large butterfly that flew amongst them before landing on Val's body and staying there long enough for them to feel this was 'a truly significant moment' before flying into the forest she had fought to protect. Bird-Rose, for whom the moment epitomised Plumwood's philosophical animism, emphasises the intentionality of the butterfly rather than 'magic' or 'co-incidence.' 'In opening one's self to others as communicative beings, one places oneself in the position of being able to experience communication.' In her work, Val Plumwood challenged 'hyperseparation' and the dualism that attributes mind exclusively to humans, and advocated 'an enriched materialism in which matter and mind are mutually forming';

a materialist spirituality grounded in gratitude, respect, and ecological belonging (Bird-Rose, 2013, p. 94-98).

Butterflies are, of course, often perceived as symbolising the liberation of a discarnate human soul from an ageing and/or wounded body by the transition we call death. In 1946, a twenty year old Elizabeth Kübler Ross visited the Nazi concentration camp at Majdanek, where her friend had lost her husband and twelve children. Walking along the rows of wooden barracks where perhaps three hundred thousand people, 'men, women, children, and entire families, spent their last days, and hours,' she found names, initials, and drawings, scratched on the walls. One image was repeated everywhere she looked. 'Butterflies. Some crude, some quite detailed.' Only after twenty-five years, having worked with hundreds of dying people and listened to many near-death experiences, did she conclude that those people must have known they would soon be leaving their bodies 'the way a butterfly leaves its cocoon' (Kübler Ross, 1997, pp. 75-76).

Kübler Ross adopted the symbol of the butterfly in her influential work on death and dying, but its analogical power derives only partly from the appalling context in which she discovered it. In Ancient Greek, *psyche* meant both butterfly and soul. The tradition associating the flight of butterflies, or birds, with the human soul comes to us freighted with problematic associations from its Platonic provenance,[18] and a considerable history of harm done in the name of spiritual transcendence (Jantzen, 1998; Brody, 2000, pp. 242-244). Variations upon a 'soul bird' motif can also be found, however, in Ancient Egypt, across the Bronze Age Middle East, in Siberian shamanism, and in many non-Western indigenous traditions (Taylor, 2012).

The apparently incommensurable discourses of Bird-David and Kübler-Ross speak to an ongoing debate around 'new' animism. The Victorian anthropologist E.B.Tylor defined animism in terms of a 'belief in souls or spirits,' interpreted as a theoretical construct designed to elucidate the difference between life and death, the appearance of dream figures, and the apparently conscious actions of natural phenomena (Tylor, 1871; Hunter, 2015). New Animism proposes a radically different relational and ecological understanding drawn from post-colonial

---

[18] For example Plato described the body as a prison to be escaped from, regarded incarnation as a fall from grace, and women as inferior because they were the agents of birth. The philosophical habit of thinking in terms of hierarchical binaries is attributed to Plato. (Jantzen 1998: 62,137-8).

ethnography and dialogue with indigenous traditions, the hallmark of which is a this-worldly focus on respectful social and ecological relationship. As Graham Harvey puts it: 'animists are people who recognize that the world is full of persons, only some of whom are human, and that life is always lived in relationship with others' (Harvey, 2005, p. xi; 2013, pp. 1-3). Whilst welcoming this development for the ethical focus it contributes, I have been concerned that 'new' animism may, once again, be marginalising extra-ordinary experience and ways of knowing, and in the process conceding vital ground to Tylorian scientism.

In *The Spell of the Sensuous* David Abram took ethnographers to task for writing extensively about shamans' relationships with 'supernatural' entities, while overlooking the ecological dimension of their craft (Abram, 1996, p. 8). Almost conversely, however, Edith Turner and others argue that anthropologists have failed to take the reality of spirits, or for instance, telepathy, seriously (Turner, 1994; Sheldrake, 2008). This inhibition can only have been encouraged by critiques of supernaturalism, however valid.

Harvey has called for the term 'spirits' to be abandoned because its association with dualistic notions of the 'supernatural' and 'meta-empirical' beings distorts perceptions of non-Western shamanistic traditions in which such beings, or 'persons,'[19] are regarded as part of 'life' or 'nature,' or simply as 'neighbours' (Harvey, 2003, pp. 9-11). While agreeing on the cultural politics and the need to develop post-dualistic understandings, my instinct is to reclaim 'spirit' and 'soul,' with due care, not least because their unambiguous designation of 'discarnate' life may be appropriate and useful, even in some non-Western indigenous contexts.[20] My background in 'mental health' self-advocacy informs a sense that the ontological status of visions, voices, or presences, is less important than their meaning and effect, the power relations surrounding them, and uses to which they are put.[21]

New animism draws heavily on Irving Hallowell and Nurit Bird

---

[19] Harvey had just introduced Irving Hallowell's neologism for the Ojibwe non-anthropocentric conception of personhood as 'other-than-human-persons', or other-than-kingfisher persons, etc. (Hallowell, 1960/2002).

[20] Darby Costello, *Desire and the Stars*, http://www.darbycostello.co.uk/-articles, accessed 6/4/15.

[21] Many of Peter Fenwick's respondents had been reluctant to talk about deathbed visions for fear of being thought mad. (Fenwick & Fenwick, 2008).

David's ethnographic insights into animism as a relational epistemology and ontology, but both describe indigenous understandings that might be recognisable to Western spiritualists (for example). Hallowell's mid-twentieth century account of Ojibwa worldviews refers to the concept of an òctcatcákwin (vital part or soul) that survives beyond death and can leave the body during dreams, when powerful other-than-human persons or 'grandfathers' can be met. He also mentions the belief that a deceased human can reappear as a ghost or animal – "often a bird" (Hallowell, 2002, pp. 93,101).

Nurit Bird-David describes Nayaka *Devaru* performances during which trance states enable communication with 'predecessors' and *devaru* ('superpersons,' including elephant-*devaru* and minor Hindu deities), and notes that 'in the modernist sense' this would be termed 'spirit possession.' She also refers to *piccacio* – the souls of people who died alone in the forest and are dangerous until helped ritually to coalesce with other ancestors and *devaru* (Bird-David 1999). According to one of her interlocutors, however, 'Bird-David tends to conflate natural phenomena ... as well as artefacts, with the spiritual beings – malevolent spirits, ancestral spirits and forest deities – that, according to the forager's religious ideology, inhabit or have their 'abode' in the forest, or are identified with certain figurines or icons ... these two aspects of the forager's life-world are distinct' (Morris, 2013). I am in no position to adjudicate, but wonder whether ethnologists themselves are qualified to evaluate such performances.

Morris's observation that binary distinctions need not be interpreted dualistically suggests a way forward in relation to contemporary animisms (Bird-David, 1999, p. 83). Patrick Curry makes a similar point in his helpful discussion of the post-secular. 'Contingent local distinctions between spiritual or mental and material ... are not the problem, any more than are either rationality or spirituality *per se*. It is their ... conversion into an ideology and programme (rationalism, spiritualism, etc.) which is pathological.' Curry juxtaposes Merleau-Ponty's conception of *flesh* as 'the wild Being of/as the world ... ' with Val Plumwood's materialist spirituality and Abram's insight that 'intelligence is no longer ours alone but ... a property of the earth; we are in it, of it, immersed in its depths ... ' (Curry, 2012, p. 4; Abram, 1996, p. 242). As an astrologer, though, Curry will also be keenly aware that the earth 'herself' is immersed within the vast yet intimately responsive body of cosmic nature, the 'responsive cosmos' of divination (Willis & Curry, 2004; Brockbank, 2011).

I wonder, therefore, whether objections to the notion of transcendence (as opposed to transcendental-*ism*) might be an anthropocentric defence? From a human existential viewpoint, nature seems riven with dualities – none more radical than the apparent chasm between 'life' and 'death' – that give rise to perceptions of complete alterity. But what seems to be *shown* to people before death is a vision of continuity, a subtle earth perhaps.

For Heidegger, Being as a whole reveals itself through *physis,* 'nature.' Woven into the etymology of *alētheia,* un-concealment, is the tradition that incarnate existence entails a necessary (error of) forgetfulness. (Farell Krell, 1993, pp. 72-4, 126, 445, 448). From the verb *phainethai,* meaning 'to show itself,' we derive both phenomenology and the 'showings' and 'appearances' of divination, a way of knowing predicated – as indeed an animist science would be/is – on respectful relationship with/in a living communicative world – whose mysterious depths are the stuff of dreams.

Questions

1. How would you tell the difference between normal encounters with birds and butterflies, and extraordinary encounters?

2. What is the 'New Animism,' and what makes it new?

3. How might dreams enable communication between the human and other-than-human worlds?

4. What would an animist science look like?

CHAPTER 14

ANIMAL ALLIES TRANSFORMED INTO ANIMAL ESSENCES: HEALING AND TRANSFORMATION WITH THE WILD EARTH ANIMAL ESSENCES

Silvia Mutterle

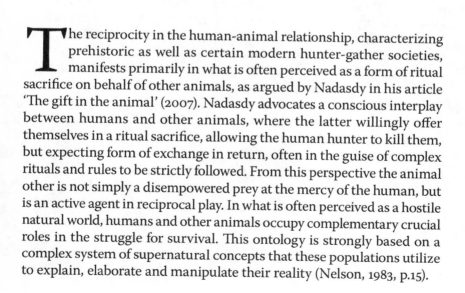

The reciprocity in the human-animal relationship, characterizing prehistoric as well as certain modern hunter-gather societies, manifests primarily in what is often perceived as a form of ritual sacrifice on behalf of other animals, as argued by Nadasdy in his article 'The gift in the animal' (2007). Nadasdy advocates a conscious interplay between humans and other animals, where the latter willingly offer themselves in a ritual sacrifice, allowing the human hunter to kill them, but expecting form of exchange in return, often in the guise of complex rituals and rules to be strictly followed. From this perspective the animal other is not simply a disempowered prey at the mercy of the human, but is an active agent in reciprocal play. In what is often perceived as a hostile natural world, humans and other animals occupy complementary crucial roles in the struggle for survival. This ontology is strongly based on a complex system of supernatural concepts that these populations utilize to explain, elaborate and manipulate their reality (Nelson, 1983, p.15).

The natural and the supernatural worlds are closely intertwined in a cross-cultural and longitudinal trait, which appears throughout human history across the most diverse geographical and cultural scenarios, from the Shuar, Mundurucu and Makuna in the South American Amazon to the Yakut and Buriat of north-eastern Siberia, to mention just a few (Rosengren, 2006 pp. 3-4; Pedersen, 2001, pp. 411-427). It is expressed through the need to entrust a carefully selected and gifted individual with the privilege and responsibility to mediate between and interpret these two closely associated realities: the shaman.

Who is the Shaman?

The figure of the shaman is very charismatic one, and is found across different cultures and throughout time. It has been a role awarded to very few individuals, selected either by birth right or through a universal initiatory period involving extenuating training processes (Herrick & Winkelman, 1993). Even though there is evidence that this role has been equally awarded to both male and female individuals, as witnessed in numerous related literature (Reinhard *et al.*, 1977, pp. 12-18; Mikhailovskii & Wardrop, 1985, p. 62), for the sake of simplicity we will refer to the shaman and his/her patients hereafter as males.

The shaman is not only 'a charismatic leader with informal political power' (Winkelman, 2002, p.3), but also represents the first healer in human history and is often entrusted with divination and assistance in hunting. Shamanism constitutes humanity's first form of theological and spiritual thought, based primarily on the biological and symbolic abilities attributed to a commonly recognized special individual (Dayle *et al.*, 1994 p. 113). What confers the shaman with his power is a peculiar ability, or gift, to access a form of trance, referred to by Eliade as 'an archaic technique of ecstasy' (Eliade in Park, 1965, pp. 1305-1306), otherwise described by Winkelman as an evolved psychobiological process which manifests itself in an Altered State of Consciousness (ASC) (Herrick & Winkelman, 1993, p. 186).

Shamanic ASC seem to be characterised by slow-wave synchronization across different brain systems, as per MacLean's three-brain theory (MacLean in Reiner, 1990, pp. 303-305). According to MacLean, the human brain is constituted of three separate but interconnected brain systems: the reptilian, the paleo-mammalian and the neo-mammalian brains, each superseding different functions. The shaman, according to Shankardass (2003), has the unique ability to elicit information from the paleo-mammalian brain, hosting emotions and insight and thereafter engaging in a vision quest or spiritual journey. The aim of the shamanic journey is to access a parallel reality of cosmic unity with all living creatures, surpassing any distinction between humans and other animals. According to Eliade, the initiatory ritual of soul dismemberment, death and consequent re-birth allowed the shaman to reinstate a lost communion with the animal others through a deep exchange and a ceremonial fusion of human and animal spirits (Eliade in Park, 1965, pp. 1340-1346). As a result, not only does the shaman acquire control over so called animal spirits, or animal guardians, that will accompany him and facilitate his vision quest, but he is also allowed a transformation to and from animal state – often referred to in the literature as 'shape shifting.'

Animal Allies and their Role

These powerful animal entities have been described in anthropological literature respectively as 'tutelary spirits' in Siberian shamanic practices (Mikhailovskii & Wardrop, 1985 p. 110), as 'nagual' in Mexico and Guatemala (Kaplan, 1956), and as 'assistant totem' beings in Australian shamanism (Madigan & Warner, 1958, p. 279). Medieval European culture would have defined these animal spirits as 'familiars,' and often associated them with folk doctors and healers, otherwise accused of being witches and burnt at the stake throughout Europe between the thirteenth and seventeen centuries (Cohn, 1975, p. 96).

Power animals, frequently referred to in shamanic practice, are pivotal figures in shamanic work, and a shaman is virtually such only because of the strong connection and collaboration with one or more of these animal allies (Harner, 1990, p. 54). At the same time, the presence of an animal spirit directly related to a human individual is not necessarily a sign of shamanic powers, because there is evidence of such 'soul animals' accompanying humans from birth, see for example the figure of the *daimon* in ancient Greek culture. Most interestingly, the philosopher Plato in both his 'Socrates' Apology' and 'Symposium,' extensively comments on the presence or *daimons* as human alter-egos in the form of different animals, both wild and domesticated, strictly connected to their human counterpart and directly influenced by their life circumstances (Stokes, 1997, pp. 175-220; Plato *et al.*, 1970, pp. 219-220).

Very similar is the figure of the *chanul* in Mayan culture. A *chanul* is a non-domesticated mammal with five fingers, which according to the inhabitants of Chamula, in the Mexican province of the Ciapas, is assigned by divine will to every individual at birth and shares this same individual's fate throughout his/her entire existence (Serpell, 2006, p. 21). According to these accounts, if anything happened respectively to the daimon or chanul, it would have had direct consequences on the human and his/her welfare. In shamanic practice, however, the shaman and his power animals are strictly related, though not as symbiotically as in the instance of these other animal figures mentioned above. The shaman frequently consults his power animal and is actually believed to shape-shift into it if needs be. The power animal remains a distinct figure that empowers the shaman during his practice and offers him help and guidance during soul journeys.

Neo-Shamanism

Neo-shamanism stems from the modern need to reconnect with nature, and animals in particular, and as Michael Harner suggests, from the need of the modern human to find a renewed form of spirituality outside of established religious practices. Neo-shamanism, however, is not a 'religion' per se, and according to Harner should instead be understood as a way of making spirituality a democratic practice that can be accessed by anyone without the need for an ecclesiastical establishment. As Harner elaborates, 'shamanism becomes a religion after politics have entered into it' (Harner, 2012), much as happened during the Middle Ages, drawing to a close traditional nature based spiritual practices.

Neo-shamanism draws syncretically from the traditional practices of different indigenous populations throughout the world, and its cross cultural development seems to be based on the need for these populations to find an effective antidote to disease and to boost to the chances of survival (Harner, 1990, p. 53). According to Harner it is more appropriate to refer to the altered state of consciousness achieved by shamans (ASC) as shamanic state of consciousness (SSC) for the simple fact that it is not simply a state of trance but an acquired knowledge of shamanic methods and techniques that can readily be accessed and learnt by non-indigenous, contemporary individuals. Shamanic states of consciousness can be explained in Harner's view as the cognitive perception of what Castaneda defines as 'non-ordinary reality' (Castaneda, 1968, p. 106), and which Lowie defines as an 'extraordinary manifestation of reality' (Lowie, 1948, p. 239).

What characterizes the shamanic ASC is the shaman's experience of a pure state of *joy* and *awe* for the vision of the beautiful realities unfolding before his eyes. There is the mental control of the shaman over the direction of his voyage, but simultaneously the absolute surprise for what he might discover in his journeying (Harner, 1990, p. 27). It is interesting to note at this point Schweitzer's notion that the 'bush doctor,' or in this context the neo-shaman, succeeds in healing for the same reason that medical doctors succeed, becaue they tap into the 'inner healer' of the individual (Schweitzer in Cousins, 1979, p. 254).

It is becoming increasingly obvious from recent developments in alternative forms of medicine that the individual's mental and emotional health are closely intertwined. Moreover, Harner argues that 'in a sense shamanism is being reinvented in the west precisely because it is needed' to face the inadequacies of an impersonal medical treatment and the widespread dissatisfaction with institutionalized modern medical practice (Harner, 1990, p. 176). Winkelman supports this assertion with his suggestion that shamanic practices operate through a subtle manipulation on unconscious brain waves, eliciting psychobiological structures of healing processes (2002, p. 10).

Daniel Mapel and the Wild Earth Animal Essences

Twenty years ago the Wild Earth Animal Essences were created by Daniel Mapel. Wild Earth Animal Essences are vibrational remedies that tap into the subtle energies surrounding and supporting the physical body. They are a non-conventional, non-chemical source of healing that can otherwise be defined as 'energetic medicine,' because it does not directly affect the physical body but rather conveys beneficial effects to it through its synergy with the emotional or etheric body (Gerber, 2001, p. 12). Vibrational medicine theories are based on notions of *vitalism* – an expression of metaphysical beliefs according to which all living organisms contain a non-physical energy, or life force, which associates and connects all lifeforms in spite of differences in physical biology (Gerber, 2001, p. 90).

This same metaphysical energy is not new to oriental philosophies and has been known under the name of Chi or QI in China, Ki in Japan, and Prana in India to mention just a few examples. Many unconventional forms of healing such as Reiki,[1] Theta healing,[2] Earthing[3] and so on, are based on the prerequisite that in order to benefit the physical body in the long term, necessary steps must be taken to first address disharmonies and imbalances in the etheric or energetic body. For this purpose, vibrational remedies such as Bach flowers[4] are a complementary source of healing, focusing directly on the improvement of the energetic field of the living organism, in this particular instance the human organism.

Wild Earth Animal Essences, according to their creator Daniel Mapel, are energetic remedies containing the vibrational imprint and energy of the animal they are connected with, but they do not contain animal parts in the slightest (Mapel, 2002, p. 13). They are almost entirely based on a spiritual connection with wild animals, for example Mapel is actually working on the creation of a dog animal essence drawing on the qualities of unconditional love and loyalty of the mixed breed domestic dog (Private conversation during the practitioner seminar at Findhorn Foundation, Scotland, May 2014).

What the shaman would have called *animal allies* or *power animals* materialize in an energetic form that is imbued into water through a simple ritual conducted in what Mapel defines as a place of power in the wilderness (Mapel, 2002, p. 25; see also question 1 below). As Mapel states in his book, 'wild animals are able to live and express their spiritual purpose from a place of grounding and power. They are perfect models of what it means to live fully in integrity, clarity and peace' (Mapel, 2002, p. 15). He further claims that the reason why the essences are effective is simply because 'everything in the universe is interconnected in an invisible whole and by using the animal essences we are able to tap directly into the gifts and powers of wild animals' (Mapel, 2002, p. 15).

Animal essences are very instinctive in their properties and purpose because they draw directly from the animal species' most outstanding characteristics and gifts. For instance, *Butterfly Essence* operates as a catalyst for transformation and is meant to offer support in times of change and emotional transition, easing the process of letting go, moving forward and trusting in inevitable life circumstances (Mapel, 2002, p. 37). *Turtle Essence*, as the shell suggests, is meant to provide psychic and emotional protection, conferring a feeling of security and safety to the individual (Mapel, 2002, p. 62). *Beaver Essence* on the other hand is supposed to facilitate clear thought, planning and programming, creating and problem solving as inspired by the beaver's mastery as a natural architect and builder (Mapel, 2002, p. 35).

Mapel has created an initial set of 32 original animal essences, followed by eight African animal ones and a growing number of 'research essences,' which include animals such as of the bumblebee and gorilla. For this reason he conducts seminars worldwide to teach the use and application of the different essences (see question 5 below). A central aspect of Mapel's work is the creation of the *Wild Child Animal Essences,* which he claims draw from the energy of a select number and species of animal offspring, such as the *Wolf Cub Essence* or the *Robin Chick Essence,* and can be utilized with young children, or to address the *Inner Child* – the most vulnerable part of the human being.

More recently Mapel has also created what are defined as *Combination Essences* and *Healing Path Essences* where the powers and gifts of different animals are combined to obtain a stronger, more immediate effect, the most popular (and perhaps most effective) one being *Saved by the Animals,* which is the equivalent in Wild Earth Animal Essence to *Rescue Remedy* in Bach flowers. This particular essence, according to Mapel, is meant to bring immediate and effective relief in cases of emotional shock, trauma or general debilitating sudden life events. The essence combines the energies of five different animals: *Eagle,* for connection with the divine source; *Dove,* for peace and calm; *Turtle,* for emotional and psychic protection; *Buffalo,* for grounding and finally *Elephant,* for deep grounding and spiritual openness (Mapel, 2002, p. 87).

The question that inevitably arises is: do the essences actually work? The simplest answer is that they have been successfully employed as alternative treatments according to numerous first person accounts and case studies for the past twenty years, and they are now moving into commercial circulation in nine different countries, including the United Kingdom (Mapel, 2002, p. 89). People evidently get something out of the essences.

The author herself is a practitioner and can offer a number of personal accounts on the empirical basis of subjective experience. My most striking experience was with the *Spider Animal Essence,* which places the spider in the role of an animal ally. Animal essences in fact work both by the law of attraction and/or repulsion to one particular animal. Since the spider is an animal the author has always been repulsed by, or even scared of, taking the essence had a very strong effect that manifested itself in dizziness, lack of balance and nausea. After working and consulting with Mapel during a later workshop, it became clear that *Spider Animal Essence* had worked very deeply on the lack of a maternal bond of the author with her mother as an infant and in early childhood. Since the spider as an animal ally is the 'weaver of the inner web,' its essence brings a nurturing sense of belonging, connection and integration at very profound levels (Mapel, 2002, p. 59). Tapping into its energy obviously triggered a deep emotional upheaval that manifested itself physically.

Discussion

Mapel does not define himself as a shaman, nor does he claim to draw from any particular shamanic tradition, which he believes are very ancient and strictly connected to indigenous populations' practices and lore. The following interview with Mapel is quite revealing of his views and inspirations:

1. Am I correct in saying that Wild Earth Animal Essences are born through a ritual that imbues simple water with a healing power? How is that possible?

The essences are made in a ceremonial process. Water is very subtle-energy-absorbent (see works by Masuru Emoto).[5] Intention infuses the water with whatever energy it is exposed to.

2. Do you access a state of altered consciousness when creating the essences?

Others might consider it altered, for me it is normal. It is a natural extension of my everyday consciousness and reality, but I do think that my general consciousness/awareness is quite different from most people.

3. Would you call yours a shamanic journey?

No. I don't use the word shaman or shamanic. I believe those words belong in the realm of those traditional cultures where there is an active shamanic tradition.

4. How do you feel while you create the essences?

Happy. It is a fun, creative process that happens easily, without any stress, it is like a form of play while also being deeply powerful.

5. Would you describe it as call or as gift? If yes, why? If not, why not?

Absolutely. From September 1995 when in a single moment I received the guidance to do this work, it has been both a constant calling that has never wavered. In terms of gifts with this work, I believe I have two, one is making the essences with consistent connection with the animals and the other is being able to teach, guide, and inspire others through traveling around the world and spreading the gifts of the animals through my teaching.

6. Would you say that the animal essences were born out of the dynamics of the healed wounded becoming a healer? How?

All I can say is that I did years and years of profound emotional healing work, and 3 weeks after completing the most important part of that work, I received the guidance to do this work (this was in 1995). So this work is a direct result of having done the deep emotional healing of the emotional and sexual abuse I experienced in childhood. It would quite simply be impossible for me to do this work had I not done that inner work first.

7. How do you know which qualities to attribute to a certain animal?

After creating an essence, I wait for the right moment to work with it. It may be a day later, a week later or a month. Then when the time is right, I take the essence and can feel how the energy works. This brings the first level of awareness of some of the major gifts that the animal offers us through the essence. Then there is further work, and allowing others to experience it as well and provide their insights.

8. Do you not fear anthropomorphizing the animals when attributing certain qualities to them?

No.

9. What is the motive behind your work?

To serve the animals, humanity, and all beings in the best way I possibly can (Mapel, 2016).

In his introductory book on the animal essences *Into the Heart of the Wild* (2002), Mapel clearly relates to a first initiation into the 'outer wild' and a second initiation into the 'inner wild.' The outer wild being his work as a 'wilderness guide' in some of the most wildest most remote locations in North America. It was during these excursions that he started to interact both physically and spiritually with a number of wild animals, such as the buffalo, the black bear and many others. The later inner wild initiation refers to his internal journey along a profound spiritual path of emotional suffering, grieving and subsequent healing as a result of the realization during psychotherapy work of having been exposed to sexual abuse by his parents in his early childhood (Mapel, 2002, pp. 18-19). Therefore, very much like in the dynamics triggered by shamanic work, the wounded shaman after undergoing life-changing experiences of despair, loss of meaning in life and a symbolic emotional and spiritual dismemberment, death and rebirth becomes himself a wounded healer (see question 6 above).

As Dayle argues, the shaman heals through a projection of symbolic models that actively engage in the healing process creating an enhanced interaction between the conscious and the unconscious mind (Dayle *et al.*, 1994, p. 113). In the same way, Mapel projects his own intent of connection and interrelation with with power animals into the creation of the animal essences. There is, then, the aspect of happiness and wonder that Mapel confirms to feel during the creation process of the essences (see question 4 above), which very much recalls the state of joy and awe ascribed by Harner to the shamanic state of consciousness.

Conclusion

Even though shamanic practices are mostly related to traditional indigenous populations, there seems to be a resurgence of interest in these practices that would appear incongruous with the sophisticated technologies and efficient chemical remedies made available by modern medicine. Shamanism was the very first response to the demand of early human communities to address physical disease and spiritual distress, which were perceived as very much interrelated. The same entanglement was reflected in the synergy between the human and the animal worlds, which survived in a complementary reciprocity.

With the dualism imposed by medieval European culture, where the healer and spiritual guide can no longer coexist in the charismatic figure of the herbalist or bush doctor, the responsibility for the physical healing of the individual moved to the medical professional and the responsibility for spiritual welfare to pastoral care. This could well be the reason behind the aversion to animal support, even in the form of love for a pet dog, manifested by most monotheistic religions. According to Menache's article 'Dogs: God's worst enemies?' (1997), dogs are bestowed with an important symbolic role of the idealized provider of unconditional love and support, challenging the protective role of pastoral care and ecclesiastical spiritual guidance.

The ever pervading cosmic energy, and the synergy between the human and animal world, clearly perceived by indigenous cultures to this day, is well expressed in the spiritual form of neo-shamanism and manifests itself in the modern need for animal allies. The Wild Earth Animal Essences, in the form of vibrational remedies, effectively embody the demand and expression of animal allies in modern society. It is almost as if the animal spirits have claimed their space in modern medicine, materializing in a bottle and acting as a medicament to ingest without the intercession of the shaman, doctor or priest. Daniel Mapel's ceremonial ritual held in a place of power can, after all, be considered a form of shamanic practice that instils in water the power of animal spirits as much as it instils in him the awe for the power of cosmic energy and the joy of serving the global community through his animal essences.

Questions

1 Can only human individuals belonging to native populations call themselves shamans? Why?

2. Why do western humans who can easily access allopathic medicine seek support from unconventional forms of healing?

3. How has the role of other animals changed in Capitalocene? Are pets our new animal allies?

4. Why might vibrational remedies work for certain people and not for others?

Notes

1. Reiki is a Japanese technique of deep relaxation and stress reduction that promotes healing through the laying of hands over the patient's body. This very ancient technique acts upon and draws from the invisible life force or life energy that permeates all living beings and aims to reduce or eliminate imbalances in the energy field. (Reikihealing.org.uk, 2011)

2. Theta Healing is a recently rediscovered healing technique obtained though a deep meditative state that allows the access and generation of theta brain waves, very similar to the altered state of consciousness practised during shamanic work. (Thetahealingcentre.co.uk, 2012)

3. Earthing is a theoretical method according to which many of the psychophysical diseases and discomforts we suffer from are directly related to our disconnectedness from the earth. The earth's magnetic field charge that used to be provided by walking barefoot or simply wearing rubber free footwear is supplied through this method of grounding though a conductive silver thread connected directly to the neutral pole of the electric plug socket. The neutral wire is the return channel for any unused static current. (Earthing-institute.net, 2013)

4. Bach flowers remedies are extremely diluted flower materials in a solution of water and brandy, developed in the early twentieth century by the English homeopath Edward Bach. He claimed that the dew particles present on flower petals would retain the healing properties of the plant. (Bachcentre. com, 2009)

5. Masaru Emoto is a Japanese researcher and author of specific literature advocating the impact of human consciousness and intent on the molecular structure of water. (Emoto, 2004; 2005)

CHAPTER 15

CRYPTOZOOLOGY IN A CHANGING WORLD

Susan Marsh

~

There are more things in heaven and earth, Horatio, than are
dreamt of in your philosophy.

—WILLIAM SHAKESPEARE

A s a child, this famous quote from Shakespeare's Hamlet always made perfect sense to me. The world was endless and unfathomable, and the vast swathes of the Amazon jungle or the North American forests seemed just as likely to be hiding new, undiscovered forms of life as the craters and plains of Mars. But as I grew older, the world got smaller, and I began to question the likelihood of undiscovered megafauna quietly thriving in even the farthest flung corners of our planet.

However, it wasn't just my perspective that grew with time. In my formative years, the world was ink and pen strokes on an oversized Atlas – a tangible, finite thing that could be categorised and knew its limitations. Now, we can use our smartphones to navigate the wildest oceans, call an Uber to cross international borders and pick up WiFi in the remotest of wildernesses. But in this new terrain of omnipotent technology, what room is there left for monsters? If the cracks in our known world are growing ever smaller, what has become of the creatures that inhabit the unknown?

Writing in 1956, the famous Belgian-French researcher Bernard Heuvelmans expressed his distaste for certain attitudes within mainstream zoology. Apparently, most experts were of the opinion that the world had already been significantly explored, and in the absence of any major new animal discoveries in recent years, they had concluded that there could be no large creatures left to be found (Heuvelmans, 1956). However, Heuvelmans disagreed. In fact, he dubbed these ideas 'fallacies' and dedicated much of his career to proving the zoologists wrong (Heuvelmans, 1956, p. 25). In the process, he became known as the founding father of cryptozoology – the oft-maligned field that studies nature's unknown, or uncategeorised, animals.

Today, the term is most commonly associated with the beasts that inhabit the hazy borderlands between the real and the unreal; the manlike hominids that stalk the North Western forests of the United States, for example, or the mysterious creature that may – or may not – lurk beneath the muddy waters of Scotland's Loch Ness.

The field of cryptozoology, then, is where we will find our monsters – if any of them remain. But if Heuvelmans' contemporaries believed that the world was already too explored, too conquered, to justify the existence of unknown animals back in 1956, what would they have made of the situation some sixty years later?

On the surface, it definitely seems as if there is little room for monsters or mystery in today's developed world. In 2017, investigators from the UK cryptozoology group the Centre for Fortean Zoology arrived in Russia to continue their research into the Almas – a yeti-like hominid said to inhabit the upper reaches of the mountains of central Asia. Ten years previously, they had found themselves on the brink of success. In fact, according to director Richard Freeman, they were on the cusp of a discovery that would change the world of cryptozoology for good.

But those ten years had been like Narnian years in farthest Russia. When the team first visited the North Caucasus republic of Kabardino-Balkaria in 2008, they found a remote, unexplored region replete with sightings of the elusive cryptid. 'We may have gotten within twelve feet of a seven-foot-plus almasty at an abandoned farm at 2:30 in the morning,' Freeman told me in an interview conducted online. But when they returned, they discovered that the population had boomed – and that the creature appeared to have made itself scarce.

Elsewhere, Freeman noticed a similar trend during his multiple trips to Sumatra investigating reports of the Orang Pendek, an alleged bipedal primate that some believe represents a missing link between humans and apes – although most experts agree that it is likely a relative of the orangutan. 'Every time I go back to Sumatra I see more and more of the Orang Pendek's habitat eaten up by coffee plantations and logging,' he explained. As a result, he believes that the elusive creature has been driven to even more remote areas in order to escape the encroachment of humans on its natural habitat.

However, if the cryptids of Sumatra and Russia have grown shy in the face of development, there is some evidence to suggest that America's most famous mystery creature might have taken the opposite approach. In 2013, NASA's Lead for Data Visualization, Joshua Stevens, used his impressive skills to map every sighting recorded by the Bigfoot Field Researchers Organization (BFRO) since 1921.

Looking at an overview of the data, it is clear that Bigfoot and Sasquatch sightings have increased in line with the growth of population in the United States. In fact, since the first concrete 'evidence' for the creature emerged in the 1950s, the number of sightings reported yearly have crept steadily upwards as the country has grown more and more populated – peaking in the early 2000s before beginning to decline around 2010 (Stevens, 2013).

However, a bivariate approach to mapping the data reveals a slightly different picture. 'There are distinct regions where sightings are incredibly common, despite a very sparse population. On the other hand, in some of the most densely populated areas Sasquatch sightings are exceedingly rare' (Stevens, 2013).

Of course, it seems logical that urban hubs such as New York City and Los Angeles are not exactly hotbeds of Bigfoot activity. But what is happening in the creature's historical stomping grounds, such as the Pacific Northwest, where fewer people results in more, not less, sightings? Although Stevens speculates that both terrain and expectations might play a role in this pattern (Stevens, 2013), might something else be at play? Could Bigfoot and his kin be growing bolder as the world around them changes, necessitating an adaptation of behaviour as well as habitat?

In pre-Columbian legend, Bigfoot-like creatures were treated with respect, viewed as spiritual beings that straddled the border between the animal and human realms (Franzoni, 1996). However, in modern times, the animals appear to have taken on an altogether more sinister edge.

In 1924, a Canadian named Albert Ostman arrived in British Columbia to take a vacation. An experienced outdoorsman, he knew that the area had its fair share of Sasquatch legends, although he was not a believer himself. However, all that changed when he was allegedly kidnapped by one of the creatures and taken to their lair many miles away. According to Ostman, he was held captive by a family of Sasquatch for six days before escaping (Storm, 2008).

For a quarter century, Ostman kept silent about his extraordinary ordeal. But as more and more people came forward to report having seen the beasts, he eventually decided to share his story. And amazingly, he is not alone. In fact, over the years, a number of witnesses have spoken up to report not just seeing but actually interacting with mystery hominids – a phenomenon that does not appear to have been reported before the late nineteenth century.

So, could Bigfoot, Sasquatch and their ilk be growing bolder as they encounter more and more humans in their natural habitats? As Stevens observed, many of the areas where mystery hominids are most commonly spotted are sparsely populated – but there are certainly more residents and visitors in the country's far flung parks and forests now than there were back in Pre-Columbian times, when these creatures remained firmly in the realms of the ethereal.

This line of thinking is perhaps best reflected in the work of David Paulides, an American cryptozoologist who believes that the amount of people disappearing in the United States' national parks might have an explanation more sinister than hikers simply overestimating their abilities and getting lost in unforgiving terrain. And although Paulides never specifically blames Bigfoot for the parks' numerous missing person reports, the implication is clear.

Meanwhile, in the United Kingdom, some might argue that the famous Loch Ness Monster – affectionately dubbed Nessie by the locals – has historically exhibited similar traits. Granted, there does not seem to be a surplus of witnesses claiming to have been kidnapped by the monster and held in an underwater den. However, the trajectory – and the very nature – of reports over the years suggest that the creature might also have changed its behaviour as its environment has altered over the years.

Like Bigfoot, reports of something strange living in the waters of Loch Ness date back to a time far wilder than today. And just as the kiosks and mountain lodges of America's national parks were once an endless No Man's Land of forests and bluffs, so too were the Nessie museums and theme pubs of Loch Ness preceded by a landscape relatively untouched by human hand. And in that environment, the monster first reared its head.

It was sometime in the 6th century A.D. when Saint Columba and his followers were apparently charged by a monster while attempting to retrieve the body of a victim from the River Ness. And by the 1970s, some 10,000 people had claimed to have spotted a similarly bizarre creature lurking beneath the surface of the vast, impenetrable loch (Williams, 2016).

However, sightings of the monster were not evenly spaced out over the years. In fact, it wasn't until the 1930s that reports of a beast in the loch became somewhat commonplace. According to the Official Loch Ness Monster Sightings Register, less than 20 sightings were recorded over the entire period of 1916 to 1932. By contrast, there were more than 50 in 1933 alone (The Official Loch Ness Monster Sightings Register, 2018). But what could have happened at Loch Ness to inspire such a sharp increase in sightings? In early 1933, drastic change was underway along the shores of a body of water that had remained largely remote over the centuries.

> The final sections of the new road down the western section of Loch Ness were being completed, with much blasting of rock and the clearing of trees and undergrowth. For the first time ever, much of the Loch could be seen from a car, and generally from a height that gave far-reaching views across the water (Williams, 2016).

Again, in this instance, development and urbanisation seems to have done little to scare off the cryptid or cryptids local to Loch Ness. However, an interesting side note comes in the experience of Mr and Mrs Spicer, a London couple who took a trip to John O'Groats in July 1933. Apparently, they were driving alongside the loch when they spotted something moving across the road approximately 150 feet in front of their vehicle.

> It was the nearest approach to a dragon or prehistoric monster that I have ever seen in my life [it] appeared to be carrying a small lamb or animal of some kind ... It seemed to have a long neck, which moved up and down in the manner of a scenic railway, and the body was

fairly big with a high back ... Length from 6 to 8 feet and very ugly (Inverness Courier, 1933).

In the annals of Loch Ness Monster history, the Spicers' sighting has remained unique as the first and only time that the creature has been spotted on land. Moreover, their encounter took place not on the newly developed Western side of the loch, but on the Eastern side, where the same ancient road has carried travellers along its shores since the eighteenth century (Williams, 2016).

Is it possible, then, that all the activity across the water may have driven the monster to take shelter in previously unexplored terrain? And if so, what does this mean for the age-old debate about the very nature of cryptids themselves?

In 1990, Jonathan Downes of the Centre for Fortean Zoology coined the term 'zooform phenomena' – a word used to describe that genus of monsters who exist outside the realms of the corporeal. Rather than flesh-and-blood creatures, these beings might look like animals, but they are more closely associated with the spirit world, being more supernatural than physical in nature.

With many cryptids, the debate over whether or not they are actual animals or some type of zooform phenomena has been raging for many years. In the peaks of the Cairngorms east of Loch Ness, for example, lurks a creature known as Am Fear Liath Mòr, or the Big Grey Man. To some, it is Scotland's answer to the Yeti or the Almas, a mysterious hominid that haunts the summit of Ben Macdui, the range's highest peak. But to others, the sinister sense of foreboding that surrounds the beast places it firmly in the non-corporeal realm.

Hundreds of miles south, on the moors of Cornwall and Devon, spectral black dogs flash their otherworldly red eyes at passing vehicles, only to disappear into the gloom. Can it really be said that these are merely an unknown species, or is something far more terrible at play? Meanwhile, on the other side of the world, cryptids such as the alien-like chupacabra continue to test the boundaries between the real and the unreal.

With this in mind, incidents of cryptids like Bigfoot and the Loch Ness Monster changing their behaviour in line with their environment adds an interesting angle to the debate. If these animals are spirits, or ghost-like reflections of another realm, one would expect material trends such as urbanisation to have little effect on their behaviour. Consider, for example, the Roman soldiers who stomp through the cellar of the Treasurer's House in York, their bodies only visible from the knees up as their feet walk along a long-buried road (Mitchell, 1974). Or the Native American wendigo, an evil cannibalistic spirit that is still said to haunt the northeast corner of North America, even as its forest habitat declines in favour of farms and fossil fuels (Ahenakew, 2011; Biello, 2010).

But if creatures like Bigfoot and the Loch Ness Monster are growing bolder, and their counterparts in Sumatra and Russia becoming more reclusive, in response to their changing environments, that would seem to suggest a nature more akin to a real flesh-and-blood animal, rather than an inhabitant of the spirit world.

Whatever the true nature of these beasts, it seems to be a common trend that the dewilding of their habitats has caused them to shift away from legend and towards a more concrete reality. Before the influx of sightings that accompanied the opening of the new road around Loch Ness, for example, many considered the monster a type of kelpie – a supernatural creature traditionally thought to inhabit large bodies of water across Scotland (Williams, 2016). But today, there are few who believe that these Celtic spirits could be responsible for the reports that continue to flood in year after year. Instead, most aficionados of the monster point to a surviving population of plesiosaurs as the most likely explanation for whatever is lurking inside the loch (Williams, 2016).

In fact, it was around the same time that the road was built that the monster, previously considered something of a shape-shifter, settled into its current long-necked, small-headed form. And even though plesiosaurs, a type of gigantic marine reptile that shared the Earth with the dinosaurs, are generally thought to have gone extinct at the end of the Cretaceous Period around 66 million years ago, their potential presence in Loch Ness is a lot easier to swallow than the idea of ethereal water spirits haunting the waters of Scotland well into the twenty-first century.

Elsewhere, the dewilding of our planet has had an even greater impact on cryptozoology. In the 1890s, the demand for natural rubber reached a peak around the world, and one of the places that had an abundant supply of the resource was the large swathe of Central Africa known as the Congo Free State. Right up until the middle of the nineteenth century, the region's impenetrable terrain, prolific diseases and fierce locals had rendered it largely immune to the slow march of European colonisation – one of the last independent bastions in a rapidly changing world.

However, in 1876, King Leopold II of Belgium announced his intentions to ramp up colonisation in Central Africa, and by 1884 he had convinced most of the world's major powers that the Congo was rightfully his to govern. And the following year, the Congo Free State was born. Unsurprisingly, Leopold wasted no time in exploiting the region's natural resources – with rubber at the top of his list.

By 1891, Leopold had taken control of the rubber plants out of the hands of the indigenous people and placed it squarely in the hands of private companies. Not only were the Congolese now obligated to hand all of their harvests straight over to the state, they also had high quotas to meet that were violently enforced by the Belgian king's own military forces.

Tragically, the humanitarian cost of Leopold's reign was great. In fact, it is estimated that as many as 15 million people might have died in the region before the state was disbanded in 1908 – with countless more mutilated by soldiers keen to prove their bloodlust to their superiors. But might the world that inspired novelist Joseph Conrad to write his seminal work *Heart of Darkness* have left another legacy?

As Leopold's unbridled exploitation of the Congo continued, the face of the region changed beyond recognition. Roads and railways were built, villages were razed to the ground and the native population numbers went into freefall. And from the ashes, one of the era's greatest cryptozoological discoveries emerged.

In 1899, in the midst of Leopold's rule, the Governor of Uganda Sir Harry Johnston encountered a group of Wambutti pygmies from the Congo's Ituri forest region. Apparently, he rescued them from being spirited away to Paris by a German showman, and eventually returned them to their homeland. Some 40 years earlier, the famous explorer Sir Henry Morton Stanley had written about his own encounter with the Wambutti and a strange, donkey like creature that he believed they called the atti. However, the Congo was not known to house wild asses, nor any animal like them, and the 'atti' became a cryptid – although it would be almost a century before the term was coined. But now, Johnston, a friend of Stanley's, had the opportunity to learn more (Heuvelmans, 1956).

> They at once understood what I meant; and pointing to a zebra-skin and a live mule, they informed me that the creature in question, which was called OKAPI, was like a mule with zebra stripes on it (Heuvelmans, 1956, p. 56).

Convinced that the okapi was a surviving Hipparion, a type of prehistoric horse thought to be long extinct, Johnston dedicated himself to proving its existence. And in 1900, he had a breakthrough, managing to acquire an okapi skin which he duly despatched to the British Museum. However, it wasn't until 1919 that a living okapi specimen made its way to a European zoo – firmly cementing the creature as one of cryptozoology's greatest success stories (Shuker, 1993).

Today, the okapi is a mainstay in zoos across the world, where the bizarre-looking animal, appearing to be somewhere between a zebra and a giraffe, continues to inspire amazement and delight. But although Johnston has been lauded for his striking contribution to the annals of zoology, few seem to have reflected on the environmental conditions that may well have enabled his discovery.

Did Leopold's unrelenting assault on the Congolese environment and people drive the okapi out of the realms of myth and towards a more traditional taxonomic definition? Or was the adoption of the creature by mainstream science just another string to the bow in the vast arsenal of colonisation? Certainly, it seems possible that the okapi might have remained a footnote in the annals of cryptozoology were it not for the arrival of cutthroat Europeans in its native habitat – although whether this was to the creature's benefit or its detriment is open to debate.

Almost twenty years later, another cryptozoological drama began unfolding some 3,000 km away in East London on the southeastern tip of South Africa. But while the changing landscape of the Congo's forests might have heralded the arrival of the okapi, it was the dewilding of an entirely different type of habitat that coincided with the coelacanth's leap into the history books.

Up until the end of the nineteenth century, the waters off the eastern coast of South Africa had largely been fished by locals looking to feed their families, as well as a few commercial enterprises. However, in the 1870s, the Mineral Revolution saw vast mining enterprises spring up across the country – bringing with them large numbers of workers who also needed sustenance as they toiled in search of diamonds and gold. In response, the state constructed a large number of fisheries, bringing in British trawlers to plumb the depths of the Indian Ocean (van Sittert, 2017).

But as South Africa changed both above and below the surface, an unlikely creature emerged that, to some at least, was worth more than the largest diamond that the country's mines had ever produced. On December 22, 1938, a museum curator named Marjorie

Courtenay-Latimer was called to inspect a catch brought in by the trawler *Nerine*. Apparently, it was customary for her to visit the wharf in order to search for specimens that might be of interest to the scientific community. And this time, she wasn't disappointed (Shuker, 1993).

What Courtenay-Latimer stumbled upon that day in East London sent shockwaves around the world. Beneath a pile of nondescript sharks she discovered a coelacanth – a monstrous looking fish that once shared the earth with the dinosaurs. And just like them, it had been believed long extinct, with the previous last fossil dating to over 60 million years ago (Shuker, 1993).

Soon, Courtenay-Latimer's discovery came to the attention of Professor J.L.B. Smith, an ichthyologist at South Africa's Rhodes University, and the academic printed thousands of leaflets in the hope that new specimens might be recovered. However, it wasn't until 1952 that one was located, over 1,000 miles away in the Comoro Islands off Africa's southeast coast (Shuker, 1993).

Eventually, it turned out that these far-flung islands were the true habitat of the coelacanth, the specimen caught in South Africa having presumably strayed far from home. However, if it wasn't for the arrival of the miners and the trawlers – and the publicity campaign launched on the back of Courtenay-Latimer's discovery – the ancient fish may well have remained in the realm of the dinosaurs for centuries to come.

But if dewilding and development around the world has driven creatures like the okapi and the coelacanth out of hiding, where they might otherwise have remained, what can that tell us about the monsters that may still lurk in the shadows? Is it only a matter of time before the predictions of Heuvelmans' contemporaries come true and 'the world has now been completely explored; no new animals have been discovered for a long time,' (Heuvelmans, 1956, p. 25). Or might there be other factors at play? After all, the summit of Mount Everest is almost a tourist trap compared to the lonely peak that Tenzing Norgay and Sir Edmund Hillary first conquered in 1953 – spotting apparent yeti footprints along the way – and yet no concrete evidence of the mysterious hominid has ever been discovered. Similarly, although the creatures previously discussed in this chapter appear to have adapted their behaviour as their environments have changed, they have yet to find their way into the cages of the world's zoos.

Could it be that some cryptids are simply better equipped at hiding and adapting than others? Or might a more complicated relationship with mankind be at work? Some insight into this might be found in the reports of an expedition that I was lucky enough to be part of back in 2006. That year, I travelled with five people to the West African nation of the Gambia in search of the Ninki Nanka, a dragon-like cryptid that has been a mainstay of the nation's folklore for generations. Except, unlike the Chinese dragon, this creature was still being spotted stalking the country's jungles and rivers right into the present day.

Perhaps unsurprisingly, we did not manage to uncover any concrete evidence of the beast. However, we did stumble across our own example of how urbanisation can negatively impact on the field of cryptozoology. Some twenty-three years before our expedition, Owen Burnham, a wildlife enthusiast who grew up in neighboring Senegal, encountered a strange creature washed up on a Gambian beach. Sixteen feet in length, it had a body similar to that of a dolphin or a whale, with a long, thick tail and a long jaw equipped with eighty teeth. Apparently, it was like nothing that Burnham had ever seen before (CFZ Expedition Report, 2006).

When Burnham and his family found two locals attempting to remove the creature's head – likely in an attempt to sell the skull to tourists – they decided that drastic action was needed. So, they dragged the animal above the high water line and buried it, hoping to return for it at some point in the future. Sadly, they were unable to, and soon all that remained of their startling discovery were some simple sketches and a rather rudimentary map.

During the expedition, we were able to follow Burnam's map to the spot where the creature was buried. But unfortunately, a nightclub had since been constructed close to – and quite possibly on top of – the mysterious creature's grave. And although we were able to conduct a cursory dig in search of remains, we achieved little more than puzzling the resident hustlers who spent their days patrolling the distinctly monster-less beach.

But although our experiences did not yield much evidence of the monster, my time in the Gambia led me to a few interesting conclusions. Most significantly, to me at least, was the fact that the people I spoke to believed wholeheartedly in the existence of the Ninki Nanka. Clearly, this was not some Bogeyman created to prevent children from wandering off – to them, it was a very real and very present threat. But why exactly was this dragon-like creature from the shadows rearing its ugly, scaled head in the twenty-first century, when the rest of the country was modernising at a startling rate?

Personally, I believe that the answer is twofold. On the one hand, it seems likely that an exceptionally large specimen of some known animal – a crocodile, for example – had begun prowling the rivers and jungles of the Gambian wilds. And somehow, these sightings had combined with the legend of the Ninki Nanka to create a spate of monster encounters. However, I suspect that there was also something else at play – a phenomenon that sheds an interesting light on the role of cryptozoology in a changing world.

When Burnham stumbled across his unknown creature on a Gambian beach, the population of the country was less than 700,000. But by the time that we arrived, that had more than doubled (Gambia Population, 2018). And with that growth came all of its associated trappings – not just the nightclub that may or may not have stood in the way of our great cryptozoological discovery, but also roads, airports and everything else that comes with a burgeoning tourist economy.

During our expedition, we travelled far from the hotels and beaches of Banjul and deep into the jungle. But even there, it was evident that the march of modernisation was on the verge of consuming even the most far-flung tribes. Could the persistence of the Ninki Nanka have been an attempt on the behalf of these people to cling to an identity that was fast disappearing? And if so, might the presence of other monsters in our ever-more explored world be an example of the same phenomenon – only failing in places where the resistance to urbanisation is less pronounced? Certainly, our relationship with the wild and the unknown has always been a part of who we are. And just as the shared archetypes of creatures like dragons and mermaids act as a common thread of humanity between disparate cultures, so too do our unique, localised cryptids and monsters come to define us. With this in mind, it seems logical that a threatened community might cling to a legend just as it clings to a dying language or tradition – bringing its beasts out to roar in the spotlight one last time. If so, it can be no surprise that the luck that befell hunters of the okapi and the coelacanth eluded us on our mission.

In conclusion, the reaction of cryptids to our changing world seems unpredictable. In some places, the dewilding of our planet seems to inspire a desperate death throe: the lake monsters walk, the coelacanths rise, and the okapis stalk on improbably long legs out of the jungle gloom. Is it a predictable result of decreasing habitats and the presence of more discerning – more inclined to document and categorise – Western minds, or is it a protest of sorts, a last ditch attempt to assert themselves in a world that deems their myth and their mystery increasingly irrelevant? And if so, what of the creatures that hide themselves as the skyscrapers march and the ever-growing cities peck at their clawed toes? Can cryptids be both less and more real in a society still struggling to define its relationship with the unknown? As always, the monsters of this world will shift and change, making Heuvelmans' belief as relevant today as it was back in 1956 – that the great days of zoology are not done.

Questions

1. Why might increased urbanisation affect cryptids differently in different parts of the world? What other factors might be at play?

2. The term 'zooform phenomena' is used to describe creatures that resemble flesh-and-blood animals, but are not. When considering the supernatural history of the world around us, how might we distinguish these from other cryptids? And how does that affect the ways in which we relate to them?

3. The okapi was once considered a mythical creature by western science. Now, it can be seen in zoos around the world. What might we stand to lose and gain from 'dewildings' such as these?

4. In the Gambia, the Ninki Nanka formed an important part of the local people's cultural identity. Think about the cryptids and legends that are local to you. What do they tell you about your own past, and how your forebearers related to the world around them?

CHAPTER 16

A HIDDEN PREDATOR: ECOLOGY AND ESOTERICISM IN THE WORK OF WHITLEY STRIEBER

Timothy Grieve-Carlson

This World is not Conclusion.
A Species stands beyond–
Invisible, as Music–
But positive, as Sound–
It beckons, and it baffles–
Philosophy, don't know–
And through a Riddle, at the last–
Sagacity, must go–

–EMILY DICKINSON,
'THIS WORLD IS NOT CONCLUSION' (FR 373, C. 1862)

The idea for this chapter emerged from a series of conversations with the author Whitley Strieber during a conference last winter. Listening to Strieber reflect on his own life and work throughout the week, I noticed a particular theme that kept coming up. One night after dinner, during a conversation in which this theme was touched upon again, I spoke up, saying, 'Whitley, your entire body of work is about ecological awareness.'

'Yes, it is,' he said immediately.

In this chapter I will describe what I meant by that, and why Strieber—an author who is well-known for horror novels and paranormal nonfiction, rather than environmental writing—confirmed my assertion without missing a beat. Whitley Strieber is an American author best known for his 1987 best-seller *Communion: A True Story*, a personal account of experiences that centered around a traumatic episode in his cabin in the Catskill region of New York state, which he and others have described as an alien abduction. In the actual text, however, the author remains surprisingly ambivalent about the precise nature of the experience, never settling on a single interpretation or explanation of the events he describes.

While the connection between extraterrestrial beings and esoteric religious ideas was already firmly established by the time of *Communion's* publication, Strieber is among its most effective popularizers in the twentieth century. Before publications by John Mack or television programs like *The X-Files* made the presence of the short, black-eyed grey aliens ubiquitous in popular culture, the cover painting of the being on the jacket of the first edition of *Communion* firmly situated what is now the popular image of an extraterrestrial in the public imagination. Strieber's own insistence on interpreting his experiences within explicitly religious, and often fully mystical and esoteric, frames of reference has further cemented the association between extraterrestrials and esotericism. While Strieber is certainly not the origin of this association, he is arguably its most influential public proponent in the last few decades.

Strieber is also well-known as the author of several best-selling novels, many in the genres of horror and science-fiction. Strieber's dual role as an author of popular fiction and profoundly religious nonfiction puts the relationship between religion and literature on vivid display in the life and work of a single author. To better understand some of the esoteric and ecological dimensions of Strieber's work, I want to turn to two of his earlier, pre-*Communion* novels, *The Wolfen* and *The Hunger*. In so doing, I hope to demonstrate that the sophisticated religious posture in *Communion*, as pointed out by scholars like Jeffrey Kripal (2015; 2014), is already on full display in Strieber's earliest work, a pair of popular horror novels.

This particular claim is not new: as the literary critic Mary Pharr (1996) and Strieber himself have each pointed out that, despite being a work of nonfiction, *Communion* is not an exception to, but rather the culmination of themes that Strieber develops in his earliest novels. Another important work which has touched on these continuous themes is Ed Conroy's *Report on Communion*, published in 1989. Indeed, Strieber himself has suggested that his earlier written corpus is actually the result of a lifetime of visitor experiences, sublimated and expressed through the form of the horror novel, with the visitors themselves appearing in the culturally mediated halloween fashions of the werewolf and the vampire. As he writes in *Communion*:

> What is most interesting to me about this story [*Communion*] is that it continues imagery that is present in my early horror novels. The visitors could be seen as the Wolfen, as Miriam Blaylock in *The Hunger* ... The theme is always the same: Mankind must face a harsh but enigmatically beautiful force that, as Miriam Blaylock describes herself, is "part of the justice of the world." This force is always hidden between the folds of experience. (2008, pp. 24-25)

In this chapter, I want to theorize this theme Strieber refers to by reading these novels along with *Communion*. In my reading, I suggest that Strieber's early period presents the sacred in the form of an ecological metaphor of predator-prey relation. Strieber's writing expresses a deep and sincere personal religious tendency, in which the human is re-imagined as both utterly submitted to and compassionately connected with the sacred. As Strieber writes above, the sacred is harsh, enigmatically beautiful, and while it is hidden, it is undeniably part of the fabric of this world. I will refer to this theme—the major theme of Strieber's early period—as the hidden predator. In addition to the brief description offered by Strieber above, there are some other features of Strieber's hidden predator that appear consistently in his writing: they are portrayed as a species which shadows humanity on earth but only reveal themselves upon the moment of encounter, which is often at night, and often in bed. The encounter culminates in an act of consumption (or communion) that may be painful or horrifying, but ultimately yields religious insight for the human as prey species.

Before turning to Strieber's fiction, it is worth beginning with a brief review of the experience with which the author begins *Communion,* in order to provide a better sense of the themes I hope to draw out of Strieber's early fiction as a foundation for the ecological insights at play in his visitation narratives. *Communion* begins with Strieber awake in his bed on December 26, 1985, to find a strange-looking being in the room with him. He is paralyzed and believes his body to be somehow floating or being carried through the window. The next thing he knows, he is lying in a small depression in the woods beyond his cabin. He notices more strange-looking humanoids around him, before suddenly seeing the spinning forest around his house rapidly recede below him. Strieber is suddenly in a dark, messy room where he is the subject of what appear to be medical experiments. At this point, the author describes a physical sensation of fear so intense that he can only describe it in terms of bodily death. 'I died, and a wild animal appeared in my place,' he writes (2008, p. 16). He is eventually shown a long needle which one of the humanoids says will be inserted into his brain. Although Strieber claims that he does not recall making any noise, another humanoid steps forward and calmly asks him, 'What can we do to help you stop screaming?' Strieber's response is strange, and he writes that he does not recall why he says it: 'You could let me smell you.' Strieber describes a scent like cardboard before hearing a bang, and a feeling that the proposed operation in his brain was complete.

Strieber's visitation on the night of the 26th concludes with a particularly violent and invasive sexual interaction, of which he writes: 'at the time I had the impression that I was being raped, and for the first time I felt anger' (2008, p. 21). He suddenly awakes the next morning with the distinct impression of a large barn owl on his windowsill. Throughout the rest of *Communion,* Strieber attempts to at first deny the reality of his experience, before a combination of therapy, hypnosis, and the corroborating reports of his family and friends at the cabin gradually lead him to accept some kind of reality behind the night of December 26 (2008, pp. 1-21).

Communion was published in 1987, when Strieber was already well known as a bestselling author. His first novel, *The Wolfen,* demonstrates that the theme of the hidden predator was already a developed concept when it was published in 1978, nearly a decade before the publication of *Communion.* The plot of *The Wolfen* revolves around two detectives with the New York Police Department who are tasked with solving a number of strange murders in the city, which they eventually attribute to an extremely intelligent and reclusive species of canine that preys on human beings. In one passage in the novel, a zoologist named Carl Ferguson turns to Montague Summers' classic book *The Werewolf* for answers. 'What marvelous beings they must be,' Ferguson muses, while reading Summers: ' ... a virtual alien intelligence right here at home ... they were a race of living ghosts, unseen but very much a part of the world' (Strieber, 1979, pp. 140-141).

The similarities here between the alien intelligence of the canine wolfen and the visitors of *Communion* are obvious enough to render further description almost redundant. In each case, humanity finds itself unknowingly accompanied by a hidden species on earth that renders human beings physically helpless in the moment of encounter. In a passage which is particularly startling for its similarity to *Communion*, Carl Ferguson reaches into the depths of his childhood to find memories of monsters:

> He remembered ... an incident that had occurred when he was no more than six or seven. They were in the Catskills, spending the summer near New Paltz in upstate New York. He was asleep in his ground-floor bedroom. Something awakened him. Moonlight was streaming in the open window. And a monstrous animal was leaning in, poking its muzzle toward him, the face clear in the moonlight. He had screamed and the thing had disappeared in a flash. Nightmare, they said. And here it was, staring at him again (1979, p.149).

It is difficult to read such a passage, written more than a decade before *Communion*, without recalling the streams of repressed traumatic memories—many of them from his own childhood—that the author would suddenly recall in the following decade. Equally evident is Strieber's troubled relationship with his own doubting superego: 'Nightmare, they said.' Indeed, when he awoke nearly a decade later in a cabin near New Paltz on the morning of December 27th, 'nightmare' is precisely what he would tell himself. As Strieber himself suggests, his own early novels appear to be unconscious expressions of the presence of a hidden predator throughout his own life, an alien intelligence in the back of his mind and on the covers of his novels.

Like humanoid visitors of *Communion*, the canines in *The Wolfen* exhibit feelings of compassion that border on the erotic for their victims. As Strieber describes the wolfen moving in on their prey, he writes, 'They loved him, lusted after him, moved closer to him' (1979, p. 61). This compassionate love between predator and prey in Strieber's writing is always somehow reciprocal. In another scene of childhood recollection after an encounter with the wolfen, the protagonist Detective Wilson recalls a childhood moose-hunting trip with his father. As his father is about to pull the trigger on an aging bull, a pack of gaunt-looking timber wolves emerge from the forest. Rather than flee or charge, the bull simply watches the wolves closing in. 'You'd never believe it. The damn wolves wagged their tails!' Wilson remembers. 'It was like they agreed together that the killing could be done. The wolves and the moose agreed.' When Detective Becky Neff asks Wilson why he is telling her this strange story, he responds with a cryptic and troubling insight: 'I'm the bull moose' (1979, p. 68). Later, Wilson asks himself what the old bull felt for the wolves: ' ... was it love, or fear so great that it mimicked love?' (1979, p. 128). There is mutual understanding and even something like love behind the violent exchange of predator and prey.

Another important aspect of Strieber's hidden predator is an uncanny, beautiful, and frightening face. Throughout *The Wolfen*, Strieber depicts victims who are humbled by the strange mixture of the beautiful and the terrible in the faces of the canines that are about to devour them. The novel describes the faces of the wolfen as 'almost serene in their deadliness. They had lips, strange sensitive lips,' 'Cruel, enigmatic, strangely beautiful,' 'Fierce, inhuman,' and 'weird, like a human.' The hidden predator with a sublime, uncanny face appears again and again throughout Strieber's fiction, compelling emotions ranging from absolute terror to sexual ecstasy. The face of Strieber's hidden predator is always human-like but not quite human, and it always has a certain ineffable quality, confounding any attempt at description. In *The Wolfen*, Strieber depicts a mauled police officer trying to describe their faces with his dying words: ' ... you'll never get it' (1979, pp. 125, 203, 254, 229).

As the descriptions from *The Wolfen* suggest, these faces seem to teeter on the edge of humanity without getting it quite right. It is a description that recalls other allusions to the uncanny valley, an aesthetic term referring to the feeling of repulsion and attraction that can accompany an image which is simultaneously recognizable as human and nonhuman. Descriptions of the uncanny valley abound in environmental writing. To provide one example, Charles Darwin describes this feeling upon looking into the eyes of a snake in a journal entry from 1845:

The expression of this snake's face was hideous and fierce ... I do not think I ever saw anything more ugly, excepting, perhaps, some of the vampire bats. I imagine this repulsive aspect originates from the features being placed in positions, with respect to each other, somewhat proportional to the human face; and thus we obtain a scale of hideousness. (1845, p. 97)

Communion is crawling with comparable descriptions of the unsettling inhumanity of the visitors: 'It is incredibly upsetting to see something that is clearly not human walking and moving about with intelligence,' Strieber writes. 'There is something that is unmistakable about the precision of consciously directed movement that is deeply frightening when seen in such an alien form' (2008, p. 121). Like Darwin looking into the eyes of a snake, Strieber's hidden predator shows a proportional similarity to the human that nauseates author and reader alike. The sickening and revolting quality of the uncanny valley is most succinctly expressed by Strieber's character Rich Fields, a photographer who, after an encounter with the wolfen, merely whispers 'Had a sort of ... face. Good Christ,' before refusing to say more (1979, p. 228).

In Jacques Derrida's 1997 address 'The Animal That Therefore I Am,' he describes his own experience of the compelling gaze of the visitors. Derrida's visitor, however, is his small cat, who watches him while he is naked in his bathroom. Derrida finds something haunting in the little cat's obvious interiority, and (for Derrida) the stunning and unavoidable conclusion that when he looks at his cat, *something looks back*. In an unabashedly prophetic and apocalyptic tone, Derrida seems to see something of both the real limits of himself, of philosophy, of the human, and of the horizon of phenomenological possibility, naked in the eyes of his cat:

As with every bottomless gaze, as with the eyes of the other, the gaze called animal offers to my sight the abyssal limit of the human: the inhuman or the ahuman, the ends of man, that is to say the bordercrossing from which vantage man dares to announce himself to himself, thereby calling himself by the name that he believes he gives himself. And in these moments of nakedness, under the gaze of the animal, everything can happen to me, I am like a child ready for the apocalypse, *I am (following) the apocalypse itself*, that is to say, the ultimate and first event of the end, the unveiling and the verdict. (Derrida, 2002, p. 381)

Strieber's second novel continues to develop many of the same themes. While *The Wolfen* saw Strieber transposing werewolf legend into a horrifying ecological reality of human predation, his 1981 novel *The Hunger* would see him do the same with the vampire, despite never using that particular word in the text. *The Hunger* follows Miriam Blaylock, an ancient being who feeds on the blood of human beings to retain her youth and remembers her birth taking place while Egyptian civilization was still young. Reading both novels today, Strieber's erotic depictions of Miriam killing and eating human beings are less shocking than some of those in *The Wolfen*, since audiences today are perhaps more used to sexualized depictions of vampiric violence. Still, the unsettling juxtaposition of sexuality, the sacred, and violent predation is present here as it is in *The Wolfen* and *Communion*.

Strieber also continues to depict the sublime, uncanny face of the predator. He writes, 'Miriam did not look a thing like a human being, but she was *beautiful* ... the face was so noble, so much at peace that just seeing it made Sarah want to sob out the petty passions of her own humanity and have done with them forever' (Strieber, 2001, p. 309). Sarah Roberts, the protagonist of the novel, wants to weep away her humanity after seeing Miriam without makeup for the first time. The fierce combination of curiosity and horror, repulsion and desire, permeates Strieber's own descriptions of the visitors' faces in *Communion*, in which he writes:

> She had those amazing, electrifying eyes ... the huge, staring eyes of the old gods ... They were featureless, in the sense that I could see neither pupil nor iris ... There was in her gaze an element that is so absolutely implacable that I had other feelings about her, too. In her presence I had no personal freedom at all. I could not speak, could not move as I wished. (2008, p. 100)

In the face of the predator, whether she takes the form of Mariam Blaylock or the visitors, Strieber and his characters (and Jacques Derrida, for that matter) are both helplessly submitted and completely enamored. As a reader, one suspects that, as we were warned by the mauled police officer in *The Wolfen*, we will 'never get it.'

One of the most striking and frightening statements from the visitors comes as a response to Strieber's protests during the initial abduction experience. In a transcription of Strieber's recollection of the night of the 26th under hypnosis, when he is informed that they are about to perform the operation on his brain with a long needle, he understandably reacts with serious distress. 'I'm not gonna let you do an operation on me. You have absolutely no right,' he declares. The visitors' response is simple and devastating: 'We do have a right' (2008, p. 76). Strieber's sense of his own personal freedom evaporating in the face of a predator is made explicit in this response. He is the mauled police officer. He is Sarah Roberts watching Miriam Blaylock remove her makeup. He is helpless.

Returning to 'The Animal That Therefore I Am,' Derrida proposes a rather simple definition of the animal, a category of being that he suggests has been more or less ignored by Western philosophy: 'The animal is a word, it is an appellation that men have instituted, a name they have given themselves the right and the authority to give to another living creature' (2002, p. 392). Rather than describing some bio-ontological reality or elegant taxonomic designation, for Derrida, 'animal' is simply a word that designates authority, the authority of one organism over another. Whitley's recognition of himself as a wild animal during that experience reinforces Derrida's notion of animality as helplessness, a power-relation of forced submission. The animal cannot resist its designator in any sustained, meaningful way. 'How odd it was,' Strieber writes, 'to find oneself suddenly under the very power that one so easily assumes over the animals' (2008, p. 103).

Much later in the book, when Strieber describes attending a support group for other abductees at the invitation of Budd Hopkins, he meets a woman named Sally who uses nearly identical language to describe her memories of the experience of being with the visitors: 'Absolute terror. I felt like an animal, totally warped and totally working on the instant,' she says of her own encounter. Hearing her, Whitley responds, 'that's how I felt' (2008, p. 261). Derrida could not have put it better than Whitley or Sally. They were both made subject to others who had given themselves the *right* to them.

Here I would like to project some insight into Whitley and Sally's shared experience of being reduced to a state of animal helplessness from the environmental feminist philosopher Val Plumwood. In Plumwood's 1995 essay 'Human Vulnerability and the Experience of Being Prey,' the author recounts her experience of being attacked by a crocodile in the paperbark wetlands of Kakadu National Park in the Northern Territory of Australia. In the moment of the attack, she describes witnessing the world, as she puts it, 'from the outside' for the first time:

The course and intensity of terminal thought patterns in near-death experiences can tell us much about our frameworks of subjectivity ... In that flash, when my consciousness had to know the bitter certainty of its end, I glimpsed the world for the first time "from the outside," as no longer my world, as raw necessity, an unrecognisably bleak order which would go on without me, indifferent to my will and struggle, to my life as to my death. (Plumwood, 1995, p. 30)

Plumwood's experience of the world 'from the outside,' that is, beyond the confines of her everyday subjectivity, resonates in interesting ways with Sally and Whitley's sensation of themselves as becoming animals during their visitation experiences. Plumwood is one of a very small number of organisms who have experienced a crocodile's death-roll and lived to tell us about it, although it is an experience she does not attempt to reduce to words. She writes, 'It is, essentially, indescribable, an experience beyond words of total terror; total helplessness, total certainty, experienced with undivided mind and body' (1995, p. 31). Plumwood's description of her experience is almost interchangeable with Whitely and Sally's memories. Sally's terror was 'absolute,' Plumwood's was 'total.' They each describe the same unyielding, monolithic sensation of physical fear that permeates the text of *Communion.* In fact, Strieber originally planned to call the book 'Body Terror' rather than *Communion,* since this overwhelming physical sensation was, to him, the overarching theme of the entire visitation experience.

But there is something significant that is present in Strieber's predator which is absent in Plumwood's crocodile. While Plumwood obviously derived some philosophical insight from her time in those spinning jaws, there was none of the reciprocity, compassion, and even love that one sees in Strieber's hidden, predatory visitors. In one passage of *Communion,* Strieber wrestles with the sense that he was simply prey, or livestock, acknowledging that his experience felt that way at times, but ultimately concluding that it was only part of the story.

Try as I might, I simply did not have the feeling that the visitors were applying the same cold ethic to their relationship with us as we did to ours with the animals. There was something of that in it though, very definitely. I had been captured like a wild animal on December 26, rendered helpless and dragged out of my den into the night. (2008, pp. 103-104)

Strieber uses the phrase 'cold ethic' in reference to the extreme subjugation of laboratory animals and livestock, and while there was 'something of that in it,' Strieber insists that there was something more to his visitation experiences. There is physical pain, there is body terror, but there is also something that moves Strieber, that compels him to seek further contact, to change the title of his book to *Communion*.

It is this compulsion which, I suggest, sets apart Strieber's corpus–in particular his early period, under consideration here–as an experiential and literary vision of the sacred within an ecological metaphor of predator-prey relation. Strieber's fixation with owls and wolves stems from a personal religious tendency in which he is both violently subjected to and utterly enamored with the appearance of the numinous in his own life. It may at first seem counter-intuitive that a person like Strieber, an American author born in San Antonio who spent much of his life in New York City, should find the interaction of predator and prey so religiously compelling. Why would a New York author in the late twentieth century, so far removed from the struggles of predator and prey, derive so much personal meaning from his interaction in his own writing, both fictional and nonfictional?

A glance at the ethnographic record makes Strieber seem less unusual in this regard. The Brazilian anthropologist Eduardo Viveiros De Castro has suggested that the religious significance of predation – both by and on human beings – appears across cultures with apparent independence from those cultures' reliance on hunting as a food source. De Castro writes, 'Horticulturalists such as Tukano or Juruna ... do not differ much from circumpolar hunters in respect to the cosmological weight conferred on animal predation' (1998, p. 472). Viveiros De Castro is referring to comparative approaches between indigenous Amazonian cosmologies, but his point remains relevant: regardless of actual food source, the religious or cosmological 'weight' bestowed on animal predation remains significant across cultures. Hunter, farmer, or urban author – everyone recognizes the religious significance of hunting, killing and eating someone else.

Indeed, the simple act of consumption – whether it is predatory, sexual, or explicitly sacramental – is itself replete with latent religious meaning. The Russian theologian Sergei Bulgakov suggests that food, and the physical act of eating, is rather obviously analogous to religious ideas and behavior:

The boundary between living and nonliving is actually removed in food. Food is *natural communion* – partaking of the flesh of the world. When I take food, I am eating world matter in general, and in so doing, I truly and in reality find the world within me and myself in the world, I become part of it. (2000, p. 103)

To expand Bulgakov's sentiment here, not only is the boundary between living and nonliving removed in the act of eating, but the boundary between the self and the world, between nature and culture, begins to blur as well. As the saying goes, you are what you eat – in Strieber's case, when this action is imbued with such an array of religious and ecological meanings, you are what eats you.

The origins of Strieber's emphasis on a sacramental religion of communion and consumption might be traced to the author's Catholic upbringing, as has been pointed out by Jeffrey Kripal (2011, pp. 304-305). It is easy to imagine something like the hidden predator gradually arising in the imagination of a young Whitley Strieber, eating the flesh of God at Mass once a week. What sets Strieber apart, of course, is the depth in which this theme appears to run in his work, and his capacity to express it repeatedly in the varied guises of vampire and visitor, fiction and nonfiction. As I suggested at the outset of this chapter, Strieber's written corpus puts the relationship between religion and literature on vivid display. As Georges Bataille famously suggested, 'Following upon religion, literature is in fact religion's heir. A sacrifice is a novel, a story, illustrated in a bloody fashion' (1962, p. 87). Strieber's personal narrative of an encounter with the numinous, written and rewritten in both novel and memoir, rings true with Bataille's claim.

Strieber's own son seemed to intuit this fact on a deeper register in a particularly touching episode in the book, with which I will conclude. In this passage, Strieber clarifies that at the time, he had never discussed the visitors or his own personal experiences with his young son. This being the case, he was understandably distressed to hear his son describing beings who would come to him at night, small bug-eyed things he called the 'thin ones.' One day, as father and son were enjoying reading to each other from a book of haiku, Strieber's young son commented on a poem: 'That was really a lot of pictures for so little words.' He goes on to say, seemingly out of nowhere: 'Dad, you know, we like the haiku and all the beautiful words. But the thin ones, it's like they are the haiku. Inside, they are haiku' (2008, pp. 221-222).

I do not want to give the sense that I have exhausted the reaches of Strieber's ecological esotericism. I have not had space to touch on Strieber's novels *Warday* and *Nature's End,* which are particularly focused on the possibility of ecological disaster following nuclear and environmental catastrophe. Both of these works predate *Communion,* and Strieber has suggested that they are his own unconscious expression of regular warnings he receives from the visitors regarding the dangers of humanity toying with its environment. Strieber's eschatological gnosis in these and other works deserves its own comprehensive treatment that I have not touched on here. Rather, I have attempted to draw out, in an abbreviated fashion, what I consider the major theme of Strieber's early period: the literary metaphor of predator and prey expressing a deeper, personal religious tendency, in which the human is imagined as both completely submitted to and compassionately connected with the sacred.

Questions

1. Whitley Strieber, Charles Darwin, and Jacques Derrida all provide examples of the uncanny valley in their writings. What are some other examples of the uncanny valley, and why do you think humans tend to find it so upsetting?

2. Whitley Strieber is a fiction author who weaves personal religious experience and philosophical themes into his fiction. What are some other examples of fiction authors (they do not have to be science-fiction or horror authors, but those are good places to start) who use the medium of fiction to elaborate personal religious or paranormal beliefs and experiences?

3. This chapter contains a few different accounts of human-animal encounters (Darwin's snake, Plumwood's crocodile, Derrida's cat, and Strieber's owl). What are the similarities and differences in the encounters themselves and in their reported effects on the humans who describe them? How are these accounts similar (or different) from the other accounts of human-animal encounters in other chapters in this book?

4. Following the chapter's argument about the religious significance of predator-prey interactions, can you think of other ecological

relationships (organism/environment, symbiosis, poisons, medicines) that take on religious meaning in certain cultural contexts?

CHAPTER 17

PSYCHIC NATURALISM

Elorah Fangrad, Rick Fehr, and Christopher Laursen

~

Meta-analyses of parapsychological studies, such as those presented by Dean Radin (1997; 2006; 2013), have shown that evidence favours the existence of psi phenomena such as telepathy and psychokinesis. But what of the *nature* of psi, particularly in how it occurs spontaneously and meaningfully in people's lives? The philosopher and parapsychologist Stephen E. Braude argues that 'the real trailblazers' who study psychical phenomena will be those who recognize that controlled parapsychological laboratory experiments tell us little about the nature of psychic functioning. Studying psi in its natural environment, particularly when it is recurrent, is best done in a way similar to a biological naturalist, he writes, to 'record and systematize the subtleties of broad ranges of organic behavior.' In this, 'the psychic naturalist' observes, documents, and analyses the nature of psi phenomena with 'perceptivity and sensitivity' (2014, pp. 174-76). In essence, the psychic naturalist examines the function of psi in its greater ecology. In this chapter, we will expand Braude's idea of 'psychic naturalism' with a proposed model of how we intend to study an active case of recurrent anomalous phenomena experienced in a rural area.

Inspired by the historian of religions Jeffrey J. Kripal (2011; 2014; 2019), we propose that the methodology of psychic naturalism be activated in the interdisciplinary humanities (where 'consciousness studies consciousness'). Humanities and social science scholars would collaborate with those who directly experience the phenomena and various experts (for example, relevant scientists). Such a collaboration would combine ongoing naturalist-inspired observation, thickly descriptive documentation, relatively inexpensive technological innovations to maintain the study, and interdisciplinary analyses that take into consideration both the physical and ontological environments of the individuals and places involved. In other words, the entire ecology around the place in which anomalous events recur are taken into consideration.

In designing the psychic naturalist model, we intend to lift barriers in how parapsychologists (and others) have defined psi to propose a larger scale re-examination of the holistic possibilities of the super natural and super consciousness (the adjective 'super,' as Kripal notes, accentuating nature and consciousness beyond current comprehension but nonetheless experienced and tangible, albeit elusive). The model provides follow through on Jack Hunter's concept of 'ontological flooding' in which all ways of being are treated as valid, even if it destabilises what is considered 'consensus reality' (2015; 2016; 2017). The psychic naturalist may collect all available data, including that considered 'paranormal,' and conduct a more holistic 'ecological' assessment of the interplay of nature and consciousness in lived realities. Initially, psychic naturalism draws from naturalist observation, oral history and testimonial collection, new humanities scholarship that integrates participant-experience, as well as technological possibilities that make it feasible.

In an upcoming study of anomalous recurrent phenomena experienced at an Ontario fishing lodge, the authors – the historian Dr. Christopher Laursen, the scholar of environmental studies Dr. Rick Fehr, and the scholar of Indigenous studies and theology and, as a worker at the lodge, participant-experiencer Elorah Fangrad – will employ the psychic naturalism model outlined in this chapter. Using the model, the authors seek to understand the interplay between anomalous phenomena, history, land, and the inhabitants. A model for psychic naturalism is outlined in this chapter.

Elusive Nature

Ideally, naturalists enter the world without preconceived ideas of the lifeways of particular species of the ecosystems they inhabit. The naturalists are open to discovery. This is not to say naturalists approach the world without methods to frame what they experience. Rather, naturalists have done their research, they have experience in the world, and they have experience with the prior literature of the world. Should the world behave as the literature predicted, naturalists can confirm the efficacy of their observational methods.

However, if the species and the ecosystems behave in ways contrary to the literature, two questions arise. Are the naturalists' observations and experiences rejected in favour of the literature? Or, do the observations and experiences inform new literature? If the inquiry is framed more by method and less by encounter, the method effectively makes the reality conform to its vision of species behaviour, the ecosystems they inhabit, and indeed the world. If, however, the findings are guided by the encounter, new dimensions of understanding are opened - not only of the species, but of the ecosystems they inhabit, the world and reality. In essence, this latter approach does not dam(n) the data, but allows the flood of information gathered to stand as part of the ecological whole, even if it does not make sense according to existing literature. There is a balance to be achieved between what is understood and what is uncertain or strange (Hunter, 2016).

One of the greatest challenges in psi research has long been the elusive nature of the phenomena not conforming to method and the repetition of experiment. Contemporary discourse on anomalistic parapsychology, for example, assumes that psi is not real – that it operates 'in terms of known (or knowable) psychological and physical factors' (French & Stone, 2014, p. 1). In classic Rhinean parapsychology still practiced by the majority of parapsychologists today, that which cannot be replicated in research settings cannot be validated as actual phenomena (Laursen, 2016).

Perhaps the problem rests with the notion of research and methods as the foundation for such inquiry. Conventional methods are effective at exploring all manner of phenomena in the realm of science, technology, and society - particularly in research addressing critical scientific and societal barriers and the ways to ameliorate them (Law, 2004). The realm of psi, however, is considerably different because of the deeply subjective and apparently illogical nature of the phenomena.

The seemingly illogical nature at play here is often described as tricksterism, and it is on full display in events at the fishing lodge. As George Hansen offers in *The Trickster and the Paranormal* (2001), there is a region of ambiguity and liminality in which expression of normalcy are inverted for brief periods of time. In the work of Victor Turner (1961/2017), this zone is described as anti-structure, and it provides the basis for the fundamental transformation of people journeying through various stages of life.

There is a fumbling occurrence that unfolds with encounter during such times of transition and in the places they occur. While it may on one level be described as extraordinary, in ecological settings it may be entirely ordinary and a part of the natural process of relationship building and sustainability with place. This encounter exists outside of the silence of words written on the page, and instead resides in the orality of relived experiences around campfires. Storytelling, therefore, as it happens in the moment, is an active yet elusive agent in moments of sharing when encounters of the day or days past are recalled. Indeed, this is foundational to mythic oral literature (Bringhurst, 2002), in which the mutable forces of nature often share characteristics with super natural experiences. Far from being confined to the spectre of the 'paranormal,' events can also manifest as apparently mundane sequences, albeit with the trickster's twist. Consider the following account from the Ontario fishing lodge. In 2017, while two members of our team visited the lodge for a natural observation exercise, there was an extended encounter among them with the lodge's staff. It was facilitated by the environment as embodied by an interplay of two trickster tropes - the rabbit and the fox - between humans and non-humans.

There was a discussion among the group about how plentiful the partridge population was that year. Staff members talked about how it was almost impossible to avoid them on the trails or in the forest, and if they ever wanted lunch, all they had to do was step outside and shoot one. A male staff member said he was going to go out and shoot one early in the afternoon, and he said the cook, a female, could clean the partridge and cook it for the team. The hunter went into the woods and only returned several hours later when the sun was close to setting, well after when he should have returned.

The hunter said he could not find a single partridge for hours. Finally, when he was about to return empty handed, he heard rustling in the fallen leaves. On aiming his shotgun, he saw a partridge and took his shot. The wounded animal scrambled around the leaves until the hunter shot again, hitting his mark, which was not a partridge at all, but a cottontail rabbit. Confused, but satisfied with his prey, the hunter left the rabbit for the cook to clean and prepare for the staff. The cook refused to clean the hunter's kill, and said she was not going to prepare the food simply because a man told her she should. She added that if he wanted the animal cleaned and cooked that badly, he could do it himself, but not to assume she should do it just because she was a woman.

The event extended to a disagreement between the two as the entire group sat around the campfire that night. As they were talking, a red fox appeared a few yards away, apparently curious and hoping for some food scraps. Some of the staff threw bits of hot dog for the animal. The fox made it clear it was not leaving anytime soon, and the staff were reluctant to feed it all of their hot dogs. But the hunter, possibly feeling conflicted about the rabbit situation, decided to offer the rabbit fur, feet, and head to the fox. The hunter set about skinning the rabbit and cleaning it, as the cook said he should have done all along. The fox was now satisfied with its meal, and the hunter successfully prepared the rabbit.

The account of the partridge, the rabbit, and the fox at the fishing lodge exemplifies how the non-human environment, in this case the animal actors, divert expectations of normalcy. The broader implications of relationship building in this case are triggered through the agency of animals in inverting human expectations about the roles of hunters / males and cooks / females. This transforms the situation. As a springboard, such zones of engagement are carried out on a scale of unexplainable phenomena at the fishing lodge. There is a blurring between what is natural and super natural, ordinary and extraordinary that speaks to the totality and interconnectedness of nature and consciousness. All of it counts as ecology.

Experiencing the Camp

The research was initiated by the experiences of co-author Elorah Fangrad, who has been employed at the lodge for five seasons. She notes that extraordinary experiences arise every season.

The majority of experiences are reported by the predominantly female kitchen and housekeeping staff. They spend most work hours indoors, and similar phenomena are reported year after year in the same buildings by different staff. Housekeepers have seen 'light' or 'dark' figures in cabins and related the figures to a male form or presence. Another recurring experience was the sudden manifestation of walls or drafts of frigid air concurrent with a deep sense of paranoia. Some staff additionally heard voices or footsteps. A standalone experience over a decade ago involved an unseen force shattering a glass light shade across a room toward a housekeeper's feet. These figures, voices, and other phenomena are always described as frightening and invasive, and experiences can be troubling to the staff for long periods.

In the 2018 season, kitchen staff experienced a new phenomenon that they termed a 'poltergeist.' They witnessed utensils, cookware, or pantry items tossed, thrown, pushed, or shaken – sometimes by distances of a few feet – apparently by an unseen force. This activity happened up to several times a week, usually in the morning, and often in front of multiple employees. It intensified directly in July 2018 before a propane dryer in an adjoining laundry room caught fire. After the fire, the poltergeist activity lessened. The poltergeist-type activity was never assigned the same level of negativity as other phenomena; it was interpreted as an ambivalent and at times positive force giving a warning. Later in the season, the poltergeist moved outside of the kitchen and into the lodge, where footsteps, voices, and opening doors (which were confirmed to be latched shut) were heard by breakfast shift staff before guests entered.

Fangrad has observed that over past seasons, dockhands and guides, more often men who spend most hours outdoors, report fewer phenomena. Their experiences tend to involve lightforms or unidentified objects, and voices heard in the forest. A dockhand taking a boat across the lake at night was followed by a green orb that kept pace with his boat for some distance, then disappeared into the trees. Soon after, he heard movement in his room one night, and items and furniture in his room were rearranged when he woke up. Two dockhands out on the lake early in the morning witnessed a 'ghost boat' speed toward them, then vanish. Before and after the experience, they heard sounds and voices in the bush surrounding their residence. Dockhands and the male lodge owner heard a female voice speaking an unfamiliar language for a sustained period as they hiked towards a nearby Indigenous ceremonial site. A hunting guide and his group reported hearing children's voices and laughter while roaming old logging trails in the same area. Dockhands have seen figures appear indoors, but in contrast to the housekeepers reporting frightening indeterminate forms, they described the figures as human males in fishing attire who may or may not have had their full body visible. They called these figures 'ghosts' and theorized them to be spirits of past guests. Generally, the dockhands do not express feelings of lasting vulnerability or danger when they encounter phenomena.

An experience shared by both the kitchen and dock staff occurred in September 2016. While out on the staff residence deck around midnight, Fangrad and a few employees witnessed lightforms in the shape of green orbs multiply in the sky over the lodge, move about erratically for minutes, then disappear into the trees on the shoreline. These orbs matched the descriptions from the aforementioned dockhand and a local ice fisherman who tried to outrun a green orb on his snowmobile. Staff collectively expressed curiosity rather than fear.

Few guests, who are predominantly male, have given reports. Longtime visitors comfortable enough to share theirs have described a variety of phenomena, from a male apparition cooking in their cabin at 3:00 a.m. to a blinding spotlight appearing over a boat to having intense paranoia and nightmares. Some guests state that they were disturbed, but others seem indifferent.

Extraordinary experiences are shared as oral stories. Around a campfire or a game of cards, employees feel enough trust in their coworkers to tell their story, or will reflect on a shared experience. At times, they hesitate to share because they previously stated that they 'did not believe in ghosts' or are 'not spiritual or religious.' Newcomers are not easily included. Many senior staff do not tell new hires of their experiences until months into the season. In an experimental attempt not to influence new hires, by 2017, Fangrad began to hold back her own campfire stories, only revealing past experiences and her academic interests when an employee came to her with their story. The same phenomena continue to be reported, and reports from herself and the other staff have increased.

Reluctance to Report

In Summer 2018, Fangrad, Fehr, and Laursen designed an anonymous questionnaire for staff to fill out. Participants were also allowed to record video or audio. While some employees initially showed interest, no surveys were submitted. The dominant reason given was that it was unclear if information would remain confidential and how it would be used. Confidentiality protocols and an overview of the research were included in the survey document, but these concerns point to a discontinuance with the oral format of describing highly personal experiences within the staff group. Staff were uncomfortable with written or recorded formats and sharing their stories with outsiders.

People who experience anomalous phenomena tend to withhold what happened to them except among a trusted circle of individuals. They do not intend for their experiences to be shared publicly. Historically, this has been a common deterrent to effectively studying psi. Recurrent anomalous events such as those at the lodge enable an opportunity to draw from multiple experiencers over an extended period of time. Even though many people experience these events together, it does not make them more open to sharing with researchers. Charles Tart (1994, and with Mishlove, 2017), Stephen Braude (2014), and Jeffrey J. Kripal (2019) are among those who have pointed out how a 'fear of psi' or of 'paranormal' events impacts the willingness of people to share, or for effective research to be completed. There is a stigma over how others will view these experiences because they do not fit consensus reality.

Field studies in particular depend on the effective collaboration between experiencers and researchers. In his 2016 study of historical poltergeist research, Laursen found that the most successful research that advanced understanding of the phenomenon was that in which field researchers deliberately employed empathy, drew on varied expertise in multidisciplinary alliances, and collaboratively observed events with experiencers. In other words, the successful outcomes of the research depended on researchers' dispositions: warmth, caring, and open-mindedness toward experiencers and phenomena, all while conducting methodical, thickly described observations and interviews to gain a holistic impression of what was happening and who was involved (Laursen, 2016, pp. 136-137, 151-161, 182).

Psychical researchers and parapsychologists often anonymized the experiencers (that is, did not reveal their real names and sometimes even excluded their locations), providing only necessary details. Personal narratives were at times adjusted as to not identify specific individuals. This could not always be avoided as media often reported these details prior to researchers' arrivals; those later cases involving media tended to be far more difficult to manage, and experiencers could be publicly harassed and even stigmatized. Just as with naturalist studies, the site should be carefully preserved, particularly to avoid 'paranormal tourism' which may exploit the delicacy of the ecosystem in which the events take place.

The authors developed the 'psychic naturalist' methodology for this investigation of the fishing lodge over a one-year period. It began with gaining permissions in October 2017. Fangrad and Fehr travelled to the lodge to speak with the owner, two dockhands, and a cook, all of whom approved sharing accounts orally. Anonymity was emphasized. However, due to the remoteness of the lodge and hectic academic schedules, only Fangrad was present during the summer of 2018; the survey was seen as a feasible way to collect descriptive first-hand accounts. Since experiencers submitted no surveys, for this chapter Fangrad compiled her own oral narratives and stripped them of features that would identify staff or locations. From lessons learned in the development of this project to date, in this chapter, Fangrad, Fehr, and Laursen refine the methodology to apply in the 2019 season which will involve Fangrad working as an insider and using oral interviewing.

Emic (or insider) approaches are most effective in gaining access to, effectively sharing, and analysing personal experiences that otherwise are inaccessible. For example, New York City firefighters have tended not to share their experiences and emotions on how they coped with the attacks on the World Trade Center in 2001. Michael Ripoll (2018) created a model as a retired New York City firefighter, demonstrating how he could interview his own colleagues as someone already known and trusted to uncover how they coped. Such a model could be duplicated by other fire service people to expand the study. As such, Fangrad, having an established place of trust among co-workers and guests at the fishing lodge, will take on the insider role as we apply our psychic naturalist methodology in 2019, on which we'll report in a second part to this chapter (to be announced on Laursen's website).

The Psychic Naturalist Collaborative Model

With the grounds for our model introduced in relation to a case study where we will actively apply it, the rest of this chapter outlines the intentions of the model itself, starting with a table summarizing it and in which we refer to ourselves as 'personnel,' moving away from the 'subject' or 'object' oriented studies to ones in which we are embedded and sensitive to the ecological context. A future follow-up to the study will demonstrate if our intentions were successful, how we refined the model, and the results. The authors hope the model will incite discussion in relation to the content of this book and welcome input that might improve it.

Table 1: Mapping the Intentions of the Psychic Naturalist
Collaborative Model

	On-Site	Off-Site
Personnel	**Participant-Experiencer(s)** Emic presence (being there)	**Interdisciplinary Scholar(s)** Etic absence (staying away)
Method of Observation	Natural: Giving things time and letting them happen as they will without expectation or seeking.	Maintain the model: Adjusting and expanding the methodology according to real-life dynamics.
Documentation	Gathering: Seamless, spontaneous documentation through oral collection from experiencers and creating perceptive, sensitive reflections as the emic observer.	Contextualizing: Historical-geographic study of human, non-human, and ecological factors. Technology: Maintaining all documentation online.
Sharing	Share: Gathering people together to talk when the moment is right (e.g. campfire conversations).	Collaborate: Ongoing cloud- and audio/video conference-based collaborative conversations and idea generation between personnel.

	On-Site	Off-Site
Analysis	Feedback: Sharing data and conceptual analyses in plain language with key people on-site. Documenting and including their viewpoints. Providing opportunities for collaborative learning.	Ecological Reconstruction: Considering the whole of the data in relation to ecology (assumed to be conscious systems) and disseminating in a way that generates both public and academic understanding and stimulates scientific curiosity.
Contribution	Enhances Quality of Local Lives: Develops a greater understanding between scholars and non-scholars, humans and non-humans, and humans in their ecological settings.	Knowledge: Expands models of how to study nature and consciousness in relation to the ecological whole, and potentially to better live in and study nature.
Next Steps	Building Better Ecological Relationships: Continuing the study depends on the continued presence of an emic observer and developing training on ecological stewardship that includes nature in all of its forms.	Advancing Interdisciplinarity: Inviting further expertise to actively analyse in a growing interdisciplinary collaboration the evidence in a way that refines the model and knowledge of the phenomena and experiences.

Table 1 maps the intentions of the psychic naturalist collaborative model. As exemplified below, in our study, Fangrad as a longstanding employee at the fishing lodge provides the crucial emic presence. Since she will be at the lodge again in 2019, she will literally 'be there.' More than fulfilling the traditional etic anthropological role of a 'participant-observer,' Fangrad is a part of the lodge community, and she has experienced, and may continue to experience, some of the phenomena in question directly. We situate emic personnel as participant-experiencers; they are a true insider.

Fehr and Laursen, while they may visit the lodge with sensitivity, largely will do their work off-site. They 'stay away.' All three collaborate together in this process. And while Fangrad also steps into the scholarly roles noted in the 'Off-Site' work column, her central role that cannot be duplicated by any etic personnel is that of emic presence, being there as an insider who has special access to the experiences of the ecology.

A porous boundary between the on-site and off-site work enables the collaboration. But there are standards in the on-site investigation to be upheld to maintain the natural conditions of ecological and social interactions in which anomalous phenomena have been experienced. In studies of paranormal cases, very often the arrival of etic researchers disrupts those conditions. Psychic naturalism approaches these environments with sensitivity not to disturb the conditions in which anomalies occur.

Below, we exemplify each element of the psychic naturalist model – the on-site and off-site work – in relation to how we intend to implement it in our 2019 study of the fishing lodge.

Natural Observation/Maintaining the Model

Natural observation has many approaches. Some naturalists choose to obscure their presence in their environments to study non-humans (for example hiding in camouflage tents to avoid frightening the animals they study). Others cordon off parts of nature into artificial grids, or remove samples of it to study off-site, which transforms nature in ways that humans can make sense of it in their own terms (Latour, 1999). Psychic naturalism takes into consideration philosophical ideas that consciousness is present beyond humans, so the interactions between humans, non-humans, and other types of phenomena are openly considered (see Kripal, 2019, Chapter 3 for an overview of the major models of consciousness). Therefore, the emic participant-experiencer as a member of the existing ecology is less prone to disturb the circumstances in which anomalous phenomena recur.

The participant-experiencer, as Fangrad has demonstrated, can be or become a direct observer of anomalous phenomena. Again, this is not about 'looking for it,' as it typical among many researchers, but 'letting it happen' when it will. Overcoming expectations that anything will be directly experienced (or won't be experienced) helps enable natural observation. The participant-experiencer's ongoing presence enables this method of observation. Fehr and Laursen's task then is to maintain the model, which is not to enforce is as it is written, but rather adjust course as required. The model must be dynamic and responsive to the ecology.

Documentation: Gathering/Contextualizing

Fangrad's co-workers at the lodge primarily interact orally. Sometimes they share experiences, at other times later, when they feel ready to share. Stories are often told in passing, when she is working with them. There is comfort between Fangrad and the lodge staff, and it is much like telling stories with friends around a campfire. Such a natural interactive approach to collecting data is crucial to psychic naturalism.

Equally important is considering the backgrounds of the experiencers. Academic research is an alien concept to most outside of the academy. At this site, most employees have focused on the trades or wildlife management versus university. In effect, participant-experiencers must 'be themselves' and empathetically relate to those around them, living with them, while subtly using their academic training to ask good questions and draw out thick descriptions of the experiences in a way that makes those in their community comfortable.

Technologies continue to advance in ways that enable psychic naturalism as a collaborative model to operate inexpensively. Smart phones enable on-the-spot recording in a non-invasive way since the majority of people are now familiar with the devices. This is different than a few decades earlier when field researchers needed to use (often bulky) audio and video recorders that even seemed more invasive. With a smart phone, the participant-experiencer can use their best judgment as to whether the person relating the experience is more comfortable with just audio or being videoed with the phone. Furthermore, notes can be taken on the same device. It enables multiple means of spontaneous documentation. The participant-experiencer's smart phone would require adequate memory and apps, increasingly standard among such devices, and having a portable power source to avoid battery depletion.

Likewise, in off-site work, digitization of existing information has revolutionized access to a wide array of materials that help contextualize places and peoples. Training in critically assessing the authorship of sources combined with collecting oral histories of places from the perspective of 'rewilding' – or thinking anew about places and peoples – updates and expands ecological knowledge. (See, for example, the websites for the Alliance for Wild Ethics and Rewild.com for more on this concept.) In other words, while Fangrad is busy on-site, Fehr and Laursen piece together a historical-geography of the fishing lodge and its surrounds, taking into consideration human interactions, non-human ecology, abiotic land (that creates desires for certain resources), and the phenomena in relation to Indigenous and non-Indigenous knowledge.

Sharing/Collaborating

Further to the spontaneous reportage of experiences to and by Fangrad herself, the methodology involves 'creating the campfire' around which stories can be gathered. The participant-experiencer, already intimately familiar with the environment and the people in it, creates spontaneous moments in which it feels right to socialize and share.

The interpersonal presence and sharing avoids the 'chasing down' that researchers and media alike tend to enact toward anomalous phenomena. It is more of a 'let's just be here and let things happen as they will.' Like how naturalists explore their environment with minimal disturbance. Being a familiar part of it, quietly observing, taking note while not concerning those around them with the research in progress.

Fangrad, Fehr, and Laursen created a space (using a cloud server, Google Drive) in which documentation is shared online on an ongoing basis between the on-site participant-experiencer and the off-site colleagues. The team can conference together via collaborative documents, video and audio conferencing, and other tools.

Analysis: Ecological Reconstruction/Feedback

The work of reconstructing the experiences of anomalous phenomena in relation to the greater ecology is, in essence, the process of writing (or creating other media). Too often scholarly studies are detached from public understanding. There is so much scholarly material produced, and scholars themselves are so busy, that information is inadequately shared. This prevents proper follow through.

We propose to remedy this in the psychical naturalism collaborative model through further steps that extend the analysis into a process of sharing the data and gaining feedback from key people from the site, which provides an opportunity for collaborative learning between the study's personnel and the community.

Contribution: Enhancing Quality of Local Lives & Knowledge-Making

Ideally, the model creates understanding between scholars and communities. The feedback and collaborative learning between the two create a better understanding of relationships between humans and non-humans, and how people live (or can live better) in their ecological settings. In turn, the knowledge created through this model expands how scholars study nature and consciousness in relation to the ecological whole.

The next steps would be to build better ecological relationships through stewardship that is perceptive, sensitive, and attentive, both to the physical/sensed elements of nature and that which is elusive, but still part of the ecology. This is taking stewardship into more complex territory where the public understanding and ongoing awareness of interconnected ecologies can be put more into daily practice. How that could happen remains to be seen.

Step by step, the model could be reapplied to deepen the interdisciplinary collaborations. More experts, who will have insights into the data collected, can investigate through the model to add knowledge. Existing knowledge created within epistemological boundaries could be applied and challenged. Allowing ontological flooding, the 'anomalous' or 'paranormal' data undammed (or 'undamned') through the psychic naturalist model creates new possibilities to understand the ecological whole as well as its components.

The ideas here may be getting lofty. We all know the realities of limited time and resources, politics, and the various obstacles encountered that block significant needs in scholarly and scientific studies. All one can expect is the unexpected. But perhaps the psychic naturalist collaborative model, with its holistic intentions of capturing the interconnectedness of ecology, will illuminate far more fruitful pathways in comprehending elusive nature.

Questions

1. How does psychic naturalism attempt to advance psi studies beyond the laboratory-based experimental model?

2. How is psychic naturalism more thorough than paranormal investigations you have seen on television or read about?

3. How would you apply a psychic naturalist methodology to another case study, not only those in wilderness settings like the lodge, but in any kind of setting, including urban settings?

4. What is the relationship between psychic naturalism and storytelling?

5. At the end of the chapter, the authors write about limitations and obstacles. Specifically, what types of obstacles might you encounter in such a study, and how could you overcome them?

BIOGRAPHIES

~

Paul Devereux is the co-founding managing editor of the peer-reviewed Routledge publication, *Time & Mind: The Journal of Archaeology, Consciousness and Culture* (www.tandfonline. com/rtam), and was a Research Affiliate with the Royal College of Art (2006-2016). He is also an author of 27 mainstream books for general readers, some of them international titles, academic papers, contributory book chapters, and numerous articles for non-specialist publications, including *Readers Digest, Time-Life, New Scientist, Focus, Financial Times*, etc. In addition, he is a columnist, UK and international freelance lecturer, occasional broadcaster, and an independent researcher.

Viktória Duda, PhD., has a doctorate in social anthropology from the University of Vienna, Austria. She devotes her work to the study of consciousness, both as researcher as well as an internationally practising hypnotherapist. Her main research areas are multidimensional experiences, archetypal experiences and the therapeutic use of past life regressions. She is member of the British Society of Clinical Hypnosis. Visit her website at www.viktoriaduda.com

Elorah Fangrad is always looking for an adventure. As a writer, artist, researcher, fishing lodge manager, and amateur bush pilot, she seeks creativity and challenges in remote locations. She graduated with a Bachelor of Theology & Religious Ethics from Western University (2016) and a diploma in Indigenous Wellness & Addictions Prevention from

Canadore College (2019), and hopes to contribute to holistic community wellness through the arts and the stories waiting to be found.

Rick Fehr, PhD., has a doctorate in Environmental Studies, and focuses much of his research on settler and Indigenous histories in the lower Great Lakes. Rick has published research on the Baldoon Mystery, Canada's most documented poltergeist, and he is working on a project with Dr. Christopher Laursen on the event. He is originally from Wallaceburg, Ontario, the community built by the surviving Baldoon settlers. Over the past couple of years, Rick has turned his attention to writing fantasy fiction.

Lance M. Foster is an anthropologist and member of the Iowa Tribe of Kansas and Nebraska, where he works in the tribal culture and history division (THPO). He received his undergraduate degree in anthropology/archaeology and Native American Studies from the University of Montana, and his graduate degrees in Anthropology and Landscape Architecture (cultural landscapes/landscape history) from Iowa State University. He has worked in cultural and historic preservation for the National Park Service and the Office of Hawaiian Affairs, as well as an instructor for the University of Montana system. He is an artist and published author of a number of works, including the book *Indians of Iowa* (University of Iowa Press, 2009) and numerous other articles on folklore, history and archaeology, such as "Haunted Archaeologies" (2012).

Jacob W. Glazier, PhD., LPC, NCC is an Adjunct Professor in the Department of Positive Human Development and Social Change at Life University and an online Adjunct Professor in the Department of Applied Psychology at New York University–Steinhardt. His work has been published in academic journals that include *Psychoanalysis, Culture & Society, Paranthropology, Subjectivity, Mortality, Critical Horizons, Rhizomes, Journal for Cultural Research*, and others. He is under contract with Bloomsbury Publishing for a forthcoming book entitled, *Arts of Subjectivity: A New Animism for the Post-Media Era* (2019).

Timothy Grieve-Carlson is a PhD student in the department of Religion at Rice University. Tim received his Bachelor's degree in cultural Anthropology and Religious Studies in 2013 from Drew University in

Madison, New Jersey. Tim holds a certificate for the study of Gnosticism, Esotericism and Mysticism (GEM) from the department of Religion at Rice, where his doctoral research focuses on ecological thought and the paranormal in early American religion.

Jack Hunter, PhD., is an Honorary Research Fellow with the Alister Hardy Religious Experience Research Centre, University of Wales Trinity Saint David, and is a Research Fellow with the Parapsychology Foundation. He is the founder and editor of *Paranthropology: Journal of Anthropological Approaches to the Paranormal* and the author of *Why People Believe in Spirits, Gods and Magic* (2012) and *Engaging the Anomalous* (2018). He is the editor *of Strange Dimensions: A Paranthropology Anthology* (2015), *Damned Facts: Fortean Essays on Religion, Folklore and the Paranormal* (2016), and co-editor with Dr. David Luke of *Talking with the Spirits: Ethnographies from Between the Worlds* (2014).

Christopher Laursen, PhD., is a social and cultural historian of religions, science, and nature focusing on modern America and the world. He teaches at the University of North Carolina Wilmington. He currently studies family lineage and psi, especially related to visitation and premonition dreams. He holds a doctorate in History from the University of British Columbia (2016) where he studied the psychologization of the poltergeist, and an MA from the University of Guelph (2009). His writing has appeared in volumes edited by Jeffrey J. Kripal, Jack Hunter, D.W. Pasulka, Simone Natale, and Sylvana d'Angelo, and in the magazine Fortean Times.

David Luke, PhD., is Senior Lecturer in Psychology at the University of Greenwich where he has been teaching an undergraduate course on the Psychology of Exceptional Human Experience since 2009. His research focuses on transpersonal experiences, anomalous phenomena and altered states of consciousness, especially via psychedelics. He has published more than 100 academic papers in this area, including seven books, most recently *Otherworlds: Psychedelics and Exceptional Human Experience* (2017). David is co-founder and director of *Breaking Convention: International Conference on Psychedelic Consciousness*. He has given over 200 invited public lectures and conference presentations and lives life on the edge, of Sussex, UK.

Susan Marsh is a freelance writer whose work focuses on forgotten histories, cosmic jokes and monsters in all their many forms. She is based in Bristol, where she helps to run an anarchist bookshop and enjoys collecting stories from the margins of life.

Cody Meyocks is a sporadic writer on the paranormal, anarchism, spirituality, and wilderness skills. He has published an essay in the British anarcho-primitivist anthology *Dark Mountain #4* titled 'Real Adventures with Unreal Creatures in Southern Oregon' in which he considers the relationship between the ecology of the unseen and the encroachment of a culture of non-believers. In other articles he has tried to glean the repercussions of modern culture's relativism, materialism, and estrangement from nature on industrial society's ability to understand and integrate some of the most profound facets of existence, which largely reside outside the framework of the modern culture's worldview – in that shifting and anomalous twilight realm of the paranormal

Silvia Mutterle, MA, was born in Italy and nourished a close rapport with birds since childhood. She is a licensed falconer, and has been working with birds of prey for the past 14 years. Over this time she has witnessed the healing produced from the interaction of humans with wild animals in natural settings. After completing a Master's degree in anthro-zoology with the University of Exeter in 2016, shas moved back to Italy and founded Falconeria ZEN, an organization that promotes Mindulfulness Based Stress Reduction through close encounters with birds of prey, combined with forest bathing. She is currently facilitating activities involving birds of prey and US veterans returning from deployment, aiming to ease PTSD and substance abuse issues.

Mark A. Schroll, PhD., is best known for his papers on ecopsychology, transpersonal psychology, and the anthropology of consciousness. He is the author of over 35 academic articles in various edited books, journals and magazines. He is the founder of the International Association for Transpersonal Ecosophy and is the editor of *Transpersonal Ecosophy Vol. 1* (2016) and *Ecology, Cosmos and Consciousness* (2018).

Amba J. Sepie, PhD., is an interdisciplinary scholar who writes, publishes, and teaches in the areas of indigenous and cultural studies, anthropology, geography, sociology, history, spirituality, and religion. Her doctorate is in Human Geography and her current research is focused on academic and social resistance to indigenous and Earth-centred ways of knowing, being, and healing.

Christine Simmonds-Moore, PhD., is a UK native. Her doctoral work with the University of Northampton explored "Schizotypy as an anomaly-prone personality." She is currently working as an Associate Professor of Psychology at the University of West Georgia. She has research interests in the psychology of exceptional experiences (including transpersonal and subjective paranormal experiences), paranormal beliefs and disbeliefs, personality and mental health correlates of exceptional experiences, synesthesia, altered states of consciousness, mind body relationships and healing and placebo effects. She is the recipient of several Bial grants to study exceptional experiences, and is currently completing a research study on ghost experiences. She is the co-author of a textbook on Anomalistic psychology and has edited a collection of chapters about Exceptional Experiences and Health.

Brian Taylor, PhD., has a doctorate in applied social sciences. His doctoral thesis was published as *Responding to Men in Crisis; Masculinities, Distress, and the Postmodern Political Landscape.* (Routledge, 2005). From the late eighties, kingfishers – and various other birds and animals – began to enter his life in a profound way, heralding and illuminating a protracted bereavement. With his partner he instigated a non-hierarchical group that celebrated the seasonal festivals for about five years, and has since been a contented solitary practitioner of what he eventually came to think of as (one of many possible varieties of) animism. He has a blog exploring animism at: https://animistjottings.wordpress.com

Maya Ward, PhD., works to foster ethical and spiritual connection to place grounded in embodied, intuitive and intellectual understanding of interdependency. Her doctorate in Creative Writing explored the ecological and evolutionary underpinning of archetypal experience, referencing neuroscience, psychology and shamanistic metaphysics, soon to be published as a book. Her memoir *The Comfort of Water: A River Pilgrimage* (Transit Lounge, 2011) is an account of her 21-day trek from the sea to the source of the Yarra River, following the length of a Wurundjeri Songline. She also works in the areas of permaculture and sustainability education and design, dance facilitation and community arts in Victoria, Australia. www.mayaward.com.au

Simon Wilson, PhD., achieved his first publication aged ten, a letter to his local paper reporting a UFO sighting. He is now a Senior Lecturer at Canterbury Christ Church University, with a long list of publications on a variety of topics, including the Grail, René Guénon, colour symbolism, Charles Fort, the visionary architecture of the Facteur Cheval, and the imaginal history of a Cambridge college. He is also the editor, with Dr. Angela Voss, of *Re-enchanting the Academy* (2017), and a member of the Institute for Orthodox Christian Studies in Cambridge.

Nancy A. Wisser was born in and lives in eastern Pennsylvania with her husband Eric. She has a passion for nature, and native wildflowers in particular. She operates the Clonehenge blog about Stonehenge replicas and also the Geopsych blog on Tumblr where she posts pictures of the places and living things she loves. She spent four years as non-member tribal secretary for the Lenape Nation of Pennsylvania. A full story of her life would be like a great and at times humorous poem, hopefully building to a satisfying ending.

References

Abram, D. (1996). *The Spell of the Sensuous, Perception and Language in a More-than-Human World*. New York: Vintage.

Ahenakew, C. (2011). 'The birth of the 'Windigo': The construction of Aboriginal health in biomedical and traditional Indigenous models of medicine.' *Critical Literacy: Theories and Practices*. Calgary: University of Calgary.

Alcock, J. E. (2003). 'Give the null hypothesis a chance: Reasons to remain doubtful about the existence of psi.' *Journal of Consciousness Studies*, 10(6-7), pp. 29-50.

Alvarado, C.S. (2009). 'Late 19th- and Early 20th-Century Discussions of Animal Magnetism.' *International Journal of Clinical and Experimental Hypnosis*, 57(4), pp. 366-381.

Ancient Egypt (2013). 'Gods and Goddesses.' [online] Ancientegypt. co.uk. Available at: http://www.ancientegypt.co.uk/gods/explore/main. html [Accessed 5 Feb. 2016].

Anderson, R. & Braud, W. (2011) *Transforming self and others through research. [electronic resource] : transpersonal research methods and skills for the human sciences and humanities*. Albany: State University of New York Press. (Suny series in transpersonal and humanistic psychology).

Anomalistic Psychology Research Unit (2019). Goldsmiths, University of London. Retrieved from https://www.gold.ac.uk/apru/

Armstrong, E. (1959) *The Folklore of Birds*. Boston: Houghton Mifflin.

Armstrong, E. (1973). *Saint Francis: nature mystic*. Berkeley: University of California Press.

Asante, M. K. (1984). 'The African American mode of transcendence.' *Journal of Transpersonal Psychology*, 16(2): 167-177.

Astley, Jeff (2002). *Ordinary Theology: Looking, Listening and Learning in Theology*. Aldershot: Ashgate.

Avatar (2009). [film] Los Angeles: James Cameron.

Azuma, R. (1997) 'A Survey of Augmented Reality.' *Presence: Teleoperators and Virtual Environments*, 6(4), pp. 355-385.

BBC (2018). 'Amazon rainforest deforestation 'worst in 10 years', says Brazil.' Available Online: https://www.bbc.co.uk/news/world-latin-america-46327634 [Accessed 30/11/2018].

Bachcentre.com (2009). 'Dr Bach's system of 38 flower remedies.' [online] Available at: http://www.bachcentre.com/centre/remedies.htm [Accessed 16 Feb. 2016].

Backster, C. (1968). 'Evidence of Primary Perception in Plant Life.' *International Journal of Parapsychology*, X(4), pp. 329-348.

Bader, C.D., Mencken, F.C. & Baker, J.O. (2017). *Paranormal America: Ghost Encounters, UFO Sightings, Bigfoot Hunts, and Other Curiosities in Religion and Culture*. New York: New York University Press.

Banissy, M.J. & Ward, J. (2007). 'Mirror-touch synesthesia is linked with empathy.' *Nature Neuroscience*, 10, pp. 815–816.

Baptista, J., Derakhshani, M. & Tressoldi, P. E. (2015) 'Explicit anomalous cognition: A review of the best evidence in ganzfeld, forced choice, remote viewing and dream studies.' In E. Cardeña, J. Palmer, & D. Marcusson-Clavertz (Eds.), *Parapsychology: A handbook for the 21st century* (pp. 192-214). Jefferson: McFarland & Co.

Barratt, B. (2010). *The Emergence of Somatic Psychology and Bodymind Therapy: Critical Theory and Practice in Psychology and the Human Sciences*. London: Palgrave MacMillan.

Barratt, E. L. & Davis, N. J. (2015) 'Autonomous Sensory Meridian Response (ASMR): a flow-like mental state.' *Peerj*, 3, p. e851. doi: 10.7717/peerj.851.

Barros, R.G., (2009). 'Message to the Younger Brother: Wisdom Teachings of the Kaggaba-Wiwa People', in L. Hogan (ed.), *The Inner Journey: Views from Native Traditions*, Morning Light Press, Sandpoint, Idaho, pp. 20-25.

Batailles, G. (1962). *Erotism: Death & Sensuality*. San Francisco: City Lights Books.

Batcheldor, K.J. (1984). 'Contributions to the Theory of PK Induction from Sitter-Group Work.' *Jounral of the American Society for Psychical Research*, 78, pp. 105-122.

Bateson, G. (1979). *Mind and Nature*. New York: E. P. Dutton.

Beilharz, P. (2001). *The Bauman Reader*. Oxford: Blackwell.

Beischel, J., Boccuzzi, M., Biuso, M. & Rock, A. (2015). 'Anomalous Information Reception by Research Mediums Under Blinded Conditions II: Replication and Extension.' *EXPLORE*, 11(2), pp. 136-142.

Belz, M., & Fach, W. (2012). 'Theoretical reflections on counseling and therapy for individuals reporting EE (exceptional experiences).' In: E. W. Kramer, E. Bauer, & G. H. Hovelmann (Eds.) *Perspectives in clinical parapsychology*. Bunnik: Stichting Het Johan Borman Fonds. (pp.267–269).

Berceli, D. (2008). *The Revolutionary Trauma Release Process: Transcend Your Toughest Times*. Vancouver: Namaste Publishing.

Bergandi, D. (2011). 'Multifaceted Ecology Between Organicism, Emergentism and Reductionism.' In A. Schwarz & K. Jax (eds.) *Ecology Revisited: Reflecting on Concepts, Advancing Science*. Dordrecht: Springer. (pp. 31-43).

Bergson, H. (1913). 'Presidential address.' *Proceedings of the Society for Psychical Research*, 27, pp. 157-175.

Berry, T. (1999). *The Great Work: Our Way into the Future*. New York: Bell Tower.

Best, S. (2017). 'Is our addiction to smartphones getting out of hand?' *Daily Mail* [online]. Available at https://www.dailymail.co.uk/sciencetech/article-5122041/7-people-checked-phone-SEX.html [Accessed 31 Dec. 2018]

Beyer, S. (2009). *Singing to the plants: A guide to mestizo shamanism in the upper Amazon*. Albuquerque, NM: University of New Mexico Press.

Biello, D. (2010). *Slash and Sprawl: U.S. Eastern Forests Resume Decline* [Online] Available at: https://www.scientificamerican.com/article/us-eastern-forests-resume-decline/?redirect=1

Bigfoot Field Researchers Organization. (2017). 'Pre-Columbian and Early American Legends of Bigfoot-like Beings.' [Online] Available from: http://www.bfro.net/legends/ [Accessed 12/11/2018].

Bird-David, N. (1999) '"Animism" Revisited, Personhood, Environment, and Relational Epistemology.' *Current Anthropology*, 40, pp. 67-91.

Bird-Rose, D. (2013) 'Val Plumwood's Philosophical Animism.' *Environmental Humanities*, 3, pp. 93-109.

Blake, W. (2010). *The Pickering Manuscript*. Whitefish, Montana: Kessinger Publishing.

Boggs, L. J., Fisher, D. & Flint, G. A. (1973) 'Technical note: The "pink" noise generator: An apparatus for inducing relaxation.' *Behavior Therapy*, 4(2), pp. 267–269.

Bohm, D. (1993). 'Science, spirituality, and the present world crisis.' *ReVision: Journal of Consciousness and Change*, 15(4), pp. 147-152.

Botelho, M.I.V., Cardosa, I.M. & Otsuki, K. (2016). '"I made a pact with God, with nature and with myself": exploring deep ecology.' *Agroecology and Sustainable Food Systems*, 40(2), pp. 116-131.

Bouchard, D.F. (1977) *Language, Counter-Memory, Practice; Selected Essays and Interviews by Michel Foucault*. Ithaca: Cornell University Press.

Boyd, C.E. & Thrush, C. (2011). 'Introduction: Bringing Ghosts to Ground.' In Boyd, C.E. & Thrush, C. (eds). *Phantom Past, Indigenous Presence: Native Ghosts in North American Culture & History*. Lincoln: University of Nebraska Press.

Bracken, P. (2002). *Trauma; Culture, Meaning, and Philosophy*. London: Whurr Publishers.

Bradbrook, G. (2019). 'Do psychedelics hold the key to social change?' *Emerge* [online]. Acailable at: http://www.whatisemerging.com/opinions/psychedelics-and-social-change

Brain Bar (2018). 'My Greatest Weakness is Curiosity: Sophia the Robot at Brain Bar.' [video]. Available at https://www.youtube.com/watch?v=Io6xuGmS5pM [Accessed Dec 1. 2018].

Bratman, G., Hamilton, J., Hahn, K., Daily, G. & Gross, J. (2015). 'Nature Experience Reduces Rumination and Subgenual Prefrontal Cortex Activation.' *Proceedings of the National Academy of Sciences*, 112(28), pp. 8567-8572.

Braude, S.E. (2014). *Crimes of Reason: On Mind, Nature, and the Paranormal.* Lanham: Rowman & Littlefield.

Brenner, E.D., Stahlber, R., Mancuso, S., Vivanco, J., Baluska, F. & Van Volkenburgh, E. (2006). 'Plant neurobiology: an integratedview of plant signalling.' *TRENDS in Plant Science*, 11(8), pp. 413-419.

Briggs, R. (1996). *Witches and Neighbours.* London: Harper Collins.

Bringhurst, R. (2002). "Mythology." In W.H. New (ed.) *Encyclopedia of Literature in Canada.* Toronto: University of Toronto Press.

Brockbank, J. (2011) 'The Responsive Cosmos: An Enquiry into the Theoretical Foundation of Astrology.' Unpublished PhD thesis: University of Kent. http://www.the9thhouse.org/theses.htm

Brody, H (2000). *The Other Side of Eden; Hunter-Gatherers, Farmers, and the Shaping of the World.* London: Faber and Faber.

Brogaard, B. & Marlow, K. (2015). *The superhuman mind: Free the genius in your brain.* New York: Hudson street press.

Brown, D. J. (2009). 'Special issue: Psychedelics and ecology.' *Bulletin of the Multidisciplinary Association for Psychedelic Studies*, 19 (1).

Brown, Jr. Tom. (1999). *The Science and Art of Tracking: Nature's Path to Spiritual Discovery.* New York: Berkley.

Buhner, S.H. (2014) *Plant Intelligence and the Imaginal Realm: Beyond the Doors of Perception Into the Dreaming of the Earth.* Rochester: Inner Traditions.

Bulgakov, S. & Evtuhov, C. (2000). *Philosophy of Economy: The World as Household.* New Haven; London: Yale University Press.

Campbell, J. (1949). *The hero with a thousand faces.* Princeton: Princeton University Press.

Camus, A. (1937). *L'envers et L'endroit.*

Caraway, R.T. (2018). 'The Spiritual Dimensions of the Permaculture Movement in Cuba.' *Religions*, 9(342), pp. 1-17.

Cardeña, E. (2005) 'The phenomenology of deep hypnosis: quiescent and physically active.' *The International Journal of Clinical And Experimental Hypnosis*, 53(1), pp. 37–59.

Cardeña, E., Lynn, S. J., & Krippner, S. (eds.) (2014). *Varieties of Anomalous Experience: Examining the Scientific Evidence*. Washington, DC: American Psychological Association.

Cardeña, E., Palmer, J., & Marcusson-Clavertz, D. (eds.) (2015). *Parapsychology: A handbook for the 21st century*. Jefferson: McFarland & Co.

Carpenter, J. C. (2004) 'First Sight: Part One, a Model of Psi and the Mind.' *Journal of Parapsychology*, 68(2), p. 217.

Carwardine, M. (2008). *Animal Records*. New York: Sterling.

Castaneda, C. (1968). *The teachings of Don Juan: A Yaqui Way of Knowledge*. Berkeley: University of California Press.

Castaneda, C. (1981). *The eagle's gift*. New York: Simon and Schuster.

Castaneda, C. (1984). *The fire from within*. New York: Simon and Schuster.

Castro, M., Burrows, R. & Wooffitt, R. (2014). 'The Paranormal is (Still) Normal: The Sociological Implications of a Survey of Paranormal Experiences in Great Britain.' *Sociological Research Online*, 19(3), pp. 1-15.

Caswell, J. M., Hunter, J., & Tessaro, L. W. E. (2014). 'Phenomenological convergence between major paradigms of classical parapsychology and cross-cultural practices: An exploration of paranthropology.' *Journal of Consciousness Exploration and Research*, 5(5), pp. 467-482.

Chaplin, J. (2016). 'The global greening of religion.' *Palgrave Communications*, 2(16047). doi: 10.1057/palcomms.2016.47.

Chapman University (2018). 'Paranormal America 2018: Chapman University Survey of American Fears.' Available Online: https://blogs.chapman.edu/wilkinson/2018/10/16/paranormal-america-2018/ [Accessed 17/01/2018].

Cheetham, T. (2015). *Imaginal Love: The Meanings of Imagination in Henry Corbin and James Hillman*. Thompson: Spring Publications.

Cheetham, T. (2005). *Green Man, Earth Angel: The Prophetic Tradition and the Battle for the Soul of the World*. Albany: State University of New York Press.

Claridge, G., Clark, K. & Davis, C. (1997) 'Nightmares, dreams, and schizotypy.' *The British Journal of Clinical Psychology*, 36(3), pp. 377–386.

Clark, J. (1998) *The UFO Book: Encyclopedia of the Extraterrestrial.* Detroit: Visible Ink Press.

Clarke, D. & Roberts, A. (2007). *Flying Saucerers: A Social History of UFOlogy.* Loughborough: Alternative Albion.

Cohn, N. (1975). *Europe's inner demons.* New York: Basic Books.

Cooper, T.W. (1998). *A Time before Deception: Truth in Communication, Culture, and Ethics: Native Worldviews, Traditional Expression, Sacred Ecology.* Santa Fe: Clear Light Publishers.

Corbin, H. (1977). *Spiritual Body and Celestial Earth: From Mazdean Iran to Shi'ite Iran.* Princeton: Princeton University Press.

Cornelius, G. (2003). *The Moment of Astrology, Origins in Divination.* Bournemouth: Wessex Astrologer.

Cousins, N. (1979). *Anatomy of an illness as perceived by the patient.* New York: Norton.

Crawley, S. E., French, C. C. & Yesson, S. A. (2002). 'Evidence for transliminality from a subliminal card-guessing task.' *Perception*, 31(7), pp. 887–892.

Creager, A. & Jordan, W. (2002). *The animal-human boundary.* Rochester: University of Rochester Press.

Curry, P (2012). 'Revaluing Body and Earth.' In E. Brady & P. Phemister (eds.) (2012). *Human-Environment Relations: Transformative Values in Theory and Practice.* Dordrecht: Springer. Available online: http://www.patrickcurry.co.uk/papers/Revaluing%20Body,%20Place%20and%20Earth.pdf

Curry, P. (2010). *Divination, Perspectives for a New Millennium.* Farnham: Ashgate.

Cutchin, J. (2015). *A Trojan Feast: The Food and Drink Offerings of Aliens, Faeries and Sasquatch.* Charlottesville: Anomalist Books.

Cutchin, J. (2018). 'The High Strangeness of Bigfoot.' *Woodknocks: Journal of Sasquatch Research*, 3, pp. 95-124.

Dams, L. (1985). 'Palaeolithic lithophones: descriptions and comparisons.' *Oxford Journal of Archaeology*, 4(1).

Daniels, M. (2005). *Shadow, Self, Spirit: Essays in Transpersonal Psychology.* Exeter: Imprint Academic.

Daniels, M. (2013). 'Three vectors of transpersonal development.' In: H. Friedman & G. Hartelius (eds.) (2013). *The Wiley-Blackwell Handbook of Transpersonal Psychology.* West Sussex: John Wiley and Sons.

Darwin, C. (1845). *Journal of Researches Into the Natural History and Geology of the Countries Visited During the Voyage of H.M.S. Beagle Round the World: Under the Command of Capt. Fitz Roy,* Volume 2. London: J. Murray.

Davis, J. (2011). 'Ecopsychology, transpersonal psychology, and nonduality.' *International Journal of Transpersonal Studies,* 30 (1-2), 89-100.

Davis. J.V. & Canty, J.M. (2013). 'Ecopsychology and Transpersonal Psychology' In Friedman, H. L., & Hartelius, G. (eds.) (2013). *Handbook of Transpersonal Psychology.* NY: Wiley-Blackwell.

Davis, W. (1999). 'San Pedro, cactus of the four winds.' *Shaman's Drum,* 52, pp. 51-60.

Davis, W. (2001). *Light at the Edge of the World: A Journey through the Realm of Vanishing Cultures.* London: Bloomsbury.

Dawkins, R. (1982). *The Extended Phenotype.* Oxford: Oxford University Press.

Dayle, J., Laughlin, C., McManus, J., d'Aquili, E., Schwartz, T., White, G. & Lutz, C. (1994). 'Brain, Symbol and Experience: Toward a Neurophenomenology of Human Consciousness.' *Anthropologica,* 36(1), p.113.

De Martino, E. (1975). *Magic: Primitive and Modern.* London: Tom Stacey.

Derr, J. S. & Persinger, M. A. (1989). 'Geophysical variables and behavior: LIV. Zeitoun (Egypt) apparitions of the Virgin Mary as tectonic strain-induced luminosities.' *Perceptual and Motor Skills,* 68(1), pp. 123–128.

Derrida, J. & Wills, D. (2002). 'The Animal That Therefore I Am (More to Follow).' *Critical Inquiry,* 28(2), pp. 369-418.

Devereux, P. (1982). *Earth Lights: Towards an Explanation of the UFO Enigma.* London: Book Club Associates.

Devereux, P. (1989). *Earth Lights Revelation: UFOs and Mystery Lightform Phenomena: The Earth's Secret Energy Force.* London: Blandford.

Devereux, P. (1991). 'Three-dimensional aspects of apparent relationships between selected natural and artificial features within the topography of the Avebury Complex.' *Antiquity*, 65.

Devereux, P. (1992). *Symbolic Landscapes: The Dreamtime Earth and Avebury's Open Secrets*. Glastonbury: Gothic Image Publications.

Devereux, P. (1996). *Re-Visioning the Earth: A Guide to Opening the Healing Channels Between Mind and Nature*. New York: Atria Books

Devereux, P. (1997). 'The archaeology of consciousness.' *Journal for Scientific Exploration*, 4, pp. 527-538.

Devereux, P. (1999). *Earth Mysteries*. London: Piatkus.

Devereux, P. (2000). *The Sacred Place: The Ancient Origins of Holy and Mystical Sites*. London: Cassell & Co.

Devereux, P. (2001). *Haunted Land: Investigations into Ancient Mysteries and Modern Day Phenomena*. London: Piatkus.

Devereux, P. (2001a/2003). *Fairy Paths & Spirit Roads*. London: Vega/Collins and Brown.

Devereux, P. (2001b). *Stone Age Soundtracks*. London: Vega

Devereux, P. (2002). *Mysterious Ancient America*. London: Vega

Devereux, P. (2008). *The long trip: A prehistory of psychedelia*. Brisbane: Daily Grail Publishing

Devereux, P. (2010). *Sacred Geography*. London: Gaia

Devereux, P. & Wozencroft, J., (2014). 'Stone Age Eyes and Ears: A Visual and Acoustic Pilot Study of Carn Menyn and Environs, Preseli, Wales.' *Time & Mind*, 7(1) http://dx.doi.org/10.1080/1751696X.2013.860278

Devereux, P., Krippner, S., Tartz, R., & Fish, A. (2007). 'A preliminary study on English and Welsh sacred sites and home dream reports.' *Anthropology of Consciousness*, 18(2), pp. 2-28.

Devereux, P., Steele, J. & Kubrin, D. (1992). *Earthmind: Communicating with the Living World of Gaia*. Rochester, Vermont: Destiny Books.

Dobkin de Rios, M. (1996). *Hallucinogens: Cross-cultural perspectives*. Prospect Heights, IL: Waveland Press.

Dossey, L. (2012) 'Fractals and the mind.' *Explore*, 8(5), pp. 263–265. doi: 10.1016/j.explore.2012.06.010.

Drengson, A.R. & Inoue, Y. (1995). *The Deep Ecology Movement: An Introductory Anthology*. Berkeley: North Atlantic Books.

Driesch, H. (1933). *Psychical Research*. London: G. Bell and Sons, Ltd.

Dychtwald, K. (1986). *Bodymind*. New York: Tarcher/Putnam.

Earthing Institute, (2013). 'Home – Earthing Institute.' [online] Available at: http://www.earthinginstitute.net [Accessed 16 Feb. 2016].

Eden, A. & Moor, J. (2012). *Singularity Hypotheses: A Scientific and Philosophical Assessment*. Dortrecht: Springer.

Eliade, M. (1964). *Shamanism: archaic techniques of ecstasy*. Routledge & Kegan Paul: London.

Emoto, M. (2004). *The hidden messages in water*. Hillsboro, Or.: Beyond Words Pub.

Emoto, M. (2005). *The true power of water*. Hillsboro, Ore.: Beyond Words Pub.

Ereira, A. (1990). *From the Heart of the World: The Elder Brothers Warning*, Film, BBC TV/Goldsmith Foundation. Available at: https://www.youtube.com/watch?v=TqokWs1q3hI

Ereira, A., (1992). *The Elder Brothers*. New York: Knopf/Random House.

Ereira, A. (2012). *Aluna: A Message to Little Brother*, Film, Colombia/UK.

Eshleman, C. (2003). *Juniper Fuse: Upper Paleolithic Imagination and the Construction of the Underworld*. Middletown: Wesleyan University Press.

Ettinger, U. *et al.* (2015) 'Cognition and Brain Function in Schizotypy: A Selective Review.' *Schizophrenia Bulletin*, 41(S1), p. S417.

Evrard, R., Hansen, G., Kennedy, J. & Kripal, J.J. (2016). 'Trickster theory panel.' In R. Nelson (Chair), *Accessing the exceptional, experiencing the extraordinary*. Convention conducted at the first combined convention of the parapsychological association (59th) and the society for scientific exploration (35th), Boulder, Colorado, USA.

Fagg, B. (1956). 'The Discovery of Multiple Rock Gongs in Nigeria.' *Man*, 56.

Farias, M., Claridge, G. & Lalljee, M. (2005). 'Personality and cognitive predictors of New Age practices and beliefs.' *Personality and Individual Differences*, 39, pp. 979–989. doi: 10.1016/j.paid.2005.04.003

Farrell K. (ed.) (1978/1993). *Heidegger: Basic Writings*. London, Routledge.

Fenwick P. (2012). 'Dr Peter Fenwick Discusses Dying, Death, and Survival.' Interview by White Crow Books: http://whitecrowbooks.com/michaeltymn/entry/dr._peter_fenwick_discusses_dying_death_and_survival (accessed 17/3/15).

Fenwick, P. (2004). 'Dying, a Spiritual Experience as shown by Near Death Experiences and Deathbed Visions.' http://www.rcpsych.ac.uk/PDF/PFenwickNearDeath.pdf (accessed 17/3/15).

Fenwick, P. & Fenwick, E. (2008). *The Art of Dying*. London: Bloomsbury.

Fenwick, P. *et al.* (2009). 'Comfort for the Dying: five year retrospective and one year prospective studies of end of life experiences.' *Archives of Gerontology and Geriatrics*. doi: 10.1016/j.archger.2009.10.004.

Fields, S. (1992). 'The crooning of crones.' Paper presented at the Union Graduate School and University Peer Day, University of Nebraska-Kearney.

Findhorn Foundation (1975). *The Findhorn Garden: Pioneering a New Vision of Humanity and Nature in Cooperation*. Findhorn Foundation: Findhorn Press.

Fleck, J. I. *et al.* (2008). 'Special issue: Research report: The transliminal brain at rest: Baseline EEG, unusual experiences, and access to unconscious mental activity.' *Cortex*, 44, pp. 1353–1363. doi: 10.1016/j.cortex.2007.08.024

Fletcher, A. & La Flesche, F. (1972/1911). *The Omaha Tribe, vol. 1*. Lincoln: University of Nebraska Press.

Foltz, B. V. (2014). *The Noetics of Nature: Environmental Philosophy and the Holy Beauty of the Visible*. New York: Fordham University Press.

Forstmann, M., & Sagioglou, C. (2017). 'Lifetime experience with (classic) psychedelics predicts pro-environmental behaviour through an increase in nature relatedness.' *Journal of Psychopharmacology*, 31(8), 975-988.

Foster, L. (2012). 'Haunted Archaeologies.' Paper given at the 2012 Montana Archaeological Conference, April 14, 2012. Online: http://paranormalmontana.blogspot.com/2012/04/haunted-archaeologies.html

Four Arrows (2016). *Point of Departure: Returning to a More Authentic Worldview for Education and Survival.* Charlotte, North Carolina: Information Age Publishing.

Fox, W. (1990). *Toward a Transpersonal Ecology: Developing New Foundations for Environmentalism.* St Mabyn: Resurgence Books.

French, C.C. & Stone, A. (2014). *Anomalistic Psychology: Exploring Paranormal Belief and Experience.* Houndsmill, Hampshire: Palgrave Macmillan.

Friedman, H. & Hartelius, G. (Eds.) (2013). *The Wiley-Blackwell Handbook of Transpersonal Psychology.* West Sussex: John Wiley and Sons.

Furst, P. (1972). *Flesh of the gods.* New York: Praeger Publishers.

Gagliano, M., Grimonprez, M., Depczynski, M. & Renton, M. (2017). 'Tuned in: plant roots use sound to locate water.' *Oecologia*, 184(1), pp. 151-160.

Gagliano, M. (2013). 'Green symphonies: a call for studies on acoustic communication in plants.' *Behavioural Ecology*, 24(4), pp. 789–796.

Gagliano, M. (2018). *Thus Spoke the Plant: A Remarkable Journey of Groundbreaking Scientific Discoveries and Personal Encounters with Plants.* Berkeley: North Atlantic Books.

Gagliano, M., Renton, M., Depczynski, M. & Mancuso, S. (2014). 'Experience teaches plants to learn faster and forget slower in environments where it matters.' *Oecologia*, 175(1), pp. 63-72.

Gell, A. (1995). 'The Language of the Forest: Landscape and Phonological Iconism in Umeda.' In E. Hirsch and M. O'Hanlon (eds.) *The Anthropology of Landscape.* Oxford: Oxford University Press.

Gerber, R. (2001). *Vibrational medicine.* Rochester, VT: Bear & Co.

Gianotti, L. R. *et al.* (2001) 'Associative processing and paranormal belief.' *Psychiatry and Clinical Neurosciences*, 55(6), pp. 595–603.

Gilligan, C. (1982). *In a different voice: Psychological theory and women's development.* Cambridge, MA: Harvard University Press.

Giovannetti, M., Avio, L., Fortuna, P. & Pellegrino, E. (2006). 'At the Root of the Wood Wide Web: Self Recognition and Non-Self Incompatibility in Mycorrhizal Networks.' *Plant Signalling and Behavior*, 1(1), pp. 1-5.

Glazier, J. W. (2016). 'Lacan, psi and the trickster: A psychoanalysis of parapsychology.' *Australian Journal of Parapsychology*, 16(2), 163-193.

Global Oneness Project (2009). *A Thousand Suns*, Film. Available at: https://www.youtube.com/watch?v=9pUofkwL8yA

Godfrey-Smith, P. (2018). *Other Minds: The Octopus and the Evolution of Intelligent Life*. London: William Collins.

Godwin, J. (1995). *Harmonies of Heaven and Earth: Mysticism in Music from Antiquity to the Avant-Garde*. Rochester: Inner Traditions International.

Goertzel, B. & Ikle, M. (2012). 'Introduction.' *International Journal of Machine Consciousness*, 4, pp. 1-3.

Goldhahn, J. (2002). 'Roaring Rocks: An Audio-Visual Perspective on Hunter-Gatherer Engravings in Northern Sweden and Scandinavia.' *Norwegian Archaeological Review*, 35(1).

Graham, R. (2017). *UFOs: Reframing the Debate*. Guildford: White Crow Books.

Grapard, A. (1994). 'Geosophia, Geognosis, and Geopiety: Orders of Significance in Japanese Representations of Space.' In R. Friedland & D. Boden (eds.) *Nowhere: Space, Time and Modernity*. Berkeley: University of California Press.

Green, C.D. (1995). 'All that glitters: A review of psychological research on the aesthetics of the golden section.' *Perception*, 24, pp. 937-968.

Greene, F. G. (2003). 'At the edge of eternity's shadows: Scaling the fractal continuum from lower into higher space.' *Journal of Near-Death Studies*, 21(4), pp. 223–240. doi: 10.1023/A:1024006114049.

Greenwood, S. (2009) *The Anthropology of Magic*. Oxford: Berg.

Grof, S. (1988). 'The shamanic journey: Observations from holotropic therapy.' In G. Doore (ed.) *Shaman's path: Healing personal growth, and empowerment*. Boston, MA: Shambhala.

Grof, S. (2012). *Healing our deepest wounds: The holotropic paradigm shift*. Newcastle, WA: Stream of Experience Productions.

Hagens, B. (2011). 'Gebser's integral/aperspectival structure of consciousness: Its implications for a new way of investigating and understanding rock art.' *Anthropology of Consciousness*, 22(1), pp. 85-98.

Hagens, B. (2014). 'Geomantic Earthmind: Practicing Earth yoga: A response to Krippner and Schroll.' *Paranthropology*, 5(4), pp. 66-69.

Hagerhall, C.M. Laikeô, T., Taylor, R, P., Kuller, M, Kuller, R. & Martin, T.P. (2008). 'Investigations of human EEG response to viewing fractal Patterns.' *Perception*, 37, pp 1488-1494.

Hallowell, A.I. (1960). 'Ojibwa Ontology, Behavior and World View.' In G. Harvey (ed.) (2002) *Readings in Indigenous Religions*. London: Continuum. pp. 17-50.

Hansen, G. P. (2001). *The trickster and the paranormal*. Philadelphia: Xlibris Corporation.

Hansen, G. P. (2016). 'The paranormal, the trickster, and structuralist concepts.' In R. Nelson (Chair), Accessing the exceptional, experiencing the extraordinary. Convention conducted at the first combined convention of the parapsychological association (59th) and the society for scientific exploration (35th), Boulder, Colorado, USA.

Haraway, D. J. (1972). *The search for organizing relations: An organismic paradigm in twentieth century developmental biology*. New Haven, CT: Yale University Press.

Haraway, D. J. (1991a). 'Introduction.' In D. J. Haraway (ed.) *Simians, cyborgs, and women: The reinvention of nature*. New York: Routledge.

Haraway, D. J. (1991b). 'The actors are cyborg, nature is coyote, and the geography is elsewhere: Postscript to "Cyborgs at Large."' In C. Penley & A. Ross (eds.) *Technoculture*. Minneapolis: University of Minnesota Press.

Haraway, D. J. (2004). *The Haraway reader*. Routledge: New York.

Haraway, D. J. (2016). *Staying with the trouble: Making kin in the chthulucene*. Durham, NC: Duke University Press.

Harding, S. (2009). *Animate Earth: Science, Intuition and Gaia*. Cambridge: Green Books.

Harner, M. (1990). *The way of the shaman*. San Francisco: Harper & Row.

Harner, M. (2005). 'Tribal wisdom: The shamanic path.' In R. Walsh & C. S. Grob (eds.) *Higher wisdom: Eminent elders explore the continuing impact of psychedelics*. Albany, NY: State University of New York Press.

Harner, M. (2012). 'The Foundation for Shamanic Studies.' [online] *The Foundation for Shamanic Studies*. Available at: http://www. shamanicstudies.com/index.php [Accessed 15 Feb. 2016].

Harpur, P. (2010). *A Complete Guide to the Soul*. London: Rider.

Harrison, K., Straight, J., Pendell, D., & Stamets, P. (2007). 'Plant spirit.' In J. P. Harpingnies (ed.) *Visionary plant consciousness: The shamanic teachings of the plant world*. Rochester, VT: Park Street Press.

Hart, T. (2003). *The Secret Spiritual World of Children*. Maui, Hawaii: Inner Ocean Publishing, Inc.

Hartmann, E. (1991). *Boundaries in the mind: A new psychology of personality*. New York, NY: Basic Books.

Hartmann, E., Harrison, R. & Zborowski, M. (2001). 'Boundaries in the mind: Past research and future directions.' *North American Journal of Psychology*, 3(3), pp. 347–368.

Hartmann, T. (2000). *The Last Hours of Ancient Sunlight: the Fate of the World and What We Can Do*. New York: Three Rivers Press..

Hartmann, T. (2009). *Threshold: The Crisis of Western Culture*. New York: Viking.

Harvey, G. (2005). 'An Animist manifesto.' *Strange Attractor Journal*, 2, pp. 124-129.

Harvey, G. (2005*). Animism: Respecting the Living World*. London: Hurst & Company.

Harvey, G. (ed.) (2013). *The Handbook of Contemporary Animism*. Durham: Acumen.

Harvey, G. (ed.) (2003). *Shamanism: A Reader*. London: Routledge.

Harvey-Wilson, S. (2001). 'Shamanism and alien abductions: A comparative study.' *Australian Journal of Parapsychology*, 1, pp. 103-116.

Havik, G., Elands, B. H. M. & van Koppen, C. S. A. (2015). 'An encounter with one's deeper self and energy: A phenomenological study among spiritually engaged individuals in the Netherlands.' *Ecopsychology*, 7(2), pp. 75–83. doi: 10.1089/eco.2015.0007.

Hay, D. & Nye, R. (2006). *The Spirit of the Child*. London: Jessica Kingsley Publishers.

Hearn, J. (1992). *Men in the Public Eye*. London: Routledge.

Heath, P.R, (2005). 'A new theory on place memory.' *Australian Journal of Parapsychology*, 5(1), pp.40-58.

Hedges, K. (1990). 'Petroglyphs in Menifee Valley.' *Rock Art Papers*, 7.

Heidegger, M. (1993). 'The question concerning technology.' In D. F. Krell (ed.) *Basic writings*. San Francisco: Harper Collins Publishers, Inc.

Hengst-Ehrhart, Y. & Schraml, U. (2013) 'Attitudes and behaviors of Neopagans toward nature.' *Ecopsychology*, 5(4), pp. 255–264. doi: 10.1089/eco.2013.0040.

Herrick, R. & Winkelman, M. (1993). 'Shamans, Priests and Witches: A Cross-Cultural Study of Magico-Religious Practitioners.' *Review of Religious Research*, 35(2), p. 186.

Heuvelmans, B. (1956). *On The Track of Unknown Animals*. London: Rupert-Davis.

Hofman, A. (1983). *LSD – My Problem Child*. Saline, Michigan: McNaughton and Gunn.

Hoffman, C. (2011a). 'Dream delay, dream decay: Dreaming in sacred places.' *Rhine Online: Psi-News Magazine*, 3(1), pp. 33-39.

Hoffman, C. (2011b). 'Introductory overview of archaeology and cultural anthropology's shifting paradigms.' *Anthropology of Consciousness*, 22(1), pp. 69-71.

Hofmann, A., Broeckers, M., & Liggenstorfer, R. (2009). 'When one lives in paradise one is in no hurry to leave.' In A. Feilding (Ed.) *Hofmann's elixir: LSD and the new Eleusis: Talks and essays by Albert Hofmann and others*. Oxford: Beckley Foundation/Strange Attractor Press.

Holiday, J. M. (2010) 'The Word, the Body, and the Kinfolk: The Intersection of Transpersonal Thought with Womanist Approaches to Psychology.' *International Journal of Transpersonal Studies*, 29(2), pp. 103–120.

Holmes, G., Smith, T.A. & Ward, C. (2018). 'Fantastic beasts and why to conserve them: animals, magic and biodiversity conservation.' *Oryx*, 52(2), pp. 231-239.

Holroyd, S. (1979). *Alien Intelligence*. Newton Abbot: David & Charles.

Holt, N. & Simmonds-Moore, C. (2008). 'Creativity, schizotypy, paranormal experiences and mental health: Developing a new cognitive-parapsychological paradigm for the assessment of psi performance in the laboratory.' Unpublished report to the Bial Foundation.

Holt, N., Simmonds-Moore, C., Moore, S. (2007). 'Psi and cognitive disinhibition: Exploring the filters of consciousness hypothesis.' *Proceedings of Presented Papers: The Parapsychological Association 50th annual convention*, pp. 192-194.

Honorton, C, (1977). 'Psi and internal attention states.' In: B. B. Wolman (ed.) *Handbook of Parapsychology*. New York: Van Nostrand Reinhold.

Honorton, C. (1993). 'Rhetoric over substance: The impoverished state of skepticism.' *Journal of Parapsychology*, 57(2), pp. 191-214

Houran, J. *et al.* (2002) 'Haunted by somatic tendencies: spirit infestation as psychogenic illness.' *Mental Health, Religion & Culture*, 5(2), pp. 119–133. doi: 10.1080/13674670210141061.

Hultman, M., 2010. 'The Known Yet Unknown Ringing Stones of Sweden.' In J. Goldhahn, I. Fuglestvedt & A. Jones (eds.), *Changing Pictures – Rock Art Traditions and Visions in Northern Europe*. Oxford: Oxbow Books.

Hunt, H. (2014) 'Implications and Consequences of Post-Modern Philosophy for Contemporary Transpersonal Studies III. Deleuze and Some Related Phenomenologies of Felt Meaning: Psychosis and Mysticism as Inherent "Structures of Thought"', *International Journal of Transpersonal Studies*, 33(2), pp. 16–32.

Hunter, J. (2012). *Paranthropology: Anthropological Approaches to the Paranormal*. Bristol: Paranthropology.

Hunter, J. (2015). 'Spirits are the Problem: Anthropology and Conceptualising Spiritual Beings.' Paper presented to the Symposium on *Afterlife Narratives; Immortality and Human Finitude, Life after Death*, University of Leeds, 20th March.

Hunter, J. (2015). '"Between Realness and Unrealness": Anthropology, Parapsychology and the Ontology of Non-Ordinary Realities.' *Diskus: Journal of the British Association for the Study of Religion*, 17(2), pp. 4-20.

Hunter, J. (2016). 'Intermediatism and the Study of Religion.' In J. Hunter (ed.) *Damned Facts: Fortean Essays on Religion, Folklore and the Paranormal*. Paphos: Aporetic Press.

Hunter, J. (2017). 'Ontological Flooding and Continuing Bonds.' In D. Klass & E.M. Steffen (eds.) *Continuing Bonds in Bereavement: New Directions for Research and Practice*. London: Routledge.

Hunter, J. (2018a). *A Study of Spirit Mediumship in the UK: Towards a Non-Reductive Anthropology of the Paranormal*. Unpublished PhD Thesis: University of Bristol.

Hunter, J. (2018b). 'Preliminary Report on Extraordinary Experience in Permaculture: Collapsing the Natural/Supernatural Divide.' *Journal of Exceptional Experiences and Psychology*, 6(1), pp. 12-22.

Hunter, J. (2019). 'Harmony and Ecology.' In N. Campion (ed). *Harmony Papers*. Bristol: Sophia Centre Press.

Hurd, R. (2011a). 'Paul Devereux live at the Rhine: Naturalizing psi as the anthropology of consciousness.' *Paranthropology*, 2(3), pp. 53-56.

Hurd, R. (2011b). 'Integral archaeology: Process methodologies for exploring prehistoric rock art on Ometepe island, Nicaragua.' *Anthropology of Consciousness*, 22(1), pp. 72-94.

Hurd, R. (2014). 'Barometers for the anomalous? Dreams as transpersonal archaeology.' *Parathropology*, 5(4), pp. 70-74..

Hurst, T. (2017). 'Catalysts that initiate embodied knowing: Reflections on individuation, synchronicity, and ritual space.' *Paranthropology*, 8(1), pp. 56-62.

Huxley, A. (1954). *The doors of perception*. London: Chatto & Windus, Ltd.

Hyde, L. (2010). *Trickster makes this world: Mischief, myth, and art*. New York: Farrar, Straus and Giroux.

Hynek, J.A. (1974). *The UFO Experience: A Scientific Inquiry*. London: Corgi Books.

IPCC (2018) 'Global Warming of 1.5 °C: An IPCC special report on the impacts of global warming of 1.5 °C above pre-industrial levels and related global greenhouse gas emission pathways, in the context of strengthening the global response to the threat of climate change, sustainable development, and efforts to eradicate poverty.' Online: http://www.ipcc.ch/report/sr15/ [Accessed 08/11/2018].

Jacobs, J. (2004). *Dark Age Ahead*. New York: Random House.

Jahn, R.G., Devereux, P., & Ibison, M. (1996). 'Acoustical resonances of assorted ancient structures.' *Journal of the Acoustical Society of America*, 99 (2).

James, W. (2004). *The Varieties of Religious Experience*. New York: Barnes & Noble.

Jantzen, G (1998). *Becoming Divine; Towards a Feminist Philosophy of Religion*. Manchester: Manchester University Press.

Jawer, M. (2005). 'Point of view: Environmental Sensitivity: A Neurobiological Phenomenon?' *Seminars in Integrative Medicine*, 3, pp. 104–109. doi: 10.1016/j.sigm.2005.10.003.

Jones, S. M. S., & Krippner, S. (2012). *The voice of Rolling Thunder: A medicine man's wisdom for walking the red road*. Rochester, VT: Bear & Company.

Jones, S. M. S., & Krippner, S. (2016). *The shamanic powers of Rolling Thunder: As experienced by Alberto Villoldo, John Barlow, Larry Dossey, and others*. Rochester, VT: Bear & Company.

Jones, S. & Hunter, J. (2018). *One School One Planet Vol.1: Climate. Education. Innovation*. Llanrhaeadr-ym-Mochnant: Psychoid Books.

Jourard, S. (1971). *The transparent self*. New York, NY: Van Nostrand Reinhold.

Jung C. G. (1987). *Flying Saucers: A Modern Myth of Things Seen in the Sky*. London: Ark Paperbacks.

Jung, C G. (1995). *Memories, Dreams, Reflections*. London: Fontana, 1963.

Jung, C. G. & Read, H. (1968). *On the psychology of the trickster figure*. London: Routledge and Kegan Paul.

Kanth, R.K. (2017). *Farewell to Modernism: On Human Devolution in the Twenty-First Century*. New York: Peter Lang.

Kaplan, L. (1956). 'Tonal and Nagual in Coastal Oaxaca, Mexico.' *The Journal of American Folklore*, 69(274), p. 363.

Kaye, R. (2006). 'The Spiritual Dimension of Wilderness: A Secular Approach for Resource Agencies.' *International Journal of Wilderness*, 12(3), pp. 4-8.

Keel, J. A. (1994). *Disneyland of the Gods*. Lilburn: IllumiNet Press.

Keel, J.A. (1970). *Strange Creatures from Time and Space*. Greenwich: Fawcett Publications.

Keel, J.A. (2013). *The Eighth Tower: On Ultraterrestrials and the Superspectrum*. Charlottesville: Anomalist Books.

Kelleher, C. & Knapp, G. (2005). *Hunt for the Skinwalker: Science Confronts the Unexplained on a Remote Ranch in Utah*. New York: Paraview.

Keller, B. (2011). 'The Twitter Trap.' *New York Times*, [online]. Available at https://www.nytimes.com/2011/05/22/magazine/the-twitter-trap.html?_r=2&src=twrhp [Accessed 1 Nov. 2018]

Kennedy, J. E. (2001). 'Why is psi so elusive? A review and proposed model.' *The Journal of Parapsychology*, 65, pp. 219-246.

Kennedy, J. E. (2003). 'The capricious, actively evasive, unsustainable nature of psi: A summary and hypothesis.' *The Journal of Parapsychology*, 67, pp. 53-74.

Kennedy, J. E. (2016). 'Coming to terms with the trickster.' In R. Nelson (Chair), Accessing the exceptional, experiencing the extraordinary. Convention conducted at the first combined convention of the parapsychological association (59th) and the society for scientific exploration (35th), Boulder, Colorado, USA.

Kimmerer, R.W. (2002). 'Weaving Traditional Ecological Knowledge into Biological Education: A Call to Action.' *BioScience*, 52(5), pp. 432-438.

Kimmerer, R.W. (2015). 'Mapping a New Geography of Hope (Keynote)', in *Women and the Land: Geography of Hope Conference*, Point Reyes, California, 13-15 March. Available at: https://www.youtube.com/watch?v=QhQKdJHLDcw

Kitzbichler M.G. *et al.* (2009). 'Broadband criticality of human brain network synchronization.' *PLoS Computational Biology*, 5(3). doi: 10.1371/journal.pcbi.1000314.

Kohn, E. (2013). *How Forests Think: Toward an Anthropology Beyond the Human*. Berkeley: University of California Press.

Kremer, J. W. (2003). 'Ethnoautobiography as a practice of radical presence: Storying the self in participatory visions.' *ReVision*, 26(2), pp. 5-13.

Kripal, J.J. (2011). *Authors of the Impossible: The Paranormal and the Sacred*. Chicago: The University of Chicago Press.

Kripal, J.J. (2011) *Mutants and Mystics: Science Fiction, Superhero Comics, and the Paranormal*. Chicago: University of Chicago Press.

Kripal, J.J. (2014). 'Better Horrors: From Terror to Communion in Whitley Strieber's Communion (1987).' *Social Research*, 81(4), pp. 897–920.

Kripal, J.J. *et al.* (2014). *Comparing Religions: Coming to Terms*. Malden, MA/Oxford: Wiley-Blackwell.

Kripal, J.J. & Strieber, W. (2016). *The Super Natural: A New Vision of the Unexplained*. New York: Tarcher-Penguin.

Kripal, J.J. (2019). *The Flip: Epiphanies of Mind and the Future of Knowledge*. New York: Bellevue Literary Press.

Krippner, S. & Friedman, H.L. (2010). *Mysterious Minds: The Neurobiology of Psychics, Mediums and Other Extraordinary People*. Santa Barbara: ABC-CLIO.

Krippner, S. & Luke, D. (2009). 'Psychedelics and species connectedness.' *Bulletin of the Multidisciplinary Association for Psychedelic Studies*, 19(1), pp. 12-15.

Krippner, S. & Schroll, M. A. (2014). 'Sacred places and home dream reports: Methodological reassessments and reflections on Paul Devereux's experiment in Wales and England.' *Paranthropology*, 5(4), pp. 56-65.

Krippner, S., Devereux, P. & Fish, A. (2003) 'The use of the Strauch Scale to study dream reports from sacred sites in England and Wales.' *Dreaming*, 13(2), pp. 95–105. doi: 10.1023/A:1023302209103.

Krishnamurti, J. (1956). *Commentaries on living*. Wheaton, IL: Theosophical Publishing House.

Kubler-Ross, E (1997). *The Wheel of Life: A Memoir of Living and Dying*. New York, Touchstone.

Kuhn, T. (1962). *The Structure of Scientific Revolutions*. Chicago: University of Chicago Press.

Lakoff, G. & Johnson, M. (1999). *Philosophy in the flesh : the embodied mind and its challenge to Western thought*. New York : Basic Books.

Lange, R. *et al.* (2000) 'The revised transliminality scale: reliability and validity data from a Rasch top-down purification procedure.' *Consciousness and Cognition*, 9(4), pp. 591–617.

Latour, B. (1993). *We have never been modern.* Cambridge, MA: Harvard University Press.

Latour, B. (1999). *Pandora's Hope: Essays on the Reality of Science Studies.* Cambridge: Harvard University Press.

Latour, B. (2017). *Facing Gaia: Eight Lectures on the New Climatic Regime.* Cambridge: Polity Press.

Laursen, C. (2016). *Reimagining the Poltergeist in Twentieth-Century America and Britain.* Unpublished PhD Thesis, University of British Columbia.

Law, J. (2004). *After Method: Mess in Social Science Research.* London and New York: Routledge, Taylor & Francis Group.

Leslie, D. & Adamski, G. (1977). *Flying Saucers Have Landed.* London: Futura.

Letcher, A. (2007) 'Mad thoughts on mushrooms: Discourse and power in the study of psychedelic consciousness.' *Anthropology of Consciousness,* 18(2), pp. 74-98.

Levin, R., Gilmartin, L. & Lamontanaro, L. (1998). 'Cognitive style and perception: The relationship of boundary thinness to visual-spatial processing in dreaming and waking thought.' *Imagination, Cognition and Personality,* 18(1), pp. 25–41. doi: 10.2190/4GBV-WAYQ-L0YR-RGCB.

Levin, T. & Suzukei, V. (2006). *Where Rivers and Mountains Sing: Sound, Music, and Nomadism in Tuva and Beyond.* Bloomington: Indiana University Press.

Levine, P.A. (2010). *In an Unspoken Voice: How the Body Releases Trauma and Restores Goodness.* Berkeley: North Atlantic Press.

Lewis, C.S. (1964). *A Grief Observed.* London: Faber & Faber.

Lewis-Williams, J. & Pearce, D. (2004). *San Spirituality.* Capetown: Double Storey Books.

Life Science (2010). 'Countdown: The World's Fastest Vehicles.' *Live Science* [online]. Available at https://www.livescience.com/32882-worlds-fastest-vehicles.html [Accessed 2 Oct. 2018]

Lilly, J. C. (1978). *The scientist.* Philadelphia: Lippincott.

Lindeman, M. *et al.* (2013) 'Is it just a brick wall or a sign from the universe? An fMRI study of supernatural believers and skeptics.' *Social Cognitive and Affective Neuroscience,* 8(8), pp. 943–949. doi: 10.1093/scan/nss096.

Lindeman, M., Riekki, T. & Hood, B. M. (2011) 'Is Weaker Inhibition Associated with Supernatural Beliefs?' *Journal of Cognition & Culture*, 11(1/2), p. 231. doi: 10.1163/156853711X570038.

Lindeman, M., Svedholm-Häkkinen, A. M. & Riekki, T. (2016) 'Skepticism: Genuine unbelief or implicit beliefs in the supernatural?' *Consciousness and Cognition*, 42, pp. 216–228. doi: 10.1016/j.concog.2016.03.019.

Linderman, F.B. (2002/1930). *Plenty Coups, Chief of the Crows*. Lincoln: University of Nebraska Press.

Linders, E. H. & Lancaster, B. L. (2013) 'Sacred illness: exploring transpersonal aspects in physical affliction and the role of the body in spiritual development.' *Mental Health, Religion & Culture*, 16(10), p. 991. doi: 10.1080/13674676.2012.728578.

Long, J.K. (1977). *Extrasensory Ecology: Parapsychology and Anthropology*. London: Scarecrow Books.

Lopez, B. (1990). *The Rediscovery of North America*. London: Vintage.

Louchakova, O. & Warner, A. S. (2003). 'Via Kundalini: Psychosomatic excursions in transpersonal psychology.' *The Humanistic Psychologist. (Transpersonal Psychology)*, 31(2–3), pp. 115–158. doi: 10.1080/08873267.2003.9986928.

Lovelock, J. (1990). 'Hands Up for the Gaia Hypothesis.' *Nature*, 344(8), pp.100-102. Available Online: https://www.uow.edu.au/~sharonb/STS300/controversy/env/artgaia.html [Accessed 05/01/2019].

Lovelock, J. (2000). *Gaia: A New Look at Life on Earth*. Oxford: Oxford University Press.

Lowie, R. (1948). *Primitive religion*. New York: Liveright Publishing.

Luberto, C. M. *et al.* (2018) 'A systematic review and meta-analysis of the effects of meditation on empathy, compassion, and prosocial behaviors.' *Mindfulness*, 9(3), pp. 708–724. doi: 10.1007/s12671-017-0841-8.

Luke, D. P. (2008). 'Psychedelic substances and paranormal phenomena: A review of the research.' *Journal of Parapsychology*, 72, 77-107.

Luke, D. (2013). 'Ecopsychology and the psychedelic experience.' *European Journal of Ecopsychology*, 4, 1-8.

Luke, D. (2017). *Otherworlds: Psychedelics and exceptional human experience*. London: Muswell Hill.

Luke, D. P. & Terhune, D. B. (2013). 'The induction of synaesthesia with chemical agents: A systematic review.' *Frontiers in Psychology*, 4. doi: 10.3389/fpsyg.2013.00753.

Luke, D. P. & Kittenis, M. (2005). 'A preliminary survey of paranormal experiences with psychoactive drugs.' *Journal of Parapsychology*, 69 (2), pp. 305-327.

Luke, D. & Zychowicz, K. (2014) 'Comparison of outcomes with nonintentional and intentional precognition tasks.' *Journal of Parapsychology*, 78(2), p. 223.

Luke, D., & Yanakieva, S. (2016). 'The transpersonal psychedelic experience and change in ecological attitude and behaviour.' Paper presented at the International Conference on Psychedelics Research, Stichting Open, Amsterdam, 3rd-5th June.

Lyons, T., & Carhart-Harris, R. (2018). 'Increased nature relatedness and decreased authoritarian political views after psilocybin for treatment-resistant depression.' *Journal of Psychopharmacology*, 32(7), pp. 811-819.

Lévy-Bruhl, L. (1935). *Primitive Mythology*. University of Queensland Press.

Mack, J.E. (1995). *Abduction: Human Encounters with Aliens*. New York: Ballantine Books.

Mack, J.E. (2011). *Passport to the Cosmos: Human Transformation and Alien Encounters*. Guildford: White Crow Books.

Maddox, J. (1981). 'A Book for Burning?' *Nature*, 293(5830), pp. 245-246.

Madigan, F. & Warner, W. (1958). 'A Black Civilization: A Social Study of an Australian Tribe.' *The American Catholic Sociological Review*, 19(3), p. 279.

Malay, M. (2014) 'Ted Hughes, Another Look at Jaguar.' *The Ted Hughes Society Journal*, 4(1), pp. 89-100.

Mancuso, S. & Viola, A. (2015). *Brilliant Green: The Surprising History and Science of Plant Intelligence*. London: Island Press.

Mander, J. (1991). *In the Absence of the Sacred: The Failure of Technology and the Survival of the Indian Nations*. San Francisco: Sierra Club Books.

Mann, J. & Patterson, E.M. (2013). 'Tool use by aquatic animals.' *Philosophical Transactions of The Royal Society B*, 368, pp. 1-11.

Mapel, D. (2002). *Into the heart of the wild*. Charlottesville, VA: Wild Earth.

Mapel, D. (2014). Animal essences practitioner seminar.

Maple, D. (2016). Interview on animal essences. [email].

Marshall, P. (2005). *Mystical Encounters with the Natural World: Experiences and Explanations*. Oxford: Oxford University Press.

Marwaha, S. B. & May, E. C. (2015) 'Rethinking Extrasensory Perception: Toward a Multiphasic Model of Precognition', *SAGE Open*, 5(1), p. 1.

Marzluff, J. & Angell, T. (2005) *In the Company of Crows and Ravens*. New Haven: Yale University Press.

Maslow, A. H. (1968). *Toward a psychology of being*. New York: D. Van Nostrand Company.

Masters, R. E. L., & Houston, J. (1966). *The varieties of psychedelic experience*. London: Turnstone.

Mathews, F. (2010). 'On Desiring Nature.' *Indian Journal of Ecocriticism*, 3.

Mathews, F. (2007). 'The World Hidden Within the World: a Conversation on Ontopoetics.' *The Trumpeter*, 23(1).

Matthiessen, P. (2009). 'Native Earth.' In L. Hogan (ed.), *The Inner Journey: Views from Native Traditions*, Morning Light Press, Sandpoint, Idaho, pp. 128-143.

McCraty, R. & Childre, D. (2010) 'Coherence: bridging personal, social, and global health.' *Alternative Therapies in Health and Medicine*, 16(4), pp. 10–24.

McDonald. M.G., Wearing, S. & Ponting, J. (2009). 'The Nature of Peak Experience in Wilderness.' *The Humanistic Psychologist*, 37(4), pp. 370-385.

McKenna, D. (2018). 'Is DMT a chemical messenger from an extra-terrestrial civilisation?' In D. Luke and R. Spowers (eds.) *DMT dialogues: Encounters with the spirit molecule*. Rochester, VT: Park Street Press.

McKenna, T. (1992). *Food of the gods: The search for the original tree of knowledge*. New York, NY: Bantam Books.

Menache, S. (1997). 'Dogs: God's Worst Enemies?' *Society & Animals*, 5(1), pp.23-44.

Merleau Ponty, M. (2002) *Phenomenology of Perception*. Routledge: Routledge Classics.

Metzner, R. (2005). 'We Are All Actors and Directors in A Giant Cosmic Drama.' In R. Metzner & D.C. Darling (eds.). *Teonanacatl: Sacred Mushroom of Vision*. Rochester, VT: Park Street Press.

Metzner, R. (1999a). *Green psychology: Transforming our relationship to the Earth*. Rochester, VT: Inner Traditions Press.

Metzner, R. (1999b). 'Introduction: Amazonian vine of visions.' In R. Metzner (ed.) *Ayahuasca: Human consciousness and the spirits of nature*. New York, NY: Thunder's Mouth Press.

Metzner, R. (2017). 'Varieties of Ritual Involving States of Consciousness.' *Confluence*, 2(2): 55-70. Retrieved from <http://youthpassageways.org/blog/2017/12/29/varieties-of-ritual-involving-states-of-consciousness>

Metzner, R. & Pinkson, T. (1994). 'Remembering the Earth.' Post-conference workshop at the 13th International Transpersonal Association conference "Toward Earth Community: Ecology, Native Wisdom and Spirituality," held in the Great Southern Hotel, Killarney, Ireland. El Cerrito, CA: Conference Recording Services.

Michell, J. (1975). *The View Over Atlantis*. London: Abacus.

Mikhailovskii, V. & Wardrop, O. (1895). 'Shamanism in Siberia and European Russia, Being the Second Part of "Shamanstvo".' *The Journal of the Anthropological Institute of Great Britain and Ireland*, 24, p.62.

Milosz, C. (1983). *The Witness of Poetry*. Cambridge, Mass. Harvard University Press.

Mishlove, J. (2017). 'Fear of Psi with Charles T. Tart.' *New Thinking Allowed*. Accessed 13 January 2019 at https://www. youtube.com/watch?v=CzoIzwSdb2Q

Mitchell, J.V. (1974). *Ghosts of an Ancient City*. York: Cerialis Press.

Mitchell, K.J. (2013). 'Synesthesia and cortical connectivity: A neurodevelopmental perspective.' In J. Simner & E.M. Hubbard (eds.) *The Oxford handbook of synesthesia*. NY, New York: Oxford University Press.

Mohawk, J. (1978). *Basic Call to Consciousness.* New York: Akwesasne Notes/Book Publishing Company.

Mohr, C. & Claridge, G. (2015) 'Schizotypy-Do Not Worry, It Is Not All Worrisome.' *Schizophrenia Bulletin,* 41(S1), p. S436.

Monbiot, G. (2014). *Feral: Rewilding the Land, Sea and Human Life.* London: Penguin Books.

Moody, RA. (1992). 'Family reunions: Visionary encounters with the departed in a modern-day psychomanteum.' *Journal of Near-Death Studies,* 11(2), pp. 83–121.

Moody, R. A. & Perry, P. (1993). *Reunions:Visionary encounters with departed loved ones.* New York : Villard Books.

Morris, B. (2013). 'Anarchism, Individualism, and South Indian Foragers; Memories and Reflections.' *Radical Anthropology,* Nov 2013, 22-37.

Morris, R. & Morris, D. (1965). *Men and snakes.* New York: McGraw-Hill.

Nasasdy, P. (2007). 'The gift in the animal: The ontology of hunting and human-animal sociality.' *American Ethnologist,* 34(1), pp. 25-43.

Naor, L. & Mayseless, O. (2017). 'How Personal Transformation Occurs Following a Single Peak Experience in Nature: A Phenomenological Account.' *Journal of Humanistic Psychology.*

Narby, J. (2006). *Intelligence in Nature: An Inquiry into Knowledge.* New York: Tarcher Penguin.

Neidjie, B. (1989). *Story About Feeling.* Broome: Magabala Books.

Nelson, M. (1998). 'A psychological impact report for the environmental movement.' *ReVision,* 20(4, pp. 37-43.

Nelson, R. (1983). *Make prayers to the raven.* Chicago: University of Chicago Press.

Nilsson, M. & Vermeule, E. (1972). *The Mycenaean origin of Greek mythology.* Berkeley: University of California Press.

Nummenmaa, L. *et al.* (2018) 'Maps of subjective feelings.' *Proceedings of the National Academy of Sciences of the United States of America,* 115(37), p. 9198.

Odum, E.P. (1966). 'The Strategy of Ecosystem Development.' *Science*, 164, pp. 262-270.

Otto, R. (1958*) The Idea of the Holy: An Inquiry into the Non-Rational Factor in the Idea of the Divine and its Relation to the Rational.* Oxford: Oxford University Press.

PEW, (2010). 'The Global Religious Landscape.' Online: http://www.pewforum.org/2012/12/18/global-religious-landscape-exec/ [Accessed 05/11/2018].

Park, W. (1965). 'Shamanism: Archaic Techniques of Ecstasy. Mircea Eliade, Willard R. Trask.' *American Anthropologist*, 67(5), pp.1305-1306.

Parra, A. (2013) 'Cognitive and emotional empathy in relation to five paranormal/anomalous experiences.' *North American Journal of Psychology*, 15(3), pp. 405–412.

Parra, A. (2013). 'What have we learned about psi? Reflections on the present of parapsychology.' *Journal of Parapsychology*, 77(1), pp. 9-13.

Parra, A. & Paul, L. E. (2009). 'Exploring the links between nocturnal hallucinatory experiences and personality characteristics.' *European Journal of Parapsychology*, 24(2), pp. 139–154.

Parsons, S.T. (2012) 'Infrasound and the paranormal.' *Journal of the Society for Psychical Research*, 76 (908), pp. 150-174.

Pavlik, S. (2014). *The Navajo and the animal people: Native American traditional ecological knowledge and ethnozoology.* Golden, CO: Fulcrum Publishing.

Peat, F.D. (1994). *Blackfoot Physics: A Journey into the Native American Universe.* London: Fourth Estate.

Pedersen, M. (2001). 'Totemism, Animism and North Asian Indigenous Ontologies.' *Journal of the Royal Anthropological Institute*, 7(3), pp.411-427.

Persinger, M. A. & Schaut, G. B. (1988) 'Geomagnetic factors in subjective telepathic, precognitive, and postmortem experiences.' *Journal of the American Society for Psychical Research*, 82(3), pp. 217–235.

Persinger, M. A., & Koren, S. A., (2001) 'Predicting the characteristics of haunt phenomena from geomagnetic factors and brain sensitivity: Evidence from field and experimental studies.' In: J. Houran, & R. Lange (eds.) *Hauntings and poltergeists: Multidisciplinary perspectives.* Jefferson, NC: McFarland and Company, Inc.

Pharr, M. (1996). 'Adam's Dream: The Gothic Imagination of Whitley Strieber.' In T. Magistrale & M.A. Morrison (eds.) *A Dark Night's Dreaming: Contemporary American Horror Fiction.* Columbia, S.C.: University of South Carolina Press.

Piaget, J. (1955). *The child's construction of reality.* London, UK: Routledge.

Pimm, S. L., Russell, G. J., Gittleman, J. L. Brooks, T. M. (1995). 'The future of biodiversity.' *Science,* 269, pp. 347-350.

Pinsent, J. (1983). *Greek mythology.* New York: P. Bedrick Books.

Planck, M. (1949). *Scientific Autobiography and Other Papers.* New York: Philosophical Library.

Plato, Groden, S., Brentlinger, J. & Baskin, L. (1970). *The Symposium of Plato.* Amherst: University of Massachusetts Press.

Plato & Stokes, M. (1997). *Apology of Socrates.* Warminster: Aris & Phillips.

Plummer, K. (1995). *Telling Sexual Stories; Power, Change, and Social Worlds.* London: Routledge.

Plumwood, V. (1995). 'Human Vulnerability and the Experience of Being Prey.' *Quadrant,* 39(3), pp. 29-34.

Plumwood, V (2002). *Environmental Culture, The Ecological Crisis of Reason.* Abingdon: Routledge.

Plumwood, V. (2010). 'Nature in the Active Voice.' *Australian Humanities Review,* 46, pp. 113-129.

Polt, R (1999). *Heidegger: An Introduction.* Ithaca: Cornell University Press.

Pope Francis (2015). *Laudato Si.* Available Online:

http://w2.vatican.va/content/francesco/en/encyclicals/documents/papafrancesco_20150524_enciclica-laudato-si.html Online. [Accessed 05/11/2018].

Popescu, P. (2016). *The Encounter: Amazon Beaming.* London: Pushkin Press.

Porteous, A. (1996). *The Lore of the Forest.* London: Random House.

Power, R. (2006). 'A place of community: "Celtic" Iona and institutional religion.' *Folklore,* 117, pp. 33-53.

Prechtel, M. (1999). *Secrets of the Talking Jaguar: Memoirs from the Living Heart of a Mayan Village*. Berkeley: North Atlantic Books.

Prechtel, M. (2014). *The Smell of Rain on Dust: Grief and Praise*. Berkeley: North Atlantic Books.

Radin, D. (1997). *The Conscious Universe: The Scientific Truth of Psychic Phenomena*. New York: HarperOne.

Radin, D. (2006). *Entangled Minds: Extrasensory Experiences in a Quantum Reality*. New York: Paraview.

Radin, D. (2013). *Supernormal: Science, Yoga, and the Evidence for Extraordinary Psychic Abilities*. New York: Random House.

Radin, P. (1972). *The trickster: A study in American Indian mythology*. New York: Schocken Books Inc.

Rao K. R & Palmer J. (1987). 'The anomaly called psi: Recent research and criticism.' *Behavioral and Brain Sciences*, 10(4), 539-551.

Ratsch, C. (1992). *The dictionary of sacred and magical plants*. Bridport, Dorset, UK: Prism Press.

Ratsch, C. (1994). 'The mead of inspiration.' Paper presented at the 13th International Transpersonal Association conference "Toward Earth Community: Ecology, Native Wisdom and Spirituality," held in the Great Southern Hotel, Killarney, Ireland. El Cerrito, CA: Conference Recording Services.

Ray, R. (2016). *The Awakening Body: Somatic Meditation for Discovering our Deepest Life*. Boulder: Shambhala.

Reddy, J. (2013). 'What Colombia's Kogi People Can Teach Us About the Environment', *The Guardian*, 29 October.

Reikihealing.org, (2011). 'Index.' [online] Reikihealing.org.uk. Available at: http://www.reikihealing.org.uk [Accessed 16 Feb. 2016].

Reiner, A. (1990). 'The Triune Brain in Evolution. Role in Paleocerebral Functions.' *Science*, 250(4978), pp.303-305.

Reinhard, J., Hitchcock, J., Jones, R. & Beegun, H. (1977). 'Shamanism and spirit possessions in the Nepal Himalayas.' *Pacific Affairs*, 50(4), pp.12-18.

Richardson, A. (1990). 'Recollections of R. Gordon Wasson's 'friend and photographer'.' In T. J. Riedlinger (ed.) *The sacred mushroom seeker*. Portland, Oregon: Dioscorides Press.

Riekki, T., Lindeman, M. & Raij, T. T. (2014). 'Supernatural believers attribute more intentions to random movement than skeptics: An fMRI study.' *Social Neuroscience*, 9(4), pp. 400–411. doi: 10.1080/17470919.2014.906366.

Ring, K. & Valarino, E. (2006). *Lessons from the Light: What We Can Learn from the Near-Death Experience.* Needham: Moment Point Press.

Ring, K. (1989). 'Near-death and UFO encounters as shamanic initiations: Some conceptual and evolutionary implications.' *ReVision*, 11(3), 14-22.

Ring, K. (1992). *The Omega Project: Near-Death Experiences, UFO Encounters, and Mind at Large.* New York: William Morrow and Company.

Ripoll, M. (2018). 'Group Reflections of 9/11: New York Firefighters Tell Their Story.' Unpublished MA thesis, University of North Carolina Wilmington.

Rockström, J., Gaffney, O., Rogelj, J., Meinshausen, M., Nakicenovic, N. & Schellnhuber, H.J. (2017). 'A Roadmap for Rapid Decarbonization.' *Science*, 355(6331), pp. 1269-1271.

Rodrigues, N. & Deuskar, M. (2016). 'A Study of the Effect of Color Meditation on Relaxation States.' *Journal of Psychosocial Research*, 11(1), pp. 13–20.

Roe C. A. (2012). 'Parapsychology in the next 25 years - still a butterfly science.' *Journal of Parapsychology*, 76, pp. 46-48.

Roll, W.G, (2008). 'Psi and the Long Body.' *Australian Journal of Parapsychology*, 8 (1), pp.6-28.

Romme, M. & Escher, S. (1993). *Accepting Voices.* London: MIND Publications.

Rootes, C. (1999) 'Environmental movements: From the local to the global.' *Environmental Politics*, 8(1), pp. 1-12.

Rosengren, D. (2006). 'Transdimensional relations: on human-spirit interaction in the Amazon.' *Journal of the Royal Anthropological Institute*, 12(4), pp.803-816.

Roszak, T. (1973). *Where the wasteland ends: Politics and transcendence in postindustrial society.* Garden City, NY: Anchor Books/Doubleday & Company, Inc.

Roszak, T. (1992). *The Voice of the Earth: An Exploration of Ecopsychology.* London: Bantam Press.

Roszak, T. (1993). 'Ecopsychology and the soul of the earth.' Keynote lecture at the 25th Anniversary Convocation of the Association for Transpersonal Psychology, Asilomar Conference Center, Pacific Grove, CA.

Rothberg, D. (1999). 'Transpersonal issues at the millennium.' *Journal of Transpersonal Psychology*, 31(1): 41-67.

Rouw, R. (2013) 'Synesthesia, hyperconnectivity, and diffusion tensor imaging.' In J. Simner & E.M. Hubbard (eds.) *The Oxford handbook of synesthesia.* New York, NY: Oxford University Press (Oxford library of psychology).

Rowland, B. (1978). *Birds with Human Souls: A Guide to Bird Symbolism.* Knoxville: University of Tennessee Press.

Russell, G.W. (1918). *The Candle of Vision.* London: MacMillan and Co., Ltd..

Sagiv, N., Ilbeigi, A., Ben-Tal, O. (2011). 'Reflections on synesthesia, perception, and cognition.' *Intellectica*, 55 (1), pp. 81–94.

Schneider, D. A. (2016).' Meeting at the thin places: Synchronicities in clinical practice.' *Smith College Studies in Social Work*, 86(2), pp. 136-155.

Schofield, K. & Claridge, G. (2007). 'Paranormal experiences and mental health: Schizotypy as an underlying factor.' *Personality and Individual Differences*, 43, pp. 1908–1916. doi: 10.1016/j.paid.2007.06.014.

Schroll, M. A. (2013a). 'From ecopsychology to a transpersonal ecosophy: Shamanism, psychedelics, and transpersonal psychology– An autobiographical reflection.' *European Journal of Ecopsychology*, 4, pp. 116-144.

Schroll, M. A. (2013b). 'Review of The voice of Rolling Thunder.' *Association for Humanistic Psychology-Perspective*, April/May, pp. 34-36.

Schroll, M. A. (2016). *Transpersonal ecosophy, Vol. 1: Reflections on sacred site dream research, the mind/body problem, parapsychology, spiritual emergency/emergence, transpersonal psychology, the anthropology of consciousness, and more.* Llanrhaeadr-ym-Mochant, U.K.: Psychoid Books.

Schroll, M. A. (2018*). Ecology, cosmos, and consciousness: Myths, comicbook lore, dreams and inquiries into various other radical transpersonal ecosophical states*. Llanrhaeadr-ym-Mochant, U.K.: Psychoid Books.

Schroll, M. A. & Rothenberg, D. (2014). 'Psychedelics and the deep ecology movement: A conversation with Arne Naess.' In R. Doblin & B. Burge (eds.) *Manifesting minds: A review of psychedelics in science, medicine, sex, and spirituality*. Berkeley, CA: Evolver Editions/North Atlantic Books, pp. 246-250.

Schroll, M. A., & Rothenberg, D. (2014). 'Psychedelics and the deep ecology movement: A conversation with Arne Naess.' In R. Doblin. & B. Burge (eds.) *Manifesting minds: A review of psychedelics in science, medicine, sex, and spirituality*. Berkeley, CA: Evolver Editions/North Atlantic Books, pp. 246-250.

Seed, J., Macy, J., Flemming, P., & Naess, A. (1988). *'Thinking like a mountain: Toward a council of all beings*. Philadelphia, PA: New Society.

Seidler, V. (1994). *Unreasonable Men, Masculinity and Social Theory*. London: Routledge.

Seidman, S. (1994). *Contested Knowledges: Social Theory Today*. Oxford: Blackwell.

Selby, D. & Kagawa, F. (2015) 'Drawing Threads Together: A Critical and Transformative Agenda for Sustainability Education.' In D. Selby & F. Kagawa (eds.) *Sustainability Frontiers: Critical and Transformative Voices from the Borderlands of Sustainability Education*. Opladen: Barbara Budrich Publishers.

Sepie A.J. (2018). *Tracing the Motherline: Earth Elders, Decolonising Worldview, and Planetary Futurity*. Unpublished PhD Thesis: University of Canterbury, Christchurch, New Zealand. Available at: https://ir.canterbury.ac.nz/handle/10092/15916

Serpell, J. (2006). *Handbook on animal-assisted therapy*. San Diego, Calif.: Academic Press.

Serpell, J.A. "Animal-assisted interventions in historical perspective." p. 21.

Severi, B. (2003). 'Sciamani e psichedelia. [Shamans and psychedelics].' *Quaderni de Parapsychologia*, 34, 36.

Shankardass, M. (2003). 'Shamanism: the neural ecology of consciousness and healing/' *Social Science & Medicine*, 57(6), pp.1144-1145.

Sheldrake, R. (1991). *The Rebirth of Nature*. Rochester, Vermont: Park Street Press.

Sheldrake, R. (2000). *Dogs That Know When Their Owners Are Coming Home: And Other Unexplained Powers of Animals*. London: Arrow.

Sheldrake, R. (2004). *The Sense of Being Stared at and Other Aspects of the Extended Mind*. London: Arrow Books.

Sheldrake, R. (2008). 'The Extended Mind, Recent Experimental Evidence.' Google Tech Talk. Available Online: http://www.sheldrake.org/videos/the-extended-mind-recent-experimental-evidence accessed 2/4/15.

Sheldrake, R. (2009). *A New Science of Life: The Hypothesis of Formative Causation*. London: Icon Books.

Shepard, P. (1998). *Nature and Madness*. Athens, GA.: University of Georgia Press.

Sherwood, S. J. (2002) 'Relationship between the Hypnagogic/Hypnopompic States and Reports of Anomalous Experiences.' *Journal of Parapsychology*, 66(2), p. 127.

Shuker, K. (1993). *The Lost Ark: New & Rediscovered Animals of the 20th Century*. Frome: Butler and Tanner Ltd.

Simard, S. & Durall, D. (2004). 'Mycorrhizal Networks: A Review of their Extent, Function and Importance.' *Canadian Journal of Botany*, 82(8), pp. 1140-1165.

Simard, S., Beiler, K., Bingham, M., Deslippe, J., Philip, L. and Teste, F. (2012). 'Mycorrhizal Networks: Mechanisms, Ecology and Modelling.' *Fungal Biology Reviews*, 26(1), pp. 39-60.

Simmonds-Moore, C. A. (2016). 'An interpretative phenomenological analysis exploring synesthesia as an exceptional experience: insights for consciousness and cognition.' *Qualitative Research in Psychology*, 13(4), pp. 303–327. doi: 10.1080/14780887.2016.1205693.

Simmonds-Moore, C. A., Alvarado, C. S. and Zingrone, N. L. (2018). 'A survey exploring synesthetic experiences: Exceptional experiences, schizotypy, and psychological well-being.' *Psychology of Consciousness: Theory, Research, and Practice*. doi: 10.1037/cns0000165.

Simmonds-Moore, C., Rice, D., O'Gwin, C. & Hopkins, R., (2017). 'Exceptional Experiences Following Exposure to a Sham "God Helmet": Evidence for Placebo, Individual Difference, and Time of Day Influences.' *Imagination, Cognition and Personality.* First Published online December 27, 2017.doi.org/10.1177/0276236617749185.

Simmonds-Moore, C.A, (2010). 'Personality variables in spontaneous psi research: Contextualising the boundary construct in its relationship to spontaneous psi phenomena.' In: C.A. Roe, W. Kramer and L. Coly (ed.) *Proceedings of an International Conference Utrecht II: Charting the future of parapsychology.* New York: Parapsychology Foundation.

Simmonds-Moore, C.A, (2012). 'Exploring ways of manipulating anomalous experiences for mental health and transcendence.' In: C. Simmonds-Moore (ed.) *Exceptional experience and health: Essays on mind, body and human potential.* Jefferson, NC: McFarland Press.

Simmonds-Moore, C.A, (2015). 'An exploration of the role of the boundary construct in exceptional experiences.' In A. Parra (ed.) *Invisible Eyes: The crusade for the conquest of the spirit.* Buenos Aires: Antigua.

Simner, J. & Hubbard, E. M. (2013). *The Oxford handbook of synesthesia.* New York, NY: Oxford University Press (Oxford library of psychology). doi: 10.1093/oxfordhb/9780199603329.001.0001.

Singer, T. & Klimecki, O. (2014). 'Primer: Empathy and Compassion.' *Current Biology,* 24(18), pp. R875-R878. https://doi.org/10.1016/j.cub.2014.06.054

Smith, H. (1976). *Forgotten truth: The primordial tradition.* New York, NY: Harper and Row.

Snyder, G. (1990). *The Practice of the Wild: Essays.* San Francisco: North Point Press.

Spadafora, A. (2016). 'Stephen Hawking Believes, AI could be mankind's Last Accomplishment.' *Beta News,* [online]. Available at https://betanews.com/2016/10/21/artificial-intelligence-stephen-hawking/ [Accessed 10 Sept. 2018]

Spehar, B, Clifford, C.W.G, Newell, B.R. & Taylor, R.P. (2003). 'Chaos and graphics: Universal aesthetic of fractals.' *Computers & Graphics,* 27, pp. 813–820.

Spencer, C. (1996). *The heretic's feast.* Hanover, NH: University Press of New England.

Spinks, C. W. (1991). *Semiosis, marginal signs and trickster: A dagger of the mind*. London: Macmillan.

Spinks, C. W. (2001). *Trickster and ambivalence: Dance of differentiation*. Madison, WI: Atwood Publishing.

Stace, W.T. (1960). *The Teachings of the Mystics*. New York: The New American Library.

Stamets, P. (2005). *Mycelium Running: How Mushrooms Can Help Save the World*. Berkeley: Ten Speed Press.

Stengers, I. (2010). *Cosmopolitics I*. Minneapolis, MN: University of Minnesota Press.

Stengers, I. (2011). *Cosmopolitics II*. Minneapolis, MN: University of Minnesota Press.

Stevens, J. (2013). 'Squatch Watch: 92 Years of Bigfoot Sightings in the US and Canada.' Online: http://www.joshuastevens.net/visualization/squatch-watch-92-years-of-bigfoot-sightings-in-us-and-canada/ [Accessed 10/11/2018].

Steward, J. (1934). 'Two Paiute Autobiographies.' *Publications in American Archaeology and Ethnology*, 33(5).

Stocking, G.W. (1982). *Race, Culture, and Evolution: Essays in the History of Anthropology*. Chicago: University of Chicago Press.

Storm, L., Tressoldi, P. E. and Di Risio, L. (2010) 'Meta-Analysis of Free-Response Studies, 1992-2008: Assessing the Noise Reduction Model in Parapsychology.' *Psychological Bulletin*, 136(4), pp. 471–485.

Storm, R. (2008). *Monster Hunt: The Guide to Cryptozoology*. New York City: Sterling Publishing

Strieber, W. (1979). *The Wolfen*. New York: Bantam.

Strieber, W. (2001). *The Hunger*. New York: Pocket Books.

Strieber, W. (2008). *Communion: A True Story*. New York: Harper.

Strochlic, N. (2016). 'A Forgotten Adventue with a Telepathic Tribe.' *National Geographic*, [online]. Available at https://www.nationalgeographic.com/magazine/plus/lost-and-found/amazon-encounter-explorer-photographer/ [Accessed 12 Dec. 2016].

Sulleyman, A. (2017). 'Stephen Hawking Warns Artficial Intelligence 'May Replace Humans Altogether.' *The Independent* [online]. Available at https://www.independent.co.uk/life-style/gadgets-and-tech/news/stephen-hawking-artificial-intelligence-fears-ai-will-replace-humans-virus-life-a8034341.html [Accessed 10 Dec. 2018]

Tarnas, R. (1991). *The Passion of the Western Mind: Understanding the Ideas That Have Shaped our World View*. London: Random House.

Tart, C. T. (2000). *MindScience: Meditation training for practical people*. Novato, CA: Wisdom Editions.

Tart, C.T. (1994). 'Fears of the Paranormal in Ourselves and Our Colleagues: Recognizing Them, Dealing with Them.' *Subtle Energies*, 5(1), PP. 35-67.

Taylor, B. (2010*). Dark Green Religion: Nature Spirituality and the Planetary Future*. Berkeley: University of California Press.

Taylor, B., Van Wieren, G. & Zaleha, B.D. (2016). 'Review: Lynn White Jr. and the greening-of-religion hypothesis.' *Conservation Biology*, Vol. 30, No. 5, pp. 1000-1009.

Taylor, B.A. (2012). 'Birds, Liminality, and Human Transformation; an Animist Perspective on New Animism.' *The Pomegranate*, 14(1), PP. 108-127.

Taylor, S. (2015) 'Energy and Awakening: A Psycho-Sexual Interpretation of Kundalini Awakening,' *Journal of Transpersonal Psychology*, 47(2), pp. 219–241.

Tedlock, B. (2006). 'Toward a theory of divinatory practice.' *Anthropology of Consciousness*, 17(2), PP. 62-77. https://doi.org/10.1525/ac.2006.17.2.62

Terhune, D. B. *et al.* (2013). 'Enhanced dimension-specific visual working memory in grapheme-color synesthesia.' *Cognition*, 129(1), pp. 123–137. doi: 10.1016/j.cognition.2013.06.009.

Thalbourne, M. A. (2009). 'Transliminality, Anomalous Belief and Experience, and Hypnotisability.' *Australian Journal of Clinical & Experimental Hypnosis*, 37(2), pp. 119–130.

Thalbourne, M. A. & Delin, P. S. (1999) 'Transliminality: Its Relation to Dream Life, Religiosity, and Mystical Experience.' *International Journal for the Psychology of Religion*, 9(1), p. 45. doi: 10.1207/s15327582ijpr0901pass:[_]6.

Thalbourne, M. A. & Maltby, J. (2008). 'Transliminality, thin boundaries, Unusual Experiences, and temporal lobe lability.' *Personality & Individual Differences*, 44(7), pp. 1617–1623. doi: 10.1016/j.paid.2008.01.022.

Thalbourne, M. A. *et al.* (2001) 'Transliminality, brain function, and synesthesia.' *The Journal of Nervous And Mental Disease*, 189(3), pp. 190–192.

Thalbourne, M.A., (1999). 'Transliminality: A review.' *International Journal of Parapsychology*, 11(2), pp.1-34.

Thayer, J. F. *et al.* (2012). 'A meta-analysis of heart rate variability and neuroimaging studies: implications for heart rate variability as a marker of stress and health.' *Neuroscience and Biobehavioral Reviews*, 36(2), pp. 747–756. doi: 10.1016/j.neubiorev.2011.11.009.

The Centre for Fortean Zoology. (2006). *Expedition Report 2006: Gambia*. North Devon: CFZ Press.

The Guardian (2013). 'Elf Lobby blocks Iceland road project.' Available Online: https://www.theguardian.com/world/2013/dec/22/elf-lobby-iceland-road-project [Accessed 18/12/2018]

The Guardian (2017). Available Online: https://www.theguardian.com/world/2017/mar/16/new-zealand-river-granted-same-legal-rights-as-human-being [Accessed 07/07/2019].

The Guardian (2017a). Available Online: https://www.theguardian.com/world/2017/mar/21/ganges-and-yamuna-rivers-granted-same-legal-rights-as-human-beings [Accessed 07/07/2019].

The Irish Times (1999). 'Fairy bush survives the motorway planners.' Available Online:

The Official Loch Ness Monster Sightings Register. (2018). 'Sightings 565 AD to 1985.' Online: http://www.lochnesssightings.com/index.asp?pageid=543532 [Accessed 12/11/2018].

The Scotsman (2014). 'Loch Ness monster is "Spiritual" say Buddhists.' Available Online: https://www.scotsman.com/news/odd/loch-ness-monster-is-spiritual-say-buddhists-1-3388747 [Accessed 18/12/2018].

Thetahealingcentre.co.uk, (2012*). Theta Healing Centre - What Is Theta Healing?* [online] Available at: http://www.thetahealingcentre.co.uk/What-Is-ThetaHealing(1111422).htm [Accessed 16 Feb. 2016].

Tompkins, P. & Bird, C. (2002). *The Secret Life of Plants.* New York: Harper.

Toynbee, A. (1971). 'The religious background of the present environmental crisis.' *International Journal of Environmental Studies*, Vol. 3, No. 1, pp. 141-146.

Trask, H.-K. (1999). *From a Native Daughter: Colonialism and Sovereignty in Hawai'i.* Honolulu: University of Hawai'i Press.

Turner, E. (1994) 'A Visible Spirit Form in Zambia.' In D..Young and J-G. Goulet (ed.) *Being Changed by Cross-Cultural Encounters, the Anthropology of Extraordinary Experience.* Peterborough Ontario, Broadview Press, pp71-98.

Turner, E. (1998). *Experiencing Ritual: A New Interpretation of African Healing.* Philadelphia: University of Pensylvania Press.

Turner, V. (2017). *The Ritual Process: Structure and Anti-Structure.* London: Taylor and Francis.

Tylor, E.B. (1871/1913). *Primitive Culture, 2 Vols.* London: John Murray.

Ullman, M., Krippner, S. & Vaughan, A. (1977). *Dream Telepathy: Experiments in Nocturnal ESP.* New York: Penguin.

Vallee, J. (1976) *The Invisible College: What a Group of Scientists has Discovered about UFO Influences on the Human Race.* New York: E. P. Dutton.

Vallee, J. (1977). *UFOs: The Psychic Solution: UFO Influences on the Human Race.* St Albans: Panther Books.

Vallee, J. (2015). *Passport to Magonia: From Folklore to Flying Saucers.* Brisbane: Daily Grail.

van der Kolk, B. (2014). *The Body Keeps the Score: Mind, Brain and Body in the Transformation of Trauma.* London: Penguin.

van der Post, L. (1962). *The Lost World of the Kalahari.* Harmondsworth.: Penguin Books.

Van Gennep, A. (1961). *The rites of passage.* Chicago, IL: University of Chicago Press. https://doi.org/10.7208/ chicago/9780226027180.001.0001. (Original work published 1909).

Van Sittert, L. (2017). 'The Marine Fisheries of South Africa.' Online: http://oxfordre.com/africanhistory/view/10.1093/acrefore/9780190277734.001.0001/acrefore-9780190277734-e-86 [Accessed 15/11/2018].

Viveiros de Castro, E. (2014). 'Who is Afraid of the Ontological Wolf?'

Viveiros de Castro, E. (1998). 'Cosmological Deixis and Amerindian Perspectivism.' *The Journal of the Royal Anthropological Institute*, 4(3).

von Werlhof, J. (1987). *Spirits of the Earth*. El Centro: Imperial Valley College Museum.

Voss, A. & Wilson, S. (2017). *Re-Enchanting the Academy*. Auckland: Rubedo Press.

Winkelman, M. (2002). 'Shamanism as Neurotheology and Evolutionary Psychology.' *American Behavioral Scientist*, 45(12), pp. 1875-1887.

WMO (2018a). 'Climate change signals and impacts continue in 2018.' Available Online: https://public.wmo.int/en/media/press-release/climate-change-signals-and-impacts-continue-2018 [Accessed 30/11/2018].

WMO (2018b). 'The State of Greenhouse Gases in the Atmosphere Based on Global Observations through 2017.' Available Online: https://library.wmo.int/index.php?lvl=notice_display&id=20697#.XAEzTOKYST8 [Accessed 30/11/2018].

WWF, (2018). 'Our Living Planet Report.' Available Online: https://wwf.panda.org/knowledge_hub/all_publications/living_planet_report_2018/ [Accessed 30/11/2018].

Wackermann, J., Pütz, P. & Allefeld, C. (2008). 'Ganzfeld-induced hallucinatory experience, its phenomenology and cerebral electrophysiology.' *Corte:; A Journal Devoted to The Study of the Nervous System and Behavior*, 44(10), pp. 1364–1378. doi: 10.1016/j.cortex.2007.05.003

Wald, G. (1984). 'Life and Mind in the Universe.' *International Journal of Quantum Chemistry*, 26(11), pp. 1-15.

Walsh, R. (2005) 'Can Synaesthesia Be Cultivated? Indications from Surveys of Meditators.' *Journal of Consciousness Studies*, 12(4–5), pp. 5–17.

Ward, M. (2011). *The Comfort of Water: A River Pilgrimage*. Yarraville: Transit Lounge.

Watson, D. (2001). 'Dissociations of the night: Individual differences in sleep-related experiences and their relation to dissociation and schizotypy.' *Journal of Abnormal Psychology*, 110(4), pp. 526–535. doi: 10.1037/0021-843X.110.4.526.

Watson, W. & Keating, D. (2000). 'The Architecture of Sound in Neolithic Orkney.' In A. Ritchie (ed.) *Neolithic Orkney in its European Context.* Cambridge: McDonald Institute Monographs.

Watson, W. & Keating, D. (1999). 'Architecture and sound: an acoustic analysis of megalithic monuments in prehistoric Britain.' *Antiquity*, 73(280).

Webb, H. S. (2012). *Yamantin and Masintin in the Andean world: Contemporary dualism in modern Peru.* Albuquerque, NM: University of New Mexico.Press.

Weiner, R. (2012). 'Where heaven and earth come closer.' *The New York Times.* Retrieved from http://www.nytimes.com/2012/03/11/travel/thin-places-where-we-are-jolted-out-of-old-ways-of-seeing-the-world.html

Weinstein, S. & Graves, R. E. (2002). 'Regular Article: Are Creativity and Schizotypy Products of a Right Hemisphere Bias?' *Brain and Cognition*, 49, pp. 138–151. doi: 10.1006/brcg.2001.1493.

Wells, H. (1922). *A Short History of the World.* London: Cassell & Co.

White, R. A. (1994). 'The need for double vision in parapsychology: The feminist standpoint..' In L. Coly & R. A. White (eds.) *Women and parapsychology.* New York: Parapsychology Foundation.

Whitehead, C. (2011). 'Altered consciousness in society.' In E. Cardena & M. Winkelman (eds.) *Altering consciousness: Multidisciplinary perspectives (Vol. 1, History, culture, and the humanities).* Santa Barbara, CA: Praeger.

Whitley, D.S. (1996). *A Guide to Rock Art Sites.* Missoula: Mountain Press.

Williams, G. (2016). *A Monstrous Commotion: The Mysteries of Loch Ness.* London: Orion Books.

Willis, R. & Curry, P. (2004). *Astrology, Science, and Culture; Pulling Down the Moon.* Oxford: Berg.

Winkelman, M. (2008). 'Psychedelics and human evolution. A view from evolutionary psychology.' Paper presented at the World Psychedelic Forum, Basel, Switzerland.

Woolf, V. (1985). *Moments of Being, A Collection of Autobiographical Writing.* Harcourt Brace & Company.

Woolley, J. (2018). 'The Wires Crossed: What dowsing reveals about environmental knowledge in Britain.' *Anthropology Today*, 34(3), pp. 22-25.

World Population Review. (2018). 'Gambian Population 2018.' Online: http://worldpopulationreview.com/countries/gambia-population/ [Accessed 05/12/2018].

Wright, P. A. (1995) 'Bringing women's voices to transpersonal theory.' *ReVision*, 17(3), p. 3.

Yogananda, P. (1975). *Autobiography of a Yogi*. Mumbai: Jaico Publishing House.

Young, D.E. & Goulet, J-G. (1998). *Being Changed by Cross Cultural Encounters; the anthropology of extraordinary experience*. Peterborough Ontario, Broadview Press.

Zaehner, R. C. (1957). *Mysticism: Sacred and Profane*. Oxford: Clarendon Press.

Zingrone N. (2004). 'Failing to go the distance. On critics and parapsychology. Skeptical Investigations.' Retrieved from http://skepticalinvestigations.org/Examskeptics/Zingrone_critics.html

INDEX